Becoming Historians

Becoming Historians

Edited by

JAMES M. BANNER, JR.,

and JOHN R. GILLIS

THE UNIVERSITY OF CHICAGO PRESS   CHICAGO AND LONDON

JAMES M. BANNER, JR., cofounder of the National History Center and the History News Service, is historian-in-residence at American University. John R. Gillis is professor emeritus of history at Rutgers University.

The University of Chicago Press,
The University of Chicago Press, Ltd., London
© 2009 by The University of Chicago
All rights reserved. Published 2009
Printed in the United States of America
18 17 16 15 14 13 12 11 10 09   1 2 3 4 5

ISBN-13: 978-0-226-03656-4 (cloth)
ISBN-13: 978-0-226-03658-8 (paper)
ISBN-10: 0-226-03656-1 (cloth)
ISBN-10: 0-226-03658-8 (paper)

Library of Congress Cataloging-in-Publication Data

Becoming historians / edited by James M. Banner, Jr., and John R. Gillis.
    p. cm.
  ISBN-13: 978-0-226-03656-4 (cloth : alk. paper)
  ISBN-10: 0-226-03656-1 (cloth : alk. paper)
  ISBN-13: 978-0-226-03658-8 (pbk. : alk. paper)
  ISBN-10: 0-226-03658-8 (pbk. : alk. paper)
  1. Historians—Biography. I. Banner, James M., 1935– II. Gillis, John R.
D14.B43   2009
907'.2022—dc22   2008032581

⊗ The paper used in this publication meets the minimum requirements of the American National Standard for Information Sciences—Permanence of Paper for Printed Library Materials, ANSI z39.48-1992.

Contents

Preface

The memoirs collected in this volume comprise a portrait of a generation born a few years on either side of the Second World War. In many ways, it was a special generation, whose members came of age after the war yet just before the upheavals of the 1960s and 1970s. While these aspiring historians did not have the wartime experiences of those senior to them and were already young adults during the Vietnam War, they reflected the racial, gender, and generational tensions that characterized the years when they began to make their way as historians. Forced to negotiate these, as well as class and religious, differences, they were to make these issues part of their professional as well as personal commitments. As a result, they were instrumental in opening up new fields of research—women's and gender history, social history, African American history, public history, and non-Western history—that fundamentally changed the landscape of American higher education.

From our present perspective, it is now possible to reflect on what was accomplished, as well as what was left incomplete or wholly ignored. The authors of these essays, many who are now approaching retirement or already formally retired, are as active as ever in their chosen fields and have a distinct view of how history has been transformed in the last half century. The essays collected here constitute a record of one of the discipline's most creative but also most contentious periods. They reveal a generation that grappled with issues for which there was no precedent. Today's younger generation faces its own dilemmas. Its members will find here the record of a multiplicity of experiences that may guide them as they forge their own relationship with the past.

One of the striking characteristics of this generation is the diversity of its members' origins, orientations, and experiences. Recognizing that there

are many ways to become a historian and many ways to be one, we had
to acknowledge from the beginning the difficulty of selecting a representative cross section of historians of our cohort. We sought out historians
whose work we admired but who had not previously published memoirs or
autobiographies of their own. While making no claims that the experiences
these historians relate are representative of the discipline as a whole, we
are confident that the collection reflects the diverse nature of history as it
is practiced today.

Much has been written about the history of history but little about historians themselves. In recruiting our contributors, we hoped that in re-
flecting on their lives they would reveal those dimensions of themselves
that they now see in retrospect to have been crucial to their becoming historians. We encouraged them to relate how they had discovered and created their vocation. To the extent that this collection reveals something
of the personal flavor of historians' lives, we believe that it captures the
variety of personalities and temperaments, origins and circumstances, as
well as the elements of chance and design that go into the making of most
practicing historians.

For all of us, the editors included, writing a memoir presented challenges
that, as historians, we had not faced before. When we set out to explain
how elements of our lives fit together to make us historians, we quickly
come up against the formidable obstacles of recall and the demands of
memoir itself. As we are now all too keenly aware, conveying any account
of the past, to say nothing of our own lives, is shot through with the unreli-
ability of memory: partial, shaped by the purposes of recall, and inherently
egocentric. All such accounts, as the essays in this volume reveal, differ
greatly by virtue of each writer's disposition, intent, and decisions about
what to include and exclude in the presentation of each one's professional
development. They differ, too, in the approaches that the authors have
adopted. While all are personal, they emphasize different elements of life
and career. Joan Wallach Scott, for instance, gives much weight to what
she calls "the internal dynamics of my psyche" and the slow growth of
her passion for history. Others stress the complicated effort involved in
coming to terms with the circumstances they encountered and the choices
they made.

What is more, telling these tales required art and artfulness as much as
accurate recall. The journey from childhood to adulthood rarely possesses,
in its humdrum details, anything like the linear progress that a storyline
suggests, but the art of memoir calls for a storyline nonetheless. Much

that is not suppressed must be omitted in the interest of space and the demands of narrative. Consequently, to assert that what is related here are tales as faithful as possible to the facts is to say little. They are tales that are faithful to the task at hand—trying to give shape to a messy reality perhaps only partially remembered and, in any case, in need of tidying up so as to create credible and decently readable accounts.

Such tidying up befits memoir, especially memoir focused on a single thread of a life, more than it does autobiography. Memoir can be, and in the cases here must be, more selective, more allusive, than autobiography. In its selectiveness, it shares much with the writing of history, in which the shards of evidence, once gathered, must be chosen among and not tumbled upon the page in promiscuous delight. Memoir must also, like history, be plausible and convincing. It must have a point of view even while steering clear of argument. Yet the memoirist cannot always indulge the scholar's practice of substantiation, verification, and citation. Though it claims to relate and represent something close to what happened (or at least the remembered part of what happened), memoir is not exactly imaginative literature; neither is it history as historians practice it.

For historians—for us—memoir can be treacherous terrain. There can be no claim in this genre to objectivity or disinterestedness; engagement in one's own life and times is necessarily its leitmotif. And the memoirists' task is to try to understand the significance of their own lives rather than the lives of others—always a sobering undertaking for professionals whose training and practice have been devoted to assessing the consequences of others' existence, decisions, and actions. To be sure, recent developments in method and theory have attuned us, more than our predecessors, to self-reflexivity. "The kind of historian I am today," Linda Gordon remarks, "determines how I see the history of my becoming a historian." The recent relaxation in the formal code of historical writing has extended to us a kind of permission to write about ourselves. Nevertheless, one senses in these memoirs the reserve about self that has traditionally attended historians' work.

Did our authors choose history, or did history choose them? Did they know early on that they wished to be historians, or did they make themselves historians? One of us, John Gillis, opens his memoir with the statement that he was not born a historian and that he long thought that "history was something that happened to other people." And a similar, gradual dawning of an affinity for knowledge of the past seems to have been the case for all but one or two of the other memoirists. Few were swept away to history as by a gift. Franklin Knight records that he became a historian indirectly, "through repeated coincidences," and that he had "a passion but not an irresistible compulsion" for the subject. Only one, Rhys Isaac, was, as he writes, "in the grip" of the past from his earliest years; only he knew from the very start that he was a votary of history's muse. And yet for some, as for Temma Kaplan, being surrounded during childhood by tales of the past, many of them of dislocation and loss, stirred in them a lasting gravitation to the sources of other people's lives and to those sources' significance and meaning.

For some contributors, like David Hollinger, becoming a historian was a matter of growing into a sense of professionalism whose direction seems to have established itself early on. It took much time for most of us to realize, in Hollinger's words, "what the practice of historical scholarship, as an act of mind, really entailed." Even so, Hollinger's own route to historical scholarship and the particular kind of scholarship he has pursued was indirect and full of unforeseeable influences. As he compresses that story, "A child of Idaho and of a small Anabaptist sect, having been inspired by an atheist's studies of New England Puritanism, found his career-defining preoccupations when connections made through a political movement brought him into contact with the work of an orthodox Jew addressing the cultural dynamics of the modernization process through a meditation on Confucian China's encounter with communism."

For most, however, becoming a historian was, as it was for Dwight Pitcaithley, more a product of the intersection of inclination, circumstance, decision, and chance and was almost always an election among other professional commitments and options. As chief historian of the National Park Service, Pitcaithley was also the one most exposed to the politics of history, a situation that contributed to his engagement with what he calls the "delicate art of public history." Only slowly and by stages did most of our memoirists awaken to their particular skills and interests and find their vocational lodging place in history. Indeed, for several contributors the discipline of history was not initially a welcoming home or one in which they ever came to feel entirely comfortable. Yet one of the most notable features of these memoirs is how much their authors did to help open up whole new areas of history, most notably women's history and public history, but also cultural, world, and social history. When they did not find ready-made roles for their talents and interests, they devoted their energies to changing institutions. They redefined the meaning of history itself to feel at home as historians. In this respect, their lives offer important lessons to younger historians assaying their own prospects as practicing historians. We hope that aspiring scholars will find models here for the kinds of changes that are inevitably required to keep the discipline vital and relevant, as well as models of the fidelity to self that makes any career satisfying.

Much else binds the authors in this collection. We think it fair to say that they constitute a generation, though this may not be their primary identification. All came of age after the Second World War, a turning point in the history both of the United States and the world at large. Although this generation did not participate in the war itself, it was deeply affected by the way that cold-war mobilization transformed the relationship between state, economy, and culture, and, in so doing, moved higher education and the academic profession from its previously marginal, though elite, status to one central to the functioning of modern mass society. This postwar generation participated in the unprecedented expansion of higher education and the incorporation of groups that had previously been denied access to the elite professions. While the struggle to integrate minorities (including religious minorities), women, and people of working-class background was always contested and continues to be fraught with difficulty, this particular generation was to be, like it or not, instrumental in the first phases of a grand, integrating experiment, which continues to this very day.

While the American branch of the discipline of history continued to focus on the American past, this was the first generation to study and undertake research abroad, principally in Europe but increasingly in non-Western regions as well. Before the Second World War, Europe had been America's main window on the world. Other regions were left to be studied by anthropologists or political scientists and rarely had a place among the subjects taught in history departments. Apart from immigrant scholars, even those who taught the history of Europe had rarely lived or done primary research there. All this changed, and quite abruptly, for this generation. Now professional qualification involved extensive research abroad, not just in Europe but in the other world regions that, for the first time, were becoming established concerns of American higher education. And as Maureen Nutting, Dwight Pitcaithley, and James Banner relate their emergence as historians, their experiences abroad also unalterably changed their perspectives on the world. Also, as Franklin Knight and Rhys Isaac suggest, coming to the United States from abroad could be transformative.

The boundaries that this generation learned to traverse were not just geographical. One of the striking features of its interests has been its interdisciplinarity. All of the contributors are beneficiaries of liberal arts educations that exposed them to a range of humanistic and social science disciplines that, in one way or another, shaped their later work. In this respect, their educations were broader than those who came before and most of those who came after them. By and large, they were not nearly so specialized or protoprofessional as today's graduate students. A generation earlier it had not always been necessary even to have an advanced degree, and Rhys Isaac was one of the last to gain access to the academy without first obtaining a doctorate or its equivalent. For the rest of us, that professional degree was essential.

Yet surprisingly little attention was given to preparation for graduate school, even at the best liberal arts colleges; our generation's entry into a world of specialization came as a distinct shock. While those entering graduate school today generally know what to expect, there was little that prepared us. Nor were most departments ready for our unprecedented numbers. Specialization was often experienced as a narrowing, even suffocating, experience. If the 1950s and 1960s were something of a golden age of American undergraduate education, the same cannot be said for graduate education in those years and for some time afterwards. Graduate preparation was just beginning to be organized in a professional way, and we were the products of its confusions, not all of which have been resolved.

In fact, one of the striking elements in a majority of these memoirs is the stories they tell of graduate education in the 1960s and early 1970s. Much of the authors' disappointment with graduate school must be seen against the way in which so many of them experienced their collegiate education. Their college years coincided with a great, confident era of the arts and sciences in American public and private education. The authors were deeply affected by their teachers, to whom many of the memoirists pay their affectionate respects. In fact, the influence of particular teachers recorded in all of the authors' memoirs is a strong and shared theme. The authors were also buoyed in college by the excitement of a broad general education and, for the youngest of them, by the intersection of learning and public realities.

And then came graduate school, with its unanticipated demands and its vastly different approach to learning. Where before one could learn with a kind of joyous abandon, now one had to apply and accept boundaries, focus on career goals, and compete. This unanticipated shift, which many contrast to their heady college years, caused more than a little anxiety and self-reflection. "How different for me," James Banner remarks, "were those sometimes searing doubts from the exciting discoveries and unbounded confidence of undergraduate days." Not surprisingly therefore, few of the accounts flatter the graduate departments in which the authors were enrolled or the approach to graduate education that was universal at the time. The authors' graduate programs seem to have been obstacles to be gotten through rather than fondly recalled sources of growth and learning. John Gillis observes that the limits of his graduate schooling required that he turn his subsequent professional work into "a continuous remediation project." Like others of this cohort, he turned to other disciplines for tools to deal with an expanding range of historical subjects.

All of the memoirists managed to survive to tell the tale, but most remained uncomfortable with the increasingly specialized, departmentalized academic world they were to inherit. Their ongoing involvement and commitment to change inside as well as outside academic walls reflects discontents that surfaced at the early stages of their careers and have been a signature of this generation's activism ever since. Their determination to expand the definition of history, to create new fields, institutions, and practices to accommodate subjects, approaches, and methods previously excluded from the professional canon—to write, as Rhys Isaac terms it, an "everybody history"—constitutes their lasting legacy.

It was the conditions of cold-war America that powerfully undermined the concept and reality of the ivory tower. The arrival on campus of minority and working class students and faculty members, together with racial and gender desegregation, were changes that this generation generally embraced as well as embodied, though there were many of its members who felt uneasy, even threatened, by this transformation. We were all drawn into the debates about affirmative action, coeducation, and gender and sexual preferences and thus forced to take stands on issues that had little resonance in academic life in earlier generations. Yet in many respects we were poorly prepared to take on the roles that were thrust upon us, often very early in our careers. Few of us, however, regret the intoxicating sense of creative engagement that we experienced during this extraordinary moment of institutional transformation in which all options seemed open to those who were willing to invest their energies in the process of change. Today's graduate students take longer to obtain their degrees and experience greater difficulties in gaining employment than we did. When they do assume their first full-time positions, they are more seasoned as historians but at the same time more conditioned to the routines of departmental and university life.

In this regard, readers of these memoirs will be struck by the serendipitous ways members of this generation gained their initial positions and published their first books and articles. One of them, Dwight Pitcaithley, even had to rappel 180 feet into a cave to win some of his professional spurs. The memoirs also testify to the discrimination that favored men over women, although the unregulated hiring system in place during the 1960s could also give an advantage to women who had the right contacts and prestigious degrees. By the 1970s this system was being challenged and replaced by the much more egalitarian policies, applied with accountability, that members of this generation in fact helped craft and enforce.

There is also much evidence in this collection of the ongoing disparities and injustices that exist within the discipline. Though Maureen Nutting has faced many obstacles and prejudices as she has pursued her unconventional career, her experience has enabled her to make contributions that have been invaluable to the discipline. It is apparent that affirmative action and civil rights statutes have gone only part way toward resolving the inequalities posed by class and race within the academy and outside it. Yet it is striking how many members of our generation came from families with no previous academic connections. Our "cultural capital" was largely achieved rather than inherited. Today, as more and more children of academics pursue higher degrees, intergenerational continuity is much more marked than before.

Yet the relative ease that attended several of the authors' searches for first employment and then professional stability came with costs. The discipline that prided itself on its ability to identify and recruit the best historical minds retained a decided, almost unthinking casualness to the manner of appointing us when we were fresh out of graduate school. The American Historical Association and Organization of American Historians had not yet developed standards and procedures for conducting searches for their open faculty positions; and departments themselves, not yet operating under mandatory federal nondiscrimination rules, followed no formal methods, including widespread public notice, in securing young historians. In addition, as Maureen Nutting's and Dwight Pitcaithley's essays illustrate, the academy did not even easily or quickly provide room for all its aspirants. Yet this did not prevent those two historians and many others from carving out deeply satisfying professional places for themselves. In doing so, they expanded for the benefit of their successors the definition of what it means to become and be a historian and made it possible for their professional heirs to rest easy in what Paul Robinson terms "history's great virtue...its tolerance for diversity, its willingness to let individual scholars pursue their demons."

These memoirs in fact raise questions about the widely held assumption, one of diminishing validity, that academic and public history have occupied and continue to occupy separate professional spheres. Dwight Pitcaithley spent his professional life principally in public service as a historian, while Maureen Nutting and James Banner were engaged in nonacademic work for much of their professional lives. But even those memoirists who found a home in the academy involved themselves throughout much of their careers, either directly or in their scholarly investigations, in issues and actions of contemporary urgency and in the creation and management of organizations that answered to public and professional needs and concerns. None of the authors was hesitant to endeavor with open eyes and lively commitment to help alter those practices and arrangements that they believed were obstacles to the realization of the nation's cherished, if often unmet, ideals. In this respect, their growth as historians had a close relationship to their civic lives and commitments. These historians would help make the future through the past.

Not that we need to spend many words in emphasizing the fact that historians have always been engaged in public affairs. Since written history's origins in the days of Herodotus and Thucydides, historians have ineluctably been implicated in the events of their times, and their histories have reflected that fact. As these memoirs suggest, part of historians' growth is built around figuring out how to make their knowledge and skills useful to society. Not one of our historians claims to have been a wholly disengaged observer. "By seeking the most compelling truths," Temma Kaplan remarks, "historians can help sustain decency against lies told to preserve the status quo and to prevent a sense that ordinary people can change history." Joan Scott observes that "becoming a historian was not a consolation for politics, but a companion to it." In fact, it may have become more difficult during the careers of members of this generation to separate the two given the spread, during their lifetimes, of communications, travel, and international exchanges.

Taken as a whole, these memoirs open some windows into the many ways that practicing historians have grown into their work and commitments and make clear that many paths can lead to a life in the discipline.

We hope, too, that they illuminate some, if not all, of the varieties of history and careers that exist today. If we have captured some of the dynamic vitality of the discipline, then we will have accomplished our goal. It is never easy to get historians to sit still long enough for a definitive group portrait. If someone were to pull together a companion collection to this one twenty years from now, one can be reasonably sure that the picture would be very different. That is not just our belief; it is our hope.

*   *   *

We have enjoyed greatly working with our colleagues at the University of Chicago Press. Our editor there, Robert Devens, saw promise in the idea for this book before it had tangible form and moved it with skill and efficiency through the steps from proposal to submission to approval. His assistant, Emilie Sandoz, has proved another marvel of good-natured efficiency in arranging for the scheduling and production of the completed work. Finally, Mara Naselli has squired the book's individual essays through their editing with good-natured aplomb, a keen eye, and a firm pen. We are grateful to them all.

James M. Banner, Jr.   John R. Gillis
Washington, D.C.   Berkeley, California

RHYS ISAAC

Toward Ethnographic History

Figures in the Landscape, Action in the Texts

"Stop the car, I see a hand axe!" my twin brother called out. Glynn was only fourteen, but—already in the grip of antiquity—he would continually scan the roadside gravels for traces of the stone-age past. We identical twins shared this orientation as we shared everything. But we had divided it between us: he would be an archaeologist, and I would be a historian. Glynn Isaac indeed became—as his 1985 London *Times* obituary declared—one of the greatest palaeoanthropologists of the twentieth century.

We two identical twins had been born in 1937 in Cape Town, South Africa. "Born at the Cape of Good Hope," I always declare. Indeed we were given a precious gift that few can have: we took our first steps in the world each with an absolute equal at his side. Our wise parents had resolutely withheld the information as to which of us was born first. Growing up as inseparable siblings was especially fortunate given that we were small in stature; anyone who took on one took on two. Our parents never had much property but lived as professional scientists off their stock of learning; and yet we twins were distinctly privileged, since we were males. There was also great privilege in the fact that we and our much younger sister were all children of the white race. There was, however, alienation and exile lurking in our circumstances since we would come of age in a South Africa where severe penalties awaited any person who resisted the apartheid regime of racial segregation. We twins left the country at age twenty-one; and our parents and sister emigrated soon after.

But my story has got ahead of itself. Soon after our birth, the world was in the grip of the Second World War, so our Welsh-born father was prevented until peace came from taking his South African wife and twin sons back to meet his own family in Britain. We could only make that exciting trip in 1947, and there in "the Old Country" we eager little boys saw great castles and cathedrals; our imaginations were stirred—the past became the foreign country we were drawn to travel in for the rest of our lives. I know also that there, unconsciously, I learned about how much more there is to any peopled landscape than meets the eye of the stranger. Our father's family was Welsh-speaking Welsh to the core. ("Isaac" is originally a baptismal given name; it thus became a patronymic—"ap Isaac"—and then, under Anglicizing pressure, it was converted to a surname.) On car rides through South Wales with John Isaac, our grandfather, we sensed indeed an insider's understanding of his own country. He was a self-taught scholar of Welsh traditions—the poetry of the bards, the singing, and the eloquent preaching in the dissenting chapels. At every turn of the winding roads, there were for our grandfather not just the slag heaps of coal mines with rows of miners' houses squeezed in beside them but the places where had been heard the lyric words of some "famous poet," or the mighty voice of a "noted preacher." There were comic stories also—the better to fix all this in impressionable young minds.

Thus when we were nine years old we had begun our matching careers in pursuit of the past. Once home in South Africa, books became our resource for pursuing what can now be seen as our vocations from childhood. Glynn pored over J. H. Breasted's *Brief History of Ancient Times* (still a very fat volume although edited and abridged by Hugh Jones), while I assiduously read Wilhelm Hedrick Van Loon's *Lives*, and Will Durant's *Age of Faith*. Writers of popular histories are frequently sneered at, but I wonder how often their work has encouraged young beginners like me. With Van Loon I dined in the company of great persons of the past, starting with his countryman, Desiderius Erasmus; with Will Durant I learned so much more about the building of those great castles and cathedrals. In time—Glynn leading the way—we began to decolonize ourselves: we came to appreciate that the significant past is not an Old Country monopoly. Glynn turned to local archaeology with its lineages of hand axes and so took first steps in what became a life-long quest for the African origins of distinctively human behavior. I learned to focus on the landscape before me and to imagine the stories of its peopling.

In the high school from which we matriculated, the A-stream was science. We went along with that and did not study history. This was fortunate, since the pure physics course put us under the spell of Arthur Jayes, a teacher who really challenged his students. I think we both were fortunate in that; certainly Glynn was, when, working at one to two million years ago, he needed all the natural science he could muster. Meanwhile history for me was being in a high-school senior's literary club where students presented papers. Mine was on medieval bestiaries, since, with my father's encouragement, I was then resolved to be a historian of science.

After high school we entered employment for half a year to pay for a ship voyage to take us back to spend the other half of the year exploring the Old Country on our own. The two weeks on shipboard as independent young men was certainly a way to get a new view of the world. We traveled with a Spanish dance troupe that had completed a tour of South Africa; they seemed to live their lives as vividly, extravagantly off stage as on. I think we were both in love with Sylvia, as with total fascination we watched her wild flirtations—although not extended to us schoolboys. We were, however, befriended by various older persons, intrigued by these bright young identical twins discovering the world. An old lady at our table took us under her wing, and her niece was to us at once half an admired belle and half a much older sister. There was an aging drunk also at our table, who had us call him "uncle"; he alarmed the old lady by his lugubrious zeal to share raunchy confidences.

We saw another as-yet-unimagined world during the ship's stopover in the anchorage off Las Palmas, on the Spanish Grand Canary Island. Churches adorned with gold reliquaries, candlesticks, and statues stood in every little plaza and the giant cathedral topped them all in the wealth of its display. Poor women in black and vendors of every description crowded the streets and alleyways. On the steep mountainsides out of town, desperately impoverished peasants carried earth in baskets to keep viable the vineyards that were their livelihood. Here was a kind of visible history in the form of a very oppressive old-world hierarchy in contrast with the colonial racial hierarchy with which we had grown up.

There were soon to be more encounters with history. Already in 1947 we had seen bomb-devastated areas of central London and heard stories of the Blitz; now we found that the widowed Welsh aunt whose home was our home whenever we were in London, had remarried to an Austrian Jewish widower. He had escaped the fate of the rest of his family by being in London when the war broke out. On the wall hung a visibly patched portrait of his grandmother; we learned that an SS man had ground it under his heel when the family was dragged from their home to death in the gas chambers. Richard Barkeley (originally Baumgarten) was a historian himself, by then employed in the university extension programs of the Workers' Education Association. And, since there was at this time a demand for fluent German speakers who could interpret British institutions to the defeated and eager-to-learn former enemy, he also made frequent lecture tours to Germany. Uncle Richard was one of the most warm and loving men we boys had ever met; himself childless, he was delighted to "adopt" us and to further our beginning steps into the world of learning.

Once in Britain, Glynn participated in a number of summer-season archaeological excavations; I enrolled in a National Trust field school on riverbank ecology, conducted at John Constable's Dedham Mill in Essex. This was memorable as my first experience of being in a coeducational class! I also did solo walking trips through romantic landscapes. Once I was able to join Glynn for a hitchhiking tour of the Salisbury plains, seeing with awe such great wonders of the Neolithic past as Stonehenge and Avebury Circle. As winter came on, we both settled in London to do university extension classes—Glynn in archaeology, I in medieval history. (I then thought—as somewhere inside me I still do—that the history of the Middle Ages was the most 'really real' of all! Indeed, I like to tell myself and others that I am still a kind of medievalist, because the American Revolution was the true end of the Middle Ages!)

*   *   *

At the start of 1956, we made the two-week return voyage home, just in time to enroll at the University of Cape Town (UCT). Glynn was doing the Bachelor of Science program he needed to prepare for research into the early fossil records of the human past; he majored in geology and zoology, with a minor in archaeology in the Arts Faculty. I had my weight on the other foot; I majored in history with enough science courses to be able to complete a Bachelor of Science degree a year after my Bachelor of Arts was done; thus I planned to be prepared to engage in the history of science. Along the way I found, however, that straight history grabbed me as nothing else. The introduction—History I—was Western Civ. Dr. Jean van der Poel took us from the kingdoms of Egypt to the end of the Middle Ages. I wrote a first essay on Charlemagne's Europe, with my father's copy of Bryce's *Holy Roman Empire* open on the desk while Beethoven's Emperor Concerto, played over and over through the frequent interruptions of changing the scratched set of 78-rpm bakelite disks on an old wind-up phonograph. In the second half of that first year Professor J. H. Mandelbrote covered the period from the Renaissance and the Reformation to the French Revolution and Napoleonic Wars.

There were no electives in that entire three-year course, run as it was by a department of five, four of whom had their research specialties in South African history. The second year—History II—was entirely conducted by Mr. Leonard Thompson (later a professor of African History, at UCLA and then Yale). In the first half we studied Imperial Expansion. We began our study with the Portuguese explorers and made our way through the rise and fall of European overseas empires to the end of the British Raj in India. At last we came to the recently proclaimed "winds of change" in Africa. In that first half-year we were given some of the framework for world history; but what really fired me up was the second half of the course—South African history. Having done the overview of empires, Leonard Thompson taught us the history of our own land as a story of settler invasions, repulses, and the slow creation of a colonial society formed by the inclusion of for-the-moment conquered peoples.

The year was now 1957; the world was in flux. The independent republics of India and Pakistan were nearly ten years old; the Gold Coast Colony in West Africa had just become the State of Ghana, a republic under the presidency of Kwame Nkruma. The rapidly changing times called forth a new historiographic ethic in that course. If I were to speculate about its sources, I would guess that the recent grim revelations of racism run riot in the Holocaust on the one hand and the positive affirmations of the United Nations' Declaration of Universal Human Right on the other hand had unsettled the old white man's historiography. Be that as it may, our forward-looking teacher fostered a strong consciousness of the histories of empire and settlement as two-sided—no longer to be told as the admirable triumph of the self-declared 'civilizing' settlers. The scarcity at that time of books and articles that presented the past in this way should have made me conscious of what a new start in historiography we were involved in. I have Leonard Thompson to thank that when I came to write colonial history myself, I took the inclusive approach as a standard in all that I did. I would strive for an everybody history with full attention to the female as well as the male, the young as well as the old, and the black as well as the white.

At the same time another form of attachment was happening that worked to give my twin and me a distinctive orientation to landscape. We had become adventurers to wild places. As members of the UCT Mountain and Ski Club we found ourselves among kindred spirits, young women and men with zest for life. With them we made expeditions to the mountain peaks and crag-bound high valleys in the sandstone ranges that form the southwestern and southern scarp of the great dry land mass of southern Africa. Those ranges beckoned us daily from our terraced varsity campus up on the eastern side of Table Mountain; later when we both saw how our published work revealed a distinctive landscape orientation, we knew one of the sources from whence it came.

Glynn was coming to know the geological origins of that rugged landscape; I was fascinated with the history of its peopling. I was reading the eighteenth-century travelers—Carl Peter Thunberg, William J. Burchell, and others—all of whom published reports of their voyaging by way of contributing to the Enlightenment description of the world and everything in it. Above all there was C. W. de Kiewiet's *History of South Africa: Social and Economic*, which, for all its textbook title, was a compelling account of conflicts in a vividly evoked landscape. I still treasure its characterization of the dispersed settlement of the seminomadic "free-burger" pastoralists. Seeking to escape the constraints of the colonial government in Cape Town, they scattered wide over the dry plains of the interior, with each man fleeing the tyranny of his neighbor's smoke. I did not say to myself that one day I would write history in matching terms—after all I was going to be a historian of science, was I not? But when I had myself written a history of colonial Virginia very explicitly set in its landscape, I could identify De Kiewiet's very distinct influence.

There had been earlier impressions that also emerged in the histories I would write of Europeans and Africans in Virginia. In 1946 we twins saw a different world to the old seaport of Cape Town and its mountainous hinterland; we went plant collecting with our botanist mother on a 600-mile camping trip to her home country in the east, where she had been born and raised. Her parents had been Scottish settlers in King Williams Town in the heart of British Kaffraria, an area then only recently annexed to the Cape Colony after fierce wars with Nelson Mandela's warrior ancestors, the Xhosa nation. Here was quite another landscape—steep-sided river valleys and the scattered dwellings of the Bapedi, Amaxhosa, and Pondo peoples. These cattle-herding farming horticulturalist peoples had very distinctive settlements made up of round thatched, wattle-and-daub huts dispersed all over the hillsides. Later in our childhood we lived for four crucial years in Grahamstown, an old garrison settlement on the edge of this world. There the sounds of Africa coming from the township and from the backyard of our house entered my psyche. When History II came to the clash of the Dutch-derived pastoralists and these densely settled warlike occupiers of all this land—the era of the so-called Kaffir Wars—I had an experiential, landscape-situated reference for the histories in the books. I had also the benefit of conversation with an expert in the cultural differences involved. Monica Wilson, professor of anthropology and distinguished ethnographer of old African traditions and changing ways among the by-then conquered peoples of the Eastern Cape, was a dear friend of the family. She was a very encouraging mentor to both my brother and to me. Later, when I aspired to play anthropologist to the past, her quiet wisdom was an important part of my inspiration.

In Grahamstown also, my twin and I—offspring of agnostic parents but with very pious Calvinist grandparents—were suddenly inducted into Anglican piety. We were put into a remarkable small boarding school that also taught us strong forms of self-reliance. I knew the value of this schooling when I found myself interpreting the contests between the Church of England as established in Virginia and the insurgent Separate Baptists who prepared the ground for an enduring evangelical hegemony in the Bible Belt South.

My second-year history studies had thus involved exciting narratives of diverse peoples and distinctive ways of occupying imagined landscapes of the past. I had a clear vision of the kind of history I wanted to practice. By contrast the third year of the course (History III) was less spellbinding, although I received strong encouragement from Mr. T. R. H. Davenport, then a young lecturer, but later a distinguished professor of modern South African history. The studies were all political history: in the first half we reviewed the later Middle Ages and in the second half the twentieth-century world to 1939. My strongest recollection is the little dismissal speech to the history majors from the soft-spoken "old prof." (J. H. Mandelbrote was the "Professor and Head of Department" in a British Imperial arrangement that irreverent Australians have called the God-Professor System.) He suggested to us that "in a few years you will have forgotten everything I've taught you!" Pause. "But at least you will have had something to forget!" He was only partly right in my case, at least. Furthermore I had in that year taken a course entitled Constitutional History and Law (English, of course) that was a prerequisite for History IV—the

honors year that seemed likely to be my next step as my commitment
to the history of science waned. There was something satisfying in the overview history of the evolving English governmental system from Anglo-
Saxon charters through the writs and assizes of King Henry II to the
unwritten conventions governing Westminster democracy in the twentieth century. Of course, we did not in the least follow the alternative trail
blazed by the thirteen rebel colonies in 1775–76; but when a need to understand those bitter disputes over the nature of the British Constitution
became central to the American history I would later write, a comprehensive grounding in the prior institutional framework was of immeasurable
value to me.

As it turned out, I neither enrolled in History IV nor completed my
Bachelor of Science, since I was advised to apply for a Rhodes Scholarship
by Leonard Thompson. He had taken pleasure in the essays he inspired
me to write, and he saw the scores I was notching up in my youthful delight at the challenges of preparing for and dashing off the brisk answers
required in the three-hour end-of-year examinations. I did apply, and I
was "elected" (their word) "Cape Province Rhodes Scholar for 1958."
The award was in the newspaper the day before the university's graduation ceremony; so, when I kneeled to have my BA degree conferred by
the university chancellor, former Chief Justice A. v. d. S. Centlivres, he
leaned forward and murmured in my ear: "Well done!" This was a kind
of send-off; the next part of my academic history education would be at
the University of Oxford.

We at UCT in this time, however, were getting history education of a
different sort, and our chancellor was playing his part. Since the general
election of 1948, the government of South Africa had been in the hands
of the Afrikaner Nationalist Party. Its leaders had two main objectives.
First, they would remake the hitherto English-dominated nation as a revived Boer republic. (The Union of South Africa was a British Imperial
creation put together in 1910, during a time of attempted reconciliation
after the bitter conflicts of the Anglo-Boer War.) Second, their revived
Boer republic would have a white-supremacy racial regime unhampered
by even the limited recognition of human rights that nineteenth- and
early-twentieth-century British liberalism had put in place. Apartheid—
segregation—was the name they gave to both the ideology and its practical implementation.

A drama was unfolding that was the reverse of more publicized events
soon to occur in Little Rock, Arkansas, and Oxford, Mississippi, where

the central government forced segregationist educational institutions to open their doors to an excluded race. One of the early targets for the Nationalist South African government were liberal universities. UCT and the University of the Witwatersrand ("Wits") insisted that the nature of a university required it to be open to recruit teachers and students regardless of race. It is easy to mock formal liberalism with its record of acceptance of the profound inequalities made by wealth and poverty and its polite methods of resisting injustice; but those in charge of UCT from the chancellor and vice-chancellor down to a majority of the largely white but nevertheless racially mixed student body felt that there were at stake sacred human rights. UCT and Wits refused to alter their open admissions policies. In 1958 the government brought in the Extension of University Education Act, which sidestepped this refusal by creating racially segregated "non-white" universities. It became a serious offense for any person not classified as "white" (there was a racial ID system by then) to enroll in a "whites-only" university.

While that iniquitous education act was a bill before the legislature, students of UCT kept twenty-four-hour vigil with a Torch of Academic Freedom at the steps leading up to Parliament House in Cape Town. (As members of the cross-country running club, my twin and I had been in a relay to carry that torch from the university campus.) On the day of a crucial reading of the bill, the university, led by its chancellor, marched gowned and capped in academic procession up the main street of Cape Town to the same steps of Parliament. But the government was resolute in its religion-derived sense of ideological righteousness; the bill became statute, as did a whole series of other measures instituting a segregationist police state. Even peaceful protest of the kind the universities had mounted became illegal and subject to violent dispersal with arrest and unlimited detention.

* * *

In September 1959, my twin and I took ship again for England; we knew this time that we would not return to live under the regime that increasingly used terror to enforce its unjust policies on its oppressed majority and on all activists in their cause. That voyage took us to opportunity and to self-imposed exile; it was also the last fortnight of our joint lives. For twenty-one years we had shared everything. Even when we started dating girls, we had done so in joyous foursomes; and for our celibate nights in those chaste times we had shared a room with bunk beds from which we would, before falling asleep, exchange the doings of the day. (We had indeed decorated that room each with the insignia of our distinct orientations to the past—Glynn had rendered on the white-washed wall a scene from the caves of Lascaux, and I had painted a version of a medieval *dies irae* showing devils stoking eternal fires with the souls of the damned!) All that was behind us now—for the next years I would be in Oxford and he in Cambridge, and after that we could expect to be scattered even farther apart. Yes—Oxbridge! We were jointly fulfilling British Empire middle-class parental ambitions. Indeed, at our birth our father had taken out an insurance policy to mature when we turned twenty-one; his intent was to fund admission to the "ancient universities." Now that the Rhodes Scholarship took care of me the entire proceeds could fund Glynn's study in the very distinguished school of prehistoric archaeology at Cambridge.

I arrived at Oxford full of great expectations—my own, and, of course, those of others. My principal mentor, Leonard Thompson, himself an Oxonian, had advised me not to think of a research degree but to do a repeat bachelor of arts in modern history. I was accepted by Balliol College and had already steeped myself in the lore of this awesome house, whose members were kept at a distance by all the rest of Oxford. "I'm at Balliol," was a sure party-conversation stopper, although I tell myself that I had not studied—have never studied—to assume the Balliol men's notorious "easy air of effortless superiority!" The choice of college was, however, a good one. Balliol had then, in Christopher Hill and R. W. Southern, two wonderful history tutors. More important than their great international eminence was their participation in the camaraderie of scholars that prevailed among Balliol students and faculty. I imagine that Christopher Hill, a long-time communist and instinctive egalitarian, had set this tone; certainly his tutorials and his once-a-term social evenings were exemplary of the ethos. The choice of study program—the modern history honors degree—was also a good one, though it would leave me with two degrees and no clear-cut onward path.

For a broad historical education—well, broad in some ways—the Oxford course was a wonderful opportunity. "Modern History" at Oxford meant everything after the fall of Rome! But modern history had become a university subject only with a certain maturing of the great Atlantic-world nation states; its core had to be national—"British History, from the beginning." And since nobody then taught Scottish, Irish, Welsh, or

British overseas history, and the only definition of "the beginning" was that the exam paper always had a first question on "Roman Britain," we did English history with compulsory exams on European history and on political theory (Hobbes and Rousseau). But to be a student under the encouragement of Christopher Hill and Dick Southern and to be free to attend lectures on a wide range of subjects, including those offered by A. J. P. Taylor and Hugh Trevor-Roper, was exhilarating in its English-history way.

In my reading for college tutorials, I got a further training—unsystematic but important—in the reading of historical documents. This became more intense when I made a bold choice. I wanted to get away from political history; probably I already wanted an anthropological history without really knowing it. In the curriculum, there was a short list of all the "Special Studies" topics defined by an extensive list of primary documents to be read: these were all political history except for "St. Augustine of Hippo" and "St. Bernard of Clairvaux." These were a kind of "intellectual" or "religious" history—but (as with all the studies) the documents must be original—and so, in Latin! I thought I had enough Latin after six years in school and two at university. St. Augustine would be my option. That was one of the most fortunate choices of my career, because, Balliol—having no don specializing in late Roman history—sent me to Peter Brown, then at All Souls College, later at Princeton. I gained a friend for life; more important, I gained a mentor who taught me the difference between reading intelligently and really reading historically—that is, really reading to understand the distinctive worldviews and cosmologies of every changing epoch. From Peter's eloquent silences as I read my essays, mapping the great Christian rhetor, sage, and eschatologist onto my mid-twentieth-century liberal worldview, I began to learn to reach for understanding of otherness and to develop a proper historian's respect for it. With so profound a historian looking on, Augustine was a very strong presence from the past to initiate such vital lessons.

In May of 1962 I came to the final exams. Alas, I had lost my beginner's assurance with the total recall of everything I set myself to learn. I felt myself now making heavy weather in the preparations. I then found that I could no longer dash off those sparkling forty-five-minute epitomes of the given subject that had carried me so high in my first time round at UCT. I don't think I came out of one exam having answered four questions properly. My result was not the expected First but a 2A. (Kind Christopher

Hill, going over his transcript of results, said I had first-class marks all over the place, but not enough of them. "You must be the top 2A!" he declared.)

Christopher's opinion, and that of others, then saved me for a career in history. I had formed a close friendship in Oxford with a remarkable bluff, burly Australian. That friendship was in itself an important extension of my education in history. Felix Raab had been born in Vienna in 1934 to a Jewish father and a convert mother. They got away in 1939 on one of the last trains allowed to take out Jews; this was also a brief interlude when Australia was giving visas to such refugees. Thereafter, Felix grew up consciously identifying as an Aussie. He learned to speak a broad vernacular and during the war would scold his parents for their continued use of Viennese German: "Why must you speak that spy language?" Indeed, I gained my command of a Melbourne vulgar tongue and a multitude of jokes to go with it while still in Oxford!

Felix had had a long and checkered career before he came to Oxford to research and write a D.Phil. thesis on the English reception of Machiavelli's political thought. I spent a lot of time enjoying hospitality and conversation at the flat he shared with his remarkable English wife, Camilla. Like Felix she was an ex-communist as well as a devotee of folksong. I learned much about both early modern and very recent Australian and European history in that warm association. My new friend's old identity and his newer one as an intellectual of the far Left, were indeed important extensions of my historical education. This was also my first intimate acquaintance with a major historical research project: I listened as Felix reported his finds in the Bodleian Library's collections of old tracts and manuscripts; I shared his anxious planning of the chapters that he determinedly wrote—one per term. The association with Felix and Camilla was, I suppose, my informal substitute for history graduate school—which is, at best, not just a period of instruction from elder scholars but also a time of interaction with fellow apprentices to the profession.

It was Felix who took me in hand as I came to the end of my Oxford course and looked uncertainly at what would be next for me. "I'll tell you what's next! You're coming to Melbourne, mate!" He knew I would have Christopher Hill's support, and that this—along with his own recommendation—would enable God-professor John LaNauze, a.k.a. Jack the Knife, to have the University of Melbourne Registrar send me a letter of appointment as a lecturer. There was nothing very unusual about this; in the British Empire of that time, young men considered promising (always men) usually went to their first appointments from the bachelor degree, provided they had an "old-boy" recommendation from their tutors. I must have been one of the last to get my start in that old Oxbridge way; soon after that an American-style insistence on professional Ph.D. certification became the rule.

So my first appointment as a historian was effected. My sweetheart and I converted a budding romance into an engagement. Colleen Malherbe and I were married in South Africa on our way to Melbourne. She became and has truly remained my constant source of encouragement in dark hours, a frequent enthusiastic research assistant, and the sternest reader of my first drafts. Coming from a mixed marriage of South African Huguenot descent on one side and the British Raj on the other, she brought in many valuable perspectives to open out my historian's tunnel vision. Besides, she has a master's degree in English and American literature and is a very talented writer of short stories.

By early 1963 when Colleen and I were headed Down Under, both my parents and my sister were part of the new-start Africa in an about-to-be-independent Kenya colony. My twin brother was there too with Barbara Miller, his English wife; Glynn and she were starting together their great work on the African origins of human society as we know it. Part of Colleen's and my honeymoon was indeed shared with my twin and his newlywed bride. Experience of the new Africa was thus part of my historian's education as I made my start as a professional in a fast-changing world.

*   *   *

My next steps from apprentice to journeyman historian did not come easily. My arrival as a tenured lecturer was a break indeed—a job for life. (In that place and time there would be no tenure review.) But I was either going to find for myself a way into publishable research work or be forever defensive about what must be a mounting if silent reproach. Once you are a lecturer you have joined the grown-ups; you must make your own way without a sponsor to depend upon. And now, suddenly, my warmest sponsor from Melbourne was gone. Felix had completed his D.Phil. and gone to Italy on holiday; while hiking, he fell off a mist-bound Calabrian mountainside. Camilla turned his dissertation into a seminal book—*The English Face of Machiavelli*—but Felix as colleague and supporter was no more; the loss was terrible. Felix's parents, Leo and Marianne Raab, welcomed Colleen and me as their children; I was a surrogate for the only son—only child—who did not return. (That was another history lesson—a window on the once-charmed world of interwar Vienna, about which Leo spoke continually with loving affection, although it had expelled him as it turned into nightmare.) My colleagues in the History Department made me most welcome, but they could only put me to work in the teaching that best matched my training. English history was well covered, so I was slotted into "Modern European"—which, in Melbourne, meant politics from the French Revolution until the outbreak of the Second World War.

I could read French, and I tried to make my intensifying knowledge of French history the basis for a research project; but after some four years spent without getting a purchase on that, my attention turned to a question that most French historians have not cared to ask. In what ways, beyond bankrupting the royal government through its participation in the War of Independence, did the bursting on the Atlantic world of the first modern republic spark off the French Revolution? Here was a researchable topic, especially if I gave it a precise focus. I had been helped to an understanding of the possibilities of this topic by the very fortunate return to Australia of Paul Bourke. He had defied the Oxford orientation of the Melbourne department by insisting on doing his further training with Merle Curti at the University of Wisconsin; he brought back something at odds with the gentleman-amateurism of the Oxbridge tradition. Paul had a strong sense of historical professionalism, together with a comprehensive knowledge of U.S. historiography. Out of my conversations with Paul, I resolved to study the role of Thomas Jefferson as a go-between from the American to the French Revolution. I was especially drawn to this topic for two reasons: it transcended "national" historiographies (R. R. Palmer's *Age of the Democratic Revolution* was my model), and it fed a theoretical interest I already had in the processes of overturn—with Thomas Kuhn's *Structure of Scientific Revolutions* supplying the paradigm.

I quickly came to the conclusion that, culminating in the work of Bernard Bailyn, American Revolution historiography had attained more sophistication than its French counterpart. Bailyn's model of a worldview with early warning system supplied an intellectual-cultural framework to explain unity in difference between the very diverse thirteen colonies. I knew that the innumerable provinces of France, with their infinitely complex cross-cutting social stratifications, posed a similar challenge that I had never seen effectively taken up by historians of the French Revolution.

I would not myself undertake the task of rectifying the deficiencies in the French explanatory systems, but I would go into Jefferson's Virginia to try to understand what sources of angst might lurk there. What conflicts might have been calling for resolution by revolutionary paradigms? In time I came to feel that the particular circumstances of my long years of upbringing and preparing to be a historian had fitted me for this task. I had learned at Oxford that I was "a colonial"—as the English called all of us, Americans included. My imagination of history had early been drawn to wide landscapes, and I empathized with what I came to call "cultural provincialism." Indeed I had lived all my life in places that perceived the center of high culture to reside in a metropolis far away—a phenomenon whose intensity most American historians of the colonial and early national periods fail to appreciate. What is more, as a student in South Africa and then as a young scholar in Australia, I had been a part of that second, post-1776 British Empire as it experienced the independence movements that have gradually, and without revolution, pulled it apart.

At last, after my awkward six-year apprenticeship of casting about for a topic, I had arrived at a focused research project, and the time was right, because in 1969, my first one-year sabbatical came due. Professor Max Crawford, esteemed builder of the greatness of the Melbourne Department and revered academic foster father to Felix Raab, put me in touch with the Newberry Library in Chicago. I was given a grant-in-aid for three months to get started in that great research collection. From there I went on to Brown University to converse with Gordon Wood, author of "Rhetoric and Reality in the American Revolution." I shared with him a draft article written out of the rich printed primary sources that had suddenly become available to me. Gordon put me in touch with Jack Greene, who also read the draft. The good fairy gives three wishes; Jack gave three commands! "First: You *must* go immediately to Virginia to do the manuscript archival work needed to make this complete and publishable! Second: I have told the American Philosophical Society that it *must* give you a grant for this purpose! And third: On your way, you *must* come by my place in Baltimore, so we can become acquainted!" Out of that did indeed come my first monograph article—"Religion and Authority"—published in the *William & Mary Quarterly* in 1973.

My induction into the company of Early American historians was already under way. There had been a bonus opportunity to get in on the ground floor of the latest initiatives. In February–March of 1970, soon after I had joined Gordon Wood in Providence, he had insisted—against organizer resistance—that he bring his young Aussie mate to a small conference organized at Brandeis. The meeting was to review the state of Early American social history on the morrow of the publication of what were simply called "the books." (The *Annales* School had lately crossed the Atlantic in the demographic inspiration of a trio of New England town studies—Kenneth Lockridge's Dedham, Philip Greven's Andover, and John Demos's Plymouth.) Once there, I met and interacted with a great assemblage of the talent in the field—and when I told Jack Greene of the excitement in it all, he devised a fourth imperative! He told Robert K. Webb, the editor of the *American Historical Review*, that he *must* commission me to write a review of "the books"!

In May 1970 commenced one of the more memorable journeys of my life: from Providence, Rhode Island, I went on my first trip to Virginia. We had no money for airfares or even Amtrak, so I rode on a series of great iron steeds—which is how I thought of the mighty Greyhound buses. Here I was, being swept along toward the land whose name and the names of the places within it had for months filled my waking and I dare say sleeping dreams. My anticipation was keen all the way and came to an excited fulfillment as that big old bus rolled over the bridge across the Potomac. Now the highway signs began to carry those place names—Pohick (George Washington's parish church), Occoquan (an early Separate Baptist meeting house in the Northern Neck), Hanover Court House (the site of Patrick Henry's Parsons' Cause speech). At Richmond I had to change and travel by a local bus down Route 5. Can I ever forget the landscape experience of the lovely low-bridge crossing of the magically named Chickahominy River? There was the oak forest with its feet in the tidewater! Then suddenly we were at the bus depot beside the old railway station of Williamsburg. Was it then or later that I took note of the great fading sign on the other side of the tracks? In my mind's eye I can see it still—an arrow pointing westward with the once black, now grey lettering underneath: "Trains—to Richmond and Beyond."

Jack Greene had called Thad Tate; I was booked into an old lodging house on Jamestown Road—once again a name! As soon as I'd checked in, I was off to see the wonders of the restored town. That was a thrill beyond my imagining. I took in the beauty of the Duke of Gloucester Street with the College of William and Mary at the end where I was lodging, and the Capitol completing the vista a short mile away to the east. I was for the moment captive to the romanticized colonial evocation that was the

Williamsburg of that time. The houses along the street and around the two great greens enchanted me for their combination of warm-colored brickwork and white-painted wooden siding and trim. My imagination had already been locked into this place before I left Providence and the John Carter Brown Library. There I had read all the colonial numbers of the weekly *Virginia Gazette*; and now the past from the pages of the old newspapers was all around me. Williamsburg was bringing on my vocation to write history as a dramaturgy imagined in the settings and the landscapes of its enactments. (In time, a close association with material-culture specialist Barbara Carson and her husband, Cary, Colonial Williamsburg's young new director of research, gave me both theoretical and practical encouragement in the use of buildings and furnishings as vital historical documents.)

Needing no encouragement, I nevertheless got much. At "the Institute," as I already knew to call what is now the Omohundro Institute of Early American History and Culture, I was warmly welcomed by the director, Stephen Kurtz, by the editor of the *William & Mary Quarterly*, Thad Tate, and by Norman Fiering, then the research fellow. (Norman would soon be editor of publications—and in time my editor.) No doubt they were amazed by this young Australian who had suddenly showed up all effervescent with excitement at being in the heart of old colonial Virginia.

I also got the welcome I absolutely needed at the research library of the Colonial Williamsburg Foundation. It was then on the corner of Francis and Henry Streets, in a house that had been built in the early-twentieth-century as the home of the superintendent of the mental hospital that had been situated just across the road since 1772. The library's rooms were stacked high with reference books, and many great steel cabinets full of microfilms. After the Rockefeller restoration and rebuilding of Williamsburg a massive project had been initiated; cameras had been sent into archives on both sides of the Atlantic wherever records relating to colonial Virginia might be found. Jack Greene had advised me to start there: the staff would give me a key to the house so I could work around the clock. Taking very little time off for meals or sleep, I combed those records before I went on to the much-less permissively managed archives that held the manuscripts themselves. I wish I could say that I now remember whose handwriting was there in brown ink on paper aged creamy yellow; but I do recall the reverential sense of a new level of deep communion with the past as I opened that first folder and gazed at that first autograph letter.

That library house in which I spent so many hours of my first stay in Williamsburg became my home for one last weekend. I had moved on to Richmond and Charlottesville; in those places I had seen and taken notes from the manuscripts relevant to my project, and I had also formed in my head the outline of the article that could finally be written at last. Now it was Thursday, I was out of time and money and due to return to Providence, where we must pack up to return to Australia. When possibly could that outline in my head become a draft on paper? I formed a desperate plan. I phoned Colleen and said I could not be back until Monday night; then I took a Friday bus back to Williamsburg, applied for the key again, and—having no money for lodgings—I camped in the library while I wrote my draft article round the clock. By the small hours of Monday it was done. Legend now has it that Cary Carson, when he became director, set up a plaque behind the door: "Rhys Isaac slept here."

My involvement at last in archival research and cutting-edge historical scholarship soon involved me in another forward leap. As I developed my first Virginia revolution research, I had been conscious of working the line between the words of the polemical printed pages and the in-real-life situations that alone gave relevance to those printed pages. I began to mutter that history until this time had been just "words about words." I wanted to break out of that closed circle and to fix rather on what—in the positive side of this Young-Turk mantra—I called "people doing things." Doubtless with the early inspiration of Monica Wilson propelling me, I sensed that this way of understanding the past would take me toward the observational methods of social-cultural anthropology. And I was soon helped forward in that. While I was away from Melbourne University, the newly founded LaTrobe University advertised some lectureships in history, fields unspecified. That was where I now wanted to go; indeed I had started attending research seminars there, and found myself drawn to the energy and camaraderie that the new department's founding chair, Allan Martin, was fostering, as he encouraged the boldness of starting something new. I applied and was promptly appointed. I returned from my year away to start at LaTrobe in the middle of the academic year; my principal assignment was to join with Greg Dening in the Theory and Method seminar offered to the department's very first History IV (honors) class. Greg was a historian newly trained in anthropology at Harvard, so I now had a mentor; I had a fellow apprentice in the person of Inga Clendinnen who had also joined this seminar. Since Inga's daily drive to work from her home in the suburb of Kew passed close by my house, she would pick me up. "Kew Taxis," we called it, and we shared and debated our readings of interdisciplinary discovery as we went; that was my second informal history graduate school.

Together in the next few years, Greg, Inga, and I worked out the principles and the practices of our distinctive versions of a generic type of "ethnographic history." It is hard to define those principles and the practices, and perhaps I favor my own formulation too much when I suggest that finding ways to observe "people doing things" in the past was at the heart of it. Certainly attention to the rhetoric of gesture was big in all our work—but then we had learned so much not just from Peter Berger and Thomas Luckmann's *Social Construction of Reality* but also from Erving Goffman's schematic ethnographies of interaction. Our quest was a search for culture as a system of conventions endlessly inflected in performances that ethnographic historians must try to appreciate as an insider might—while knowing that they never can attain such an insider understanding. The genre of the work we came out doing was recognizable enough for the late Clifford Geertz to use it as a talking point in an essay he wrote on "History and Anthropology." He called us "the Melbourne Group," and he even signed the off-prints that he sent us of that article: "Your man in Princeton."

At LaTrobe also I was caught up in endeavors to find new and more effective ways of educating our undergraduates. Many were from recent-migrant backgrounds; soon others were mature-age women and men. (After its election in 1972, Gough Whitlam's dynamic Labor government introduced funding reforms, including free university tuition; this enabled LaTrobe to invite persons over twenty-five to enroll as part-time students so as to take the college courses denied them in the more austere economic environment of their youth.) I thus spent this part of my professional life trying, in conversation with my colleagues and students, to develop ways of teaching that would bring to our classes the special sense of inclusive history that we were seeking in our research. We hoped to make history a vital study in the busy and troubled world from which our students certainly came. Could I help them return to that world better prepared for further participation? We academics make much of research—and rightly so, for it is what makes the university *be* what it *must* be—but I am ready to assert that our real social product is ultimately not so much our research as our students.

Meanwhile, on the research front, my zeal for a history that was not just words about words was already strong when I got an assignment to participate in a Williamsburg conference on religion and the American Revolution. Here was the first great opportunity to apply my version of the action-observation ethnographic approach. I would explore the clash of cultures that was mounting in Virginia as an invasion of religious radicals from New England started to set the backcountry on fire. I would show the distinctive insurgent New Light Baptist forms of action and implied cosmology; I would show the traditional gentry-led, old ways with a very different cosmology. This essay was crucial since it served as the launching pad for the larger ethnographic history of the religious and political revolutions in Virginia that I was now resolved to write.

In the course of writing that essay, I came to a realization of what must be the paradigm for the larger ethnographic history that would be my first book. I would not just observe people doing things, I would proceed as though I was writing the stage directions for the actions: the set, the costumes, the props must be specified. And so as I entered that project, I arrived at a paradigmatic understanding that all particular settings were situated in a larger, comprehensive past landscape. I came to the view that the most revealing document of itself that any society creates is its built environment—its total organization of terrain to create the settings for the forms of action by which it both lives and understands itself. That was the model—or rather the metaphor—that began to direct the assemblage of pencil-drafts-become-typescripts that would be melded eventually into *The Transformation of Virginia, 1740–1790*. My first book was at last published in 1982. Landscape in this paradigm is not mere terrain; it is terrain shaped and reshaped by changing culturally specific uses.

Landscape in the usage I was establishing resides less in physical forms than in the meanings that those culturally shaped forms have for the inhabitants. The first part of the book showed the colonial landscape that the English (and the Africans) made, largely in erasure of the one from which the Algonquian Indians had been expelled. The focus was on the stage settings created for characteristic rituals and social dramas—the church, the courthouse, and indeed all the homes of the gentry, the common planters, and the enslaved. In the second part I engaged with the profoundly changed meanings that any real revolution must produce. I would strive to show novel settings such as the New Light preachers' stumps in the fields where the great mass revivals began; I would also show how the old settings acquired new meanings from new forms of action—such as the courthouses of the monarchy becoming the places of republican elections that had become expressive of the sovereignty of the people. Finally

I added a "Discourse on the Method." This explained systematically the "dramaturgic ethnography" that has been my way of being anthropologist to the past. I had deliberately not obstructed with methodology the narratives designed to be a user-friendly history.

Looking back now, I can also see how much the book was of its time; it was a history of a previous great revolution that reflected the making-the-world-anew revolutionary optimism of the civil rights era and the movement against the Vietnam War. In 1969, while I was at the Newberry Library just starting my American research, Colleen and I, with our toddler daughters in back-carry-packs, had stepped out in the Chicago Moratorium March.

Then there was an unexpected moment for my book in the Australian limelight. LaTrobe University had its moment of glory out of the distinctive kind of history that it had early fostered. The Columbia School of Journalism was not in the way of lavishing its Pulitzer endowment funds on phone calls or telegrams to the recipients of its prizes; the awards are mostly in journalism, and so the School lets the news networks of the world carry the tidings. Thus it was that one day in April 1983, the Public Relations Office of my university got a call from the Channel 10 newsroom saying that one Rhys Isaac of LaTrobe University was listed as winner of the "Prize in History." I was teaching a class when the chair of my department came to fetch me. This really started as a bad moment. I thought as he hovered in the open door that he must be bringing news of some disaster to my family. But no: he called me out, told me of the award, told my class, and then dismissed the cheering students. Next he told me to scrub up fast—the Channel 10 Eye-Witness-News helicopter would be landing on campus within minutes for an interview. Soon—with news anchorman mediating—I had my less-than-fifteen minutes of fame! I had even to learn about "noddies"—the footage of the interviewee just nodding in response to nothing; a crew with only one camera must shoot these after the interview for later insertion as needed in the editing process.

*   *   *

My brother and I seemed to reach a career pinnacle almost simultaneously at this time. Glynn had just been appointed to a prestigious chair at Harvard, and was on a train in Europe going to give an important lecture in the Netherlands when, reading the Paris edition of the *Herald Tribune*, he learned of the award. He was thus immediately able to send ecstatic

congratulations. That was to be the last such communication. Not long after, when his global connections in the field of human evolution took him
to visit important fossil sites in China, he succumbed to a sudden flare
up of a virulent form of malaria contracted in tropical Africa. Harvard
enlisted the U.S. Secretary of Defense to have him airlifted toward the
most advanced medical aid, but it was too late. He left a stricken wife and
daughters, as well as devastated old parents, and the grieving sister who
had had to break the news to them. I was in the air, having been suddenly
informed of the crisis and involved by Harvard in last attempts to pull
Glynn through. But I could not reach him in time to join his wife Barbara
at his side. Our last communication had been by phone. The shock to us all
was overwhelming. For weeks, feeling cut in half, I found that every time
I talked I heard his voice in mine. (Our speech had been truly identical;
even our wives could not tell us apart if they only heard but did not see.)

All Glynn's dearest ones have continued on in the way that people
can who are inspired by the one they lost. For me, the way forward was
slow and very difficult. *The Transformation of Virginia* was a hard act to
follow—although I had already embarked on my new project when the
Pulitzer was announced. I have to acknowledge that my own next project
took me into an approach that could be decried as words about words and
certainly as the history of an elite dead white male. Like other historians
of Revolutionary Virginia, I had found and used the eccentric but very
revealing narratives in an extraordinary diary kept by a planter grandee
in Northern Virginia from 1752 to 1778. Unlike those other historians I
resolved that I would not just use little pieces of Colonel Landon Carter's
diary for immediate purposes; I would study the diary in its entirety for
the ethnography of its author's world that might then be carefully pieced
together. In that way I hoped still to be faithful to my calling as an anthropologist to the past.

I had begun my Landon Carter researches during a year in Princeton
as a Shelby Cullom Davis Fellow. There was the mighty Clifford Geertz,
whose essays in *The Interpretation of Cultures* had so inspired the Melbourne Group and me in our early steps toward a historical ethnography.
Of more consequence for the trajectory of this next work was the introduction Geertz gave me to Alton Becker. Pete, as his acquaintances call
him, was a linguist specializing in Burmese, Javanese, Malay, and Balinese,
ancient and modern; more important he was a profound thinker about the
nature of language and the work of translation—which we might acknowledge to be at the heart of everything that historians seek to do. "Words

about words?"—Pete taught me about really reading that complex diary. He made me attentive to genres and rhetorical forms, not least the art of the storyteller in which the diarist excelled. Those concerns involved me in a critical review of action-oriented ethnographic history. I do still affirm its value; but I came to know that I must also acknowledge that historians see nothing for themselves. They *make* their stories from the stories (told or implied) that they *find* in the archives. We thus need to be very attentive to the versions of the world that organized the stories in the past, and to the corresponding versions organizing the historians' recycling of those stories in their own present time.

With digressions to undertake other assignments, I spent twenty years learning to read that diary so as to plot its stories against histories of its own fast-moving times. To start with, I became at last a historian of science. The plantation diary, from its inception in 1757 with the words "Farming Observations etc.," was an Enlightenment natural philosophy of daily and seasonal work in the fields. Considerations of health and sickness must also loom large in the operation of a country estate with a complex household at its center. With some hundred enslaved men, women, and children in the vicinity, and with a scientifically minded record keeper, the diary was also a very extensive record of medical practice. I did a great deal of research into mid-eighteenth century cosmologies—the theories of sun, rain, earth, and the growth of plants. Likewise I made a study of the medical diagnoses and therapies of this period. All that had to be boiled down into two small but important chapters, although I could enlarge somewhat in a third chapter that cried out to be written. Alongside the diary itself there was a heavily annotated library that had survived in the big estate house whose construction Colonel Carter had overseen in the 1730s when he commenced housekeeping and farming on his own. From the marginalia in that precious set of books there could be richly reconstructed the learned cosmology of this very literary provincial gentleman.

As I entered into the possibilities opened by the close study of this assemblage of texts, I followed out an ethnographic historian's imperative to attend closely to the numerous stories I found. These included frequent sometimes folkloric, sometimes novelistic narratives of family quarrels and outrageous betrayals; there were also endless stories of enslaved workers' delinquencies and conspiracies. I subjected them all to systematic readings for genre, tradition, and mode of discourse; I even discovered the hitherto unnamed genre of "gentrylore"—the stories that lords of labor have told each other for eight or nine thousand years, ever since the beginnings of agriculture inaugurated the hierarchies, inequalities, and oppressions of civilization. (In this I was, I believe, subjecting the WASP male to the anthropological analysis that has most usually been applied only to the poor and powerless. Were I to be naming the genre now, I would use a designation less narrowly English in its allusions—"masterlore.")

In the course of the long time of my work on this body of documents, I also came to the realization that the twenty-year series of diaries had an unconscious overall narrative structure that synchronized with the diarist's participation in the bringing on and climaxing of the American Revolution. In 1765–66—the year of the Stamp Act—Colonel Carter and his peers went into revolt against the government of their king; in that year his diary began for the first time to be interlarded with outraged narratives of revolts in his own little plantation kingdom. When, in 2004, Oxford University Press published my *Landon Carter's Uneasy Kingdom: Revolution and Rebellion on a Virginia Plantation*, I hoped I had done something to extend anthropologizing history into the ethnography of those paper artifacts we call "documents"—the written performances that are the historians' principal access to the forms of past human social life.

During the time of completing the Landon Carter book I retired from my teaching post at LaTrobe University; new possibilities opened up. My graduate student teaching had been limited—although I had enjoyed my many opportunities informally to mentor generations of mainly Australian history research students. Over all those years I had been able to supervise only two doctoral students—Gwynedd Hunter and Ronald Southern, both very challenging and rewarding scholars to work with. I now had opportunities to extend mentoring relationships through more frequent appointments in the United States. This happened during a fellowship at the John Carter Brown Library and then—more long-term—through an appointment in the College of William & Mary's History and American Studies programs. During this time the fire of my zeal for the history of Virginia has not diminished; I have involved myself with colleagues in a Colonial Williamsburg Foundation project to write what we call the Big Book of Williamsburg. The aim is to draw on the vast research the museum has done over some eighty years to tell the eighteenth-century role of this place as center of power and oppression, of fashion, aesthetics, and ideas. This work has also brought me very special new friends—such as George and Joan Morrow—with whom I delight in sharing my undiminished zeal.

My 2002 Williamsburg appointment was actually due to a Congressionally funded National Institute of American History and Democracy, jointly operated by William & Mary and the Colonial Williamsburg Foundation. In this working environment I have become more deeply involved in an aspect of being a historian that I believe to be scandalously neglected by academic historians—when it is not even more scandalously scorned—namely "public history." This is the professional endeavor of those who seek to bring the findings of academic historians to interested fellow citizens and their children. I have worked the last five years in an intermediary role between the old college and the big museum. My teaching has thus lately engaged me intensely with history as stories that museum educators and documentary filmmakers find to popularize, drawing on the stories we academic historians have taken from the archives. This engagement has also involved me and my students more explicitly with the moral aspects of doing history.

*   *   *

Becoming and practicing as a historian, I could only "get by with a little bit of help from my friends"—actually a lot of help. I have been most fortunate in the doors that were opened to me by generous persons who believed in what I might do. I have also been fortunate in the excitements I found behind those doors in the chambers of the many-mansioned house of history. Though retired from any appointment in the academy, I mean still to research and write and to find whatever ways I can to open doors for younger aspirants now coming forward. Furthermore, I find that the issues of public history have an increasing urgency for me. How shall we academics so tell the inspiring and the terrible deeds that appear in the record as to render our work a contribution to the making of a better future for our world?

JOAN WALLACH SCOTT

Finding Critical History

There are so many ways to tell this story, so many reasons I could give for having ended up in history. But one thing is certain: I was never in love with Clio. Facts, events, causality weren't compelling. I wasn't one of those kids who devour books about wars or the lives of the famous, though I read my share of exemplary biographies borrowed, along with novels and fairy tales, from the Eastern Parkway branch of the Brooklyn Public Library. History was something I learned well, but so also were biology and algebra and most other subjects. I was a good student and I usually got high grades, more because of a need to be good than because of the appeal of any particular body of knowledge. I don't think I knew, in those days, what intellectual passion meant; school was about the acqui-sition of skills and information and the ability to use them to prove some-thing about myself: that I was bright, capable, smart, that I could excel at most things and so please my parents, make them proud, earn their love.

*　　*　　*

It might be said that since my parents were high school history teachers it was inevitable that I would become a historian, moving up the profes-sional ladder they had begun to climb as children of East European im-migrants. They had college degrees, I got a Ph.D.; they taught history, I wrote history; their love of the subject nurtured mine. But I don't think that's exactly right. My father taught history and economics because he'd been told as a student at Brooklyn Technical High School that there wouldn't be jobs as engineers for Jews. At City College in New York in the late 1920s, it was Marxism that called. The story of the past served to illuminate the theory. And it was the theory—a way of seeing how economic relations determined social ones—that he wanted to instill in me, along with his faith in inevitable progress, in the redemptive power of history. I don't know why my mother chose history. All I remember is that she loved to teach. Her stories at the dinner table were about how she'd finally won over a sullen girl or figured out how to explain some difficult idea to a skeptical boy. Or about how she'd thwarted mischief; rescued a favorite but troubled student; converted a bigot; convinced a colleague to join the union. From my mother's example I learned that teaching was a form of activism: the transmission of knowledge for a purpose beyond itself, a purpose animated by caring relationships and politics, shaping the way kids thought about the world in order to make it a better place.

*   *   *

Surely, then, it was politics that drew me to history. Perhaps that's true, but only if you stretch the connection, only if you think that I took literally the injunction to change the world. In our family doing politics was the most obvious way to "make history." Long before my father was fired in 1953, he told us bedtime stories about bunny rabbits (black and white together) on strike. My lullabies were "Joe Hill" and "Union Maid." If his firing was meant as a warning to other radicals in the heat of the cold war, for us his refusal to name names, his proud invocation of the democratic ideals of the American Revolution, made him a hero to emulate. In response to a reporter's question after his testimony at a House subcommittee hearing: "Don't you know that you placed your job in jeopardy?" he famously replied, "Those guys placed the Constitution in jeopardy; that worries me more." The moral imperative in many Red Diaper families was to vindicate one's parents by following in their political footsteps. One of my persistent fantasies was that I would be, as I put it on the psychological personality assessment questionnaire I filled out as a freshman at Brandeis, "a leader of men."

*   *   *

Perhaps, you might say, writing history was a fallback position, what one reached for when politics turned out to be disappointing or thwarted or too hard; when it became clear that power would resist our yearnings for peace and justice and equality (always my wishes as I blew out my birthday candles); when progress no longer seemed inevitable and revolutionary struggle yielded results more complex than our utopian imaginings had promised. I don't think that's right either. Not only because I decided to become a historian in the heat of my own political activism in the 1960s, but also because I continue to think of myself as politically engaged. Becoming a historian was not a consolation for politics, but a companion to it. Though not an inevitable one.

*   *   *

So then, why history? It might just as well have been literature. The first real excitement I remember as a student was in an AP English class at Midwood High School. Mr. Schlakman taught us how to read. Using the classic texts of the New Criticism, Brooks and Warren's *Understanding Poetry* and *Understanding Literature*, we learned about metaphors and symbols, the ways language could signify and figures represent. Deciphering those texts was the hardest work I'd ever been asked to do. I didn't do it well at first, but learning how to do it was the most fun I'd ever had. There were secrets to be uncovered, mysteries to be solved, meanings to be unraveled. And no answer was final. There was always something more to ponder. The joy was in the chase. Now I can say that this was a formative moment in the linking of knowledge and desire; then I said I loved my English class.

The next class I loved was Frank Manuel's. The legendary historian of ideas at Brandeis thundered his interpretations of the great moments of Western civilization. The tone was authoritative, but I somehow understood there was more to uncover where he worked. Manuel was a terrifying figure. His empty trouser leg—we speculated endlessly about how he'd lost his leg—swaying as he led us down intricate and difficult pathways. I followed one course after another. We read the canonical texts of European political thought line by line. And though I never dared speak in class or to him, I was hooked. In what might have been a challenge to my father's teachings, I began to see the importance of ideas. It was less their world historical import that mattered to me than it was the pleasure of pursuing them. Alice following the rabbit into unknown, unforeseen territory. Thrilled.

The courses at Brandeis I still remember were like that, the ones where doors opened and new ideas emerged. Most of these were in history or sociology; few were in literature—the accident of who was teaching there at the time. At home, Oedipal battles were fueled by ideas. When I had outargued my father he'd resort to moralism. I knew even then that moralism was the enemy of desire.

In those days of distribution requirements and the early declaration of majors, I chose history. Even in courses I didn't like, I picked research topics that were about the history of ideas. Except for my senior thesis, a silly, banal study of the Revolution of 1848 in France, offered to me by a professor who preferred diplomacy and politics to intellectual history. I arrived at Brandeis with French as my foreign language, having had a particularly good teacher in junior high school. In European history courses I tended to research French topics because I could read the language. In retrospect, I don't fully understand my passivity. Many of my fellow students wrote on the likes of Nietzsche, Marx, and Freud. That I didn't suggests that I hadn't fully realized that the pleasure I found in certain courses was mine to pursue. I attributed it to the courses; I didn't see how it could come from me, how I could choose it.

Anyway, my calling in those years was politics. I was still the dutiful daughter of political parents, seeking my fulfillment in their pleasure (or someone who was a substitute for them), or finding mine in an extension of theirs. I wrote for the student newspaper, joined picket lines at Woolworths, organized ban the bomb petitions and rallies–became that "leader of men" I'd said I wanted to be. During one of the international crises of the early 1960s, Herbert Marcuse thrust some money into my hands, urging me to "organize something," which, with my equally activist roommate, I did.

*   *   *

But what I've said about parental pressures to engage in politics isn't exactly right either. If there was an expectation that I'd act to hasten history's inevitable forward motion, there was also an assumption that I'd acquire a profession, and not just any profession. Because I was raised, too, with a reverence for scholarship and learning that dedicated teachers inspire

in their own children as well as in their students. That was part of the reason I'd always been a good student; the value placed on academic achievement was very high. Even higher, perhaps, in families like mine (many
teachers were, like my father, fired in the 1950s), because the child's success was seen as a vindication of the father's principles; the deprivation of
his vocation would be rectified by the accomplishment of hers.

I had always expected to become a high school teacher, a career that
became less appealing, less inevitable, as I glimpsed worlds of scholarship I hadn't been aware of before college. The possibilities for women
in higher education were opening in 1962—the year of my graduation. In
fact, much later when I was doing research for an article on American
women historians, I realized that my choices were determined in large part
by the circumstances of those years. An expanding economy and a growing population led to forecasts of a huge increase in college students. To
meet the anticipated demand for teachers, it became clear that women
would have to be recruited. To recruit us, there were some token fellowships and lots of informal advice. The professor who had supervised my
senior thesis suggested I consider graduate school in history. And, lacking
any other serious options, *faute de mieux*, as they say in French, I com-
plied. My acceptance of history had some of the features of an arranged
marriage: wiser adults, whose judgment I had no reason to doubt, urged
me on. There was nothing repellent or unworthy about the match; indeed
I had already glimpsed its pleasurable possibilities. But pleasure was not
passion; that would take many years of learning, both about history and
myself.

*   *   *

Although I applied to the University of Wisconsin blindly and for reasons having little to do with professional ambition, it turned out to be a
wise choice. Madison was a thriving center of political thought and action.
The journal *Studies on the Left* was edited there; courses offered by William Appleman Williams drew graduate students who wanted a radical take
on American foreign policy; since the days of John R. Commons Wisconsin had been a center for the study of labor relations; and the legal scholar
Alexander Meiklejohn had, well before my time, identified the school
with advocacy for civil liberties and academic freedom. I didn't know
much of this when I decided to go there and I was startled, and even a
little disappointed, when I arrived to find it teeming with the children of

trade unionists, socialists, and communists. I had hoped to leave home in some definitive way and this felt too much like home. Still, I joined the ranks of activists. There was a lot to do in those years from 1962, when I got there, until 1967, when I left to do dissertation research in France. We organized to support Freedom Riders in the south, rallied against the Vietnam War, spent hours arguing about strategy and tactics in demanding and sophisticated ways, and balanced our course work with our politics. At Wisconsin I saw more clearly that scholarship and politics could be linked: it was especially Williams's course and the graduate students in his seminar who set the example. And yet I did not become a Williams student.

Part of the reason was that I was assigned to a seminar in French history by the chair of the department, American historian Merrill Jensen. Jensen thought that women would destroy the collegiality he so enjoyed with his male students and so he took few of them and, I suspect, he acted to protect his fellow Americanists from having their seminars corrupted by the disturbing presence of the fair sex. When in our initial interview I responded to his question about languages that I had French and had written a senior thesis on 1848, he put me in the modern French history seminar. In those days, one was assigned to the same seminar for the entire time in grad school; getting into a different one was difficult and, political activist that I was, I was still remarkably passive about scholarly choices.

But that's not the only reason. I think I wanted to stay away from American history because my parents had done it, because there was a family line I knew I would be expected to toe. Independence would be easier to achieve on different soil, in a different language. So I did not take up French history for love of it, which is not say it wasn't rich and compelling as a field of study.

What I did love in those years were the classes in American intellectual history taught by William R. Taylor. Himself influenced by New Criticism and by Ruben Brower's courses at Amherst that emphasized interpretive reading, Taylor led us through one hermeneutic circle after another. We read novels and philosophical texts always attending to language: to the way metaphors were deployed and narratives woven, to the symbolic work of figures of speech and the manner in which tension and contradiction were managed. I can still remember how I felt confronting some of his exam questions: invited to explore, excited at what I could see, filled with a rush of creativity that didn't happen anywhere else. In retrospect I think this is the true experience of sublimation, not so much a substitute for physical sex as an erotics of knowledge for its own sake. That I married one of Taylor's graduate students seems no accident, even though the reasons for romance are many and overdetermined: we were both turned on by the pleasures of Taylor's way of thinking and teaching, something we still share though we are no longer husband and wife.

Taylor's pedagogy made a difference too; his questions were open-ended and he sought to elicit students' reactions to texts. He was more provocative than authoritative; it was not mastery, but discovery that he was after. His teaching assistants were instructed in the method—teaching was an intellectual challenge on a par with their own research—and they became remarkably skillful at creating communities of interpretation among their undergraduates. The best teaching I've done has been modeled on those courses.

*   *   *

I didn't become a Taylor student, but his influence had an important effect on the direction of my work in French history. It happened the year my dissertation advisor, Harvey Goldberg, was on leave. In Goldberg's seminar we were all being trained to be biographers of French socialist and labor leaders, following in Harvey's footsteps—he had written a biography of Jean Jaurès. We met in a stifling, windowless room in the basement, with stark white walls and harsh neon lights. The combination of Goldberg's narcissism and the heroic narratives we were expected to produce week after week made me restless and rebellious. For my paper on Paul Lafargue (Marx's son-in-law and the author of *The Right to be Lazy*), I attempted a textual exegesis à la Taylor, which won only scorn from the professor. Goldberg walked into the room, threw my paper down on the table and commented caustically that this was an example of how not to write history. I was not completely crushed; instead I was confirmed in my wish to somehow escape, but not entirely. I wanted Harvey's approval despite my fury at his response to my paper. The psychology was complex: I was seeking approval for behavior that defied the conditions upon which love and approval were based.

The opportunity for something different came the following year when Goldberg was on sabbatical. Bill Taylor organized a comparative social history seminar in 1964–65 with a colleague who taught British History, and he invited me to join it. The seminar was the highpoint of my graduate career. We read all the new social history as it was published: E. P. Thompson's *The Making of the English Working Class*, Eric Hobsbawm's *Primitive Rebels*, Stephan Thernstrom's book on Newburyport, Massachusetts, the work of Herbert Gutman and Eugene Genovese, Charles Tilly's study of the Vendée, and much more. It was then that I became aware of the work of the *Annales* school and read some of its historians. When Stanley Elkins came to class, we grilled him relentlessly about his use of psychoanalysis to characterize slaves as Sambos. And we designed our own studies of communities and social movements. Week after week the group argued about interpretation and method, about theory and historical practice. This was a moment of disciplinary reformation and we were eagerly participating in it. The limits of this disciplinary reformation became apparent to me only years later: we did not read anything by Michel Foucault, whose epistemological bomb shells were published in the same years as the English New Left historians and their American counterparts whose work we avidly consumed.

Inspired by the seminar, I dropped my project on Paul Lafargue and set out to find a community study. By the time Goldberg came back from his sabbatical, all he could do was suggest places and events I might look at. Carmaux was a mining town in the south of France, in the department from which Jaurès had been elected. There were glass bottle blowers there too. I applied for and received a cross-disciplinary research training fellowship from the Social Science Research Council. Under the guidance of a mentor, graduate students were to employ methods not usually associated with their disciplines; the result would be a cross-fertilization that enriched all sides. The historical sociologist Charles Tilly was designated my advisor and so began my excursion into sociological theory and quantitative methodology. The attempt to quantify the reasons for the collective behavior of social groups was engaging, as was the exploration of the relationship between family, occupation, and politics. Though in rereading some of my correspondence with Chuck, I'm startled to find how fiercely resistant I was to sociological classifications that didn't take account of what I referred to as historical process. My project became a study of the political effects of proletarianization on the glassworkers of Carmaux. The rest, as we might say, is history.

Or was it? To be sure, undertaking that dissertation established my identity as a historian of modern France and a labor historian; it also made me one of the early practitioners of the emerging field of social history.

But to assume continuous linearity would be to miss both the external contingencies of my trajectory (the jobs I got, the friends I made, the scholars I interacted with, the pressures—political and intellectual—I confronted, the changing problematics of my areas of study, the challenges posed by students along the way) and the internal dynamics of my psyche.

One thing that was continuous, though, was my connection to France and French history. It's taken me years to learn to read the culture and to make genuine friendships, not just professional contacts, but from the beginning—during my months of dissertation work in the archives at Albi—I knew this was a place I wanted to keep coming back to. Not only because the aesthetics of food and wine and clothes and conversation were so appealing, but also because France offered both an intriguing history of its own, and another way of thinking about History—one infused with philosophical questions and interpretive approaches that weren't part of what the French would call my "formation." It's no accident, I think in retrospect, that I was so drawn to French poststructuralism; it seemed a continuation of the critical influences I already associated with "France."

                                    *   *   *

I'm trying not to write this as an account in which language is the persistent undercurrent, pulling me toward it even as I get sidetracked by quantitative history and a certain behaviorism. But some of that seems unavoidable. One of the insights I still remember vividly about *The Glassworkers of Carmaux* (1974) came when I was revising the chapter on mechanization. It had to do with the way the leaders formulated their demands for protection of this once highly skilled craft. They wanted apprenticeship to be regulated. Why I wondered was a system that was inherently regulated in need of regulation? I remember thinking then that this was a quintessentially "Taylor" question and it stirred a familiar excitement. Answering it enabled me to get at the nature of the changes that new technologies of production had created, to the ways in which the union conceived of its role, and to the ultimately unresolvable contradiction that conception contained. One of the readers of my dissertation wondered why I had gone so deeply into the language union leaders employed. I don't remember how I replied, but I didn't drop the pages. There was too much pleasure invested in grappling with the meanings conveyed by the union leaders' words.

But (there will always be "buts" in this necessarily imperfect recollection, which depends on memory, full of tricks of its own), there was pleasure too in simply figuring things out, learning about something I hadn't known before—not just to acquire more information but to make sense of it, see not more, but differently, in ways I hadn't imagined before.

And there was, too, and I don't want to underestimate it, the political resonance of the work many of us were doing, following the lead of Tilly's Vendée study and Thompson's book on the English working class. The aim, in the heated context of riots in urban ghettos in the late 1960s, was not just to study working class and other protest movements, but to demonstrate their logic and reasonableness: apparently angry, sometimes violent actions were strategic, driven by real interests; they were coherent, even organized; one could read their aims and motives if one understood the economic and social pressures, and the cultural repertoires on which they relied, what Thompson called the "moral economy." The influences operated to create or mobilize groups who were—however unfamiliar or nonnormative the forms might be—eminently political in their behavior. We were rewriting some of the meanings of politics in these studies, with an eye to legitimating the movements of social protest that were taking shape around us. And we were lending weight to arguments about the need for more equitable distribution of resources, for an end to discrimination based on class or race (gender hadn't yet come into it), for social policies based on considerations of justice and moral right. The sense that this was *relevant* history made it somehow more interesting and purposive than those dry exegeses of constitutional development or imperial diplomacy we had to read to prepare for prelims.

In 1983, at a conference on "representations of work" at Cornell University, the French philosopher-historian Jacques Rancière delivered a scathing critique of our burgeoning field. In a paper called "The Myth of the Artisan," he called into question the reigning premise of much of our research, insisting that studies of the proletarianization of highly skilled craft workers, which linked technical change to political militancy, were a misrepresentation. He questioned the motives of those of us writing this history, unconscious though they might be. He argued that what was at stake in what we were doing was the perpetuation of a socialist myth in which all workers shared a common experience, a common artisanal "culture," which their political movements sought to protect against the ravages of technology and Taylorization. This myth he attributed to struggles within labor movements of the time that sought to protect one faction's version of labor militancy, which maintained that only it represented the authentic artisanal culture at the origin of working class politics, against the claims of others. In other words, we were reproducing a political position, taking sides in a past political struggle, as if it were a more or less accurate and dispassionate recounting of the past. Moreover, those of us using demographic and other statistics were lending an aura of objectivity to the project. In place of the story we were telling, Rancière offered one that insisted on contradiction and on attention to it in the writings—the language—of those we studied. His book, translated as *The Nights of Labor,* gave evidence of some workers' longing to be poets, not craftsmen—they toiled only in order to eat—and they aspired to a bourgeois life of ease and artistic fulfillment. Here was a serious challenge to the homogenous artisans of our mythology, an insistence on the complexity of experience. It was more than relations of production, more than work or class culture, but a host of influences and responses to them—the desire for change might, for example, take the form of emulation instead of political militancy. Rancière's critique replaced a field of closed determination—artisan culture transformed by capitalist industrialization leads necessarily to socialist politics—with a set of questions premised on the unknown effects and paths of experience. It opened the history we had studied to readings we hadn't entertained. At the time, I didn't know about Rancière's pedigree as a student of Althusser and Derrida, but I was persuaded that his critique made sense and that I needed to rethink the grounds of my own historical investigations. My response was undoubtedly influenced by the fact that I was deeply immersed in poststructural readings at Brown, where I taught from 1980 to 1985, but that gets too far ahead of my story.

Rancière was right about the mythologizing effect of our studies, but his critique underestimated another of our aims: to insist that there were good reasons for the kinds of uprisings (strikes, riots, revolutions) that governments and employers (then as now) characterize as irrational. We wanted to demonstrate, as well, that these mobilizations constituted a legitimate form of politics, one that called into question prevailing assumptions about what counted not only as politics, but as history. Here Charles Tilly's notion of collective action was important because it brought into focus an array of militant behaviors previously deemed in official histories and contemporary accounts disruptive, riotous, violent, and, if not immoral, certainly impolitic. Beyond giving reason to what once seemed excessive and dangerous kinds of action, the expansion of the notion of politics surely made possible the reevaluation of women's role as historical actors and even the idea that "the personal is the political."

*   *   *

I entered the job market in 1969 just as the feminist movement was exploding on campuses and I eventually took one of those "turns" that continues to mark my career. As students clamored for "her-story," those of us sympathetic to the idea of including women in the history curriculum agreed to try to tell the tale. Most of us were women; those of us with jobs were usually the only woman in our department. Whether we volunteered or not, we were expected to acquire and transmit knowledge of women's history. In the process, I became a feminist historian.

That's not exactly right. I was, in one sense, already a feminist, having been raised by parents who treated women no differently from men. In my father's lessons about the idiocy of religion, one of the clinching points was that Genesis was a discriminatory tale, a plot (Eve created from Adam's rib!) concocted by men to keep women in an inferior place. Even if there was a traditional sexual division of labor in our family (my mother cooked, my father ruled), the ideology was one of equality and my mother had a respected professional career. So I had long been prepared to press for the recognition of women's part in history, even if not of their right to a separate her-story.

But in another way, the politics of feminism was not part of my political heritage. It was one thing to treat women as partners in the quest for social justice, quite another to seem to put what was always represented in socialist history as a bourgeois campaign for individual rights before the collective struggles of workers and blacks. As I became more involved in agitating about women on committees on the status of women at universities where I taught and in the professional associations to which I belonged, as well as on committees to establish Women's Studies programs, my father expressed doubt about the enterprise. "What are the women up to these days?" he would ask, looking for an opening through which he could pour cold water on my enthusiasm. Mostly I refused to engage the argument I knew was coming about the superiority of the class struggle to all others. Thinking his views were a relic of the Old Left, I was surprised to find his attitude alive and well in the labor history circles in which I then traveled. Today, you can still find scholars on the left who attribute the downfall of Marxism to feminist deviations. To feminists and, what they insist on calling, postmodernists.

Before I get to poststructuralism (the more accurate designation) though, I have to talk more about feminism and the extraordinary moment of the mid-1970s and 1980s. It was then that the various aspects of my activity—scholarly, personal, and political—came together in ways that were both logical (everything was geared to a similar end) and amazing, because we were not only inventing a—for us—new politics, we were also producing new knowledge. That's why, when I finally began to read Foucault, the notion of power/knowledge seemed to make so much sense. The production of knowledge made possible the conceptualization of problems and the emergence of subjects in ways previously unseen; agency was not inherent in individuals, but a socially created possibility. It is not, as I eventually formulated it, individuals who have experience, but subjects who are constituted through experience. And that's what we were doing in a gloriously rebellious and furious political campaign that was also an academic treasure hunt and a large and noisy theoretical debating society. We announced new discoveries only to learn we had foremothers who had already said similar things; we circulated reading lists like so much *samizdat* literature, crudely photocopied, mailed in bulky packages, passed from hand to hand at conferences with promises to send one's material in return—there was no email in those days; we organized and attended conferences, astonished at the numbers of students and colleagues who turned up; listened to papers for every fact and interpretive nuance we could glean; fought furiously over which theory—if any—made the most sense; faced painful challenges to the presumed universality of the category "women," seeking to pluralize the term while retaining something of its unity; and we worried about whether politics would compromise the quality of our history. At the same time, we challenged the standards by which quality was judged and also the bias of the judges, linking questions about what counted as history to questions about who counted as historians. We learned first hand that those with power had the ability to define the rules of the game, including dismissing as unacceptably "political" or "ideological" the call for the inclusion of women in history. Formulating a critique of that power was a demanding intellectual task: where did some notion of "quality" figure in the writing of women's history? Was it wise or even legitimate to focus exclusively on women? Would "gender" dilute or strengthen our analysis? What would be the measure of our success? And though there were many bitter moments I can recall—

denunciations, accusations, exclusions, tears—they are outweighed by the excitement generated in a search for answers not yet known and by the camaraderie one could find along the way.

That's how I met Louise Tilly. I had already seen her in Cambridge and then Toronto, when, as a graduate student with an SSRC fellowship, I visited her husband Charles Tilly to study social theory and method. Louise had decided to return to graduate school—her four children were now all in school—to pursue a Ph.D. in history, inspired by Natalie Davis, then also at Toronto. As I recall, she brought sandwiches for our lunch and joined the conversation. We discussed her dissertation topic and mine. The real beginning of our collaboration though came during a meeting of the Society for French Historical Studies in 1972, when we compared notes on our teaching of women's history and discussed a paper that Edward Shorter had written about illegitimate births during the Industrial Revolution.

Louise and I disagreed with that paper because of its facile deduction of motive from behavior. Shorter attributed increased rates of illegitimacy to a newfound emancipation among young women exposed to the "market values" (independence, autonomy, rejection of tradition and parental authority) that accompanied the industrial revolution. Bastards were a consequence of women's sexual liberation, the sign of a search for individual self-fulfillment and self-expression. Shorter was not alone in representing industrialization as a story of progress instead of exploitation, but he had a particularly sensationalist way of inferring changes in values from statistical findings: heightened illegitimacy was a sign of women's liberation; high rates of infant mortality were indicators of a deficit of maternal love. As we heatedly countered his arguments, it became clear—Louise suggested it—that we had to write a paper contesting not only Shorter's ideas, but what we considered to be a short-sighted position of the feminist movement on the issue of women's work. That paper began the collaboration that led to our book, *Women, Work, and Family* (1978).

We steeped ourselves in historical materials: monographs, government reports, memoirs, social investigations, newspaper accounts, novels, trade union records, socialist meetings, and feminist congresses. The point was to counter, with evidence from the past, the easy equation of paid work with liberation and the idea that women's entry into the wage labor market was the source or the consequence of the acquisition of political rights. We disputed the idea that women's work outside the home was an invention of capitalist industrialism that was to universalize nineteenth and twentieth century middle class experience. Among craftspeople, manual laborers and peasants, women had long engaged in productive activity; the pressure to work and the jobs women did were a function of a family economy which depended for survival on everyone's contribution. The family economy was at once a practical institution and a set of cultural values. In place of schematic representations of change, we offered historical process. We objected to studying the past through the lens of the present, insisting that our notions of sexual self-realization, for example, were inappropriate for thinking about the lives of eighteenth- and nineteenth-century working women. The advent of industrialization and urbanization changed the context in which the family economy operated, we argued, even as young women continued to understand themselves in its terms. So, to return to Shorter, illegitimacy might well result from a loss of family protection, or an attempt to recreate a family in a new urban context rather than be a sign of a newfound desire for sexual self-realization.

But I don't want here to summarize the arguments of "Tilly/Scott." The point of this essay is to reflect on my relationship to history. In that connection, I want to emphasize that we used history to complicate feminist political theorizing, working against the grain of prevailing assumptions in order to refine the theory. Although we didn't think about it in quite the terms I'm about to use, we were insisting that the category of "woman" needed not only to be pluralized, but also historicized. This tacking back and forth between current political preoccupations and empirical history was exhilarating and demanding. But there was more to it: we were also making women, ourselves included, visible as historical subjects within the discipline of history.

And though social history made the job easier, having identified a whole series of actors whose lives and politics needed to be included in the story, whether of nationhood or class formation or economic development, establishing the case for women's inclusion was trickier, since women were assumed to be either already included in the idea of "man" or irrelevant to the narratives of public events because attached to the private or domestic or sexual sphere. It was made even more difficult because of pressure from feminist political activists, many of them students sitting in our classes or colleagues in women's studies programs, to write "herstory" as an analysis of patriarchy in terms the movement prescribed. How to resist herstory as a form of present-focused consciousness-raising and yet make women visible agents, past and present? Politics at once enriched our work, making research an engaged enterprise, and it tried to set limits to the insights we produced. The resulting tension was, however, not crippling but enormously productive. In one way or another, I have worked best negotiating this kind of tension, perhaps because it resonates with that complicated stance I mentioned before: a critical refusal to accept the rules (the terms of identity) set by someone (or some group) I nonetheless care about, indeed whose aims I share and whose approval and affection I also seek. For me, that constitutes what—perhaps—might be labeled the psychodynamic of critique. About which more later.

But there was another aspect to my feminist turn that also bears mentioning: the tremendous pleasure I found working with women. My collaboration with Louise Tilly was a remarkable lesson in professional deportment. Until then, I tried to separate the realms of my life: in public I was a professor and a scholar, in private a wife and mother and I tried never to let the demands of the latter impinge on the former. Certainly, I'd never admit to a professional colleague that I hadn't finished a paper or couldn't attend a meeting because one of my children was sick or that I couldn't concentrate on a topic we had to discuss because I was upset about how someone in the family was behaving. If there had been maternity leaves available, I would probably not have taken one, so anxious was I to prove that having children would not impede my intellectual productivity. And, yet, of course, I also very much needed to prove that my femininity had not been compromised by my intellect. Yet here was Louise writing that she hadn't had time to finish her share of one of our chapters because she'd been up all night with a vomiting daughter or that the washing machine had broken down or the car needed to be serviced. None of this prevented her from going to the library and eventually completing her assignment or from wrestling with a particularly difficult interpretation we were trying to sort out; it was her willingness to avow the interconnections between the two parts of her life that allowed me to acknowledge that my own life was a lot like hers. What a relief!

But there was more. I was no longer engaged in battles that were mine alone; Louise and I shared a similar stance in regard to the feminism we both supported and critiqued. This mutuality was different from what I'd experienced in the brotherhood of labor and social historians—an openness that permeated the rigid boundaries between public and private I had tried to maintain for myself. And there was still more: beyond my collaboration with Louise, the company of women with whom we exchanged

papers and ideas, hardly a homogeneous or coherent assemblage, but one
not governed by prevailing disciplinary and professional norms, gave me
a new perspective not only on myself, but on ways to think about the
present and the past. If I was already inclined to work against the grain of
disciplinary orthodoxy, it was still a lot easier with allies.

*   *   *

And yet there were questions about women's history I couldn't seem
to answer, let alone pose, within the terms of social history. How to explain the persistence of the oppression of women after political equality
had been achieved? Why did reforms seem only to superficially address
wage disparities and gender hierarchies? If sheer male enmity didn't explain the persistence of patriarchy, if masculine self-interest wasn't a good
enough reason, and if social roles and customs didn't do it either, then
how to account for what seemed to be the foundational place of sexual difference in the organization of societies across time and place? It wouldn't
do to pile up examples of the subordination or mistreatment of women as
proof of a timeless patriarchy. For one thing, there were warnings from
medievalists, as well as historians and anthropologists of non-Western cultures, not to read apparent similarities as reflections or confirmations of
the urban, industrialized patterns that first- and now second-wave feminists challenged. For another, if we wanted to argue for change, we had to
show that it could take place, not only through social protest movements,
though these were undoubtedly important, but also by some alteration of
the very meaning of the concepts "women" and "men." Beyond that was a
question about the recalcitrance of the discipline to our efforts. What difference did it make for understanding the French or American Revolutions,
the noted male historians of those events demanded, that women had participated in crowds or even claimed inclusion as citizens? The "so what?"
question demanded answers more informed than accusations of bias. In
what ways did women's history challenge not only the storyline of mainstream history but also the rules of the discipline and the image of the disciplinary practitioner? Feminists were insisting that we would do exactly
that—it wouldn't work just to add women and stir. But staying within established disciplinary frameworks made it hard to fulfill the promise of
radical transformation. How did being a historian of women or, for that
matter, a woman historian, change the way we thought about history, both
in the sense of the record of the past and of the craft we practiced? How

to avoid the essentialist answer that made women "natural" historians of the fair sex?

* * *

Those were the questions nagging at me when I arrived at Brown University to take up the Nancy Duke Lewis chair, a chair for a scholar in women's studies. My appointment was in the history department. In the wake of a sex discrimination suit brought by anthropologist Louise Lamphere and with an eye to increasing gift-giving by alumnae of Pembroke College, the coordinate institution that had been incorporated into Brown in 1971, the university wanted to improve its record on women. The terrain was open and there was a group of women ready to work it with me. It matters a great deal for the turn I took at Brown that most of these women were literary scholars, schooled in theories I had had little exposure to before. Not only poststructuralism (Barthes, Foucault, Derrida, de Man), but psychoanalysis (Freud, Lacan, Laplanche) and "French feminism" (Irigaray, Cixous, Kristeva) provided the frames within which they wrote; they were (some still are) forging feminist theory in remarkably creative ways.

I cannot say that I instantly recognized the value of theory for my own thinking. Not at all. I was confused, intimidated, resistant, dismissive. And anyway, my attention was claimed initially by the institutional work I had signed on for: fund-raising to complete the financing of my chair, the creation of a woman's studies program, and the founding of the Pembroke Center for Teaching and Research on Women–still my proudest institutional accomplishment. It wasn't just my accomplishment. My fellow architect and co-conspirator was Elizabeth Weed, whose gifts as a reader of institutional politics are matched only by her abilities to read even the most difficult of philosophical texts.

If my collaboration with Louise Tilly had been built on a shared formation as social historians, my work with Elizabeth had to negotiate mutual philosophical incomprehension. Of course, as with Louise, we shared a commitment to making women visible and to legitimizing their presence as objects of scholarship and subjects of inquiry. And there was for me, again, pleasure in feminist company, in a joint endeavor that was at once political and scholarly. But as Elizabeth and I wrote grant proposals and designs for a women's studies curriculum, we found ourselves having to translate key words, explain our basic assumptions to one another, and spell out the meanings of things we each took for granted in very different ways. This process of institution building wasn't just practical, it was the beginning of my intellectual reorientation. Looking back on that early encounter, I think it enabled me to begin to relate my history to her theory. I already cared too much about history to leave it: the archival surprises; the awareness of contingency; the puzzling over influence, cause, and effect; the telling of stories; and the use of the past to bring the present into relief. But some of the theory also made sense, not because it provided me with a reliable explanation for why things happened, but precisely because it didn't. Rather, it enhanced my ability to read differently and made me conscious that I was not just discovering, but producing knowledge. Thinking about myself in those terms brought politics and scholarship together in a new way; it enabled me to begin to address the questions that my earlier work in women's history had left unresolved.

But, as I've said, it didn't happen all at once. And here, the role of institutions in scholarly directions matters a great deal. Having secured external foundation funding, the Pembroke Center came into existence in 1981 and, with it, an interdisciplinary seminar that remains one of the premier intellectual venues in academe. Over the course of the next four years, I read books I'd not encountered, listened to and sometimes argued with scholars in fields I'd never traversed, and found myself forced to examine and explain the presuppositions of the work I did. There were moments of frustration so great that I wished I'd never gotten involved; some ideas were so difficult that I found myself unable at first to absorb them. It was like squinting in the face of light that was too bright. Some of what was said was scary because it challenged the premises upon which I had learned to rely, notions of experience, agency, structure, reality. But there was, too, the stirring of that enormously pleasurable sensation I had long associated with attention to language and exposure to completely different ways of thinking—that early linking in high school between desire and knowledge as the pursuit of the unknown. Not unknown facts, but unknown meanings; a readiness to think the not-yet-thought required an openness that my disciplinary training precluded. Of course, thinking needs discipline in the sense of rigor and hard analysis, but not the application of inflexible rules about what counts as history and what doesn't. Or maybe it's better to say we at once need those rules *and* the ability (the right?) to challenge them; against the closure that orthodoxy seeks to maintain the lure of the unknown provides resistance, the desire to keep moving on.

In those years my feminism acquired its intellectual rationale, the philosophical underpinnings for my work as a historian. That kind of work now has a name: critical history. But then I improvised, applying critique not only to events of the past, but also to the interpretive practices of the discipline. Poststructuralist theory gave me a language for articulating a feminist critique and for conceiving of how history might serve it. In those years, too, I developed an increased sense of trust in the connection between the pleasure I felt and the knowledge I produced.

I've been accused by more than one outraged historian, especially historians of women, of following fads instead of sticking to the tried and true. In a strange evocation of patriotism, they've ridiculed my attraction for "fancy French theory," suggesting it was easier to deal in abstraction than to go to the dusty archives in pursuit of truth. As if one canceled the other; philosophy or history, but not both. These were the charges leveled against Carl Becker and Charles Beard in the 1930s; the opposition between philosophy and history is one of the ways that the orthodox idea of history's objectivity has been protected. For me, philosophy only improved my ability to do history by analyzing the past in a new way, by clarifying what it meant to be doing history, and by throwing important light on the reasons that mainstream or traditional historians resisted the validity of, for example, women as subjects of history and objects of historical investigation. It provided both a diagnosis and a way of addressing the problem. Reading the work of Michel Foucault—critically engaged, philosophically driven history—was the earliest and probably the most important, though not the only, influence on my "linguistic turn."

My first encounter with Foucault was *The Order of Things*, the book that begins with an analysis of Velazquez's *Las Meninas* and goes on, dizzyingly, to uncover an "archaeology of the human sciences," and, with it, the emergence of "the age of history," and concludes by reminding us that "man is an invention of recent date. And one perhaps nearing its end ... like a face drawn in the sand at the edge of the sea." If I wondered at the triumphant harshness of that final image, it was the historicizing of History that left me breathless: "History, as we know, is certainly the most erudite, the most aware, the most conscious, and possibly the most cluttered area of our memory; but it is equally the depths from which all beings emerge into their precarious, glittering existence. Since it is the mode of being of all that is given us in experience, History has become the unavoidable element in our thought."

It hadn't always been this way, Foucault argued. History had become both a form of knowledge and "the mode of being of empiricity" only in the nineteenth century. We were "still caught inside" the momentous conceptual change that it signified, so it was "largely beyond our comprehension." Yet, of course, Foucault aimed to produce that comprehension by interrogating the categories we took for granted as analytic tools: not only history, but—among others—reason, truth, event, sexuality, Man and man. These categories weren't fixed and reliable instruments for discovering truth; instead they were malleable and mutable terms by which understanding was organized and knowledge produced. I've taught and reread that text many times, but I haven't forgotten my initial impression: a combination of enormous anxiety and great temptation (the two often go together), which I didn't do much to resist. If it is possible to pinpoint the moment at which passion entered my arranged marriage with history, it was in that reading group at Brown in 1981 or 1982 when I was introduced to the writing of Michel Foucault.

It's astonishing to me that many historians today cite Foucault and claim to be inspired by him and yet refuse the epistemological challenge he posed. They refer to discourse as if it meant simply words and they treat the topics of his research thematically as about prisons, asylums, or sex, without grasping his subversive intent: to call into question the taken-for-granted aspect of the institutions and concepts that organize our existence; to unveil the discursive regimes of truth that pass themselves off as objective descriptions of nature or ethics or the essence of the human. And above all, to write what he called a "history of the present," a history that "serves to show how that-which-is has not always been," and so to show "why and how that-which-is might no longer be that-which-is." Genealogy was Foucault's name for this critical history. "Criticism is no longer going to be practiced in the search for formal structures with universal value but, rather, as a historical investigation into the events that have led us to constitute ourselves and to recognize ourselves as subjects of what we are doing, thinking, saying." Events were not revolutions, elections, or wars, but discursive shifts, changes in concepts that created values, meanings, and subjects. People and their societies came into being through discourse; it was not words attached to preexisting realities, but the construction of those realities themselves. Discourse was not about conflicts of ideas or opinions—the stuff of ordinary intellectual history—it was about the shared premises that established the very grounds on which debate could occur: reason as the primary attribute of Man or sovereignty as the inherent right of the individual or freedom as his desired condition. Or sexual difference as the referent "in nature" for social and political hierarchies.

For Foucault, discourse was about the relationship between knowledge and power, the ways in which things acquired words to define them, the ways in which people came into existence as subjects by becoming objects of knowledge. Knowledge was a field—but not the only one—upon which power was enacted. Becoming a subject meant being placed in certain positions in relationships of power (men and women, teachers and students, workers and employers, rulers and ruled, doctors and patients, immigrants and natives, sane and insane) and through that positioning acquiring agency—agency taken not as an inherent capacity of humans, but as an attribution of traits and responsibilities upon which subjects are expected to act.

Here was a way to interrogate the attributions to biology of the social assignment of sex roles, to ask how feminine and masculine subjects were constructed, how normative systems operated, and how people were able to imagine themselves outside prevailing rules of behavior. Instead of thinking of resistance as innate, one had to ask what the specific discursive resources of such oppositional agency were. It was the possibility of putting these kinds of political questions to historical materials, the linking through them of feminist critique and feminist history, that led me to hail gender as "a useful category of historical analysis."

Of course, it was not only Foucault that inspired that claim. The Brown feminist theory reading group, a name I've retrospectively assigned to it, also devoured its share of Derrida, Kristeva, Irigaray. Through these authors I learned how to think about difference, to be alert to its operations, its variability, its symbolic power and its instability. Through contacts with scholars who came to the center—Denise Riley was prominently among them—I was able to articulate an approach to history that took conceptualizations of difference to be its focus. I learned that meanings are always sliding even as they are being declared inviolate. To get at what is happening requires a different kind of attention—to language, its figures of speech, its allusions and symbolism—from that usually paid by historians. To take things literally usually misses the point, making historians party to ideological systems whose terms they ought to analyze. Describing what women did or what was said about them is not the same as asking how their subjectivity is being constituted and in what relationships; pointing out that "class, race, and gender" are all part of a woman's identity is not the same as asking how those attributes are used to identify and position women in specific relationships and contexts. To assume that there is something universal about "women" or "men" is essentializing and ahistorical, no different in the end from the attribution of inevitable sexed traits to anatomy; it obscures the fact that the terms themselves, and the subjects who inhabit them, have a history. Gender is a useful category only if differences are the question, not the answer, only if we ask what "men" and "women" are taken to mean wherever and whenever we are looking at them, rather than assuming we already know who and what they are. In this sense, my appropriation of poststructuralism is relentlessly historical—there are no women or men, no classes, no races, outside of the relationships established between them and the ways those relationships are understood. Even deviations from the norm refer to normative understandings, indeed they find the possibilities for nonnormative behavior in the negative terms with which norms are constructed, and upon which they invariably lean.

This is where Derrida comes in. It was his theorization that provided me with a set of analytic tools (his metaphor is levers) by which the operations of difference could be unearthed and examined in all their elusive complexity. Elizabeth Weed, Naomi Schor, Gayatri Spivak, and, perhaps most of all, Barbara Johnson helped me to understand what deconstruction meant and how to make it work for feminism. The exciting thing about our appropriations of this critique of metaphysics was that it never had to end; it was not a matter of becoming a doctrinaire follower of a particular school, but rather the deployment of a theory of signification that made language the object of our inquiry, the way in to historically specific analyses of subject construction, social organization, and relations of power. Indeed, it was the insight into politics that, for me, was crucial.

It's important, I think, to stress the appeal of critique here, since the term is so often misused and misunderstood. At the moment that I discovered it, poststructuralism—both as exemplar and mode of analysis—provided a critical intervention in the disciplined way I had practiced history. Critique is not a criticism, nor the proposal of alternatives. Rather it is an interrogation of the very premises upon which things we take to be foundational are based. In the translator's introduction to Derrida's *Dissemination,* Barbara Johnson puts it succinctly:

A critique of any theoretical system is not an examination of its flaws and imperfections. It is not a set of criticisms designed to make the system better. It is an analysis that focuses on the grounds of the system's possibility. The critique reads backwards from what seems natural, obvious, self-evident, or universal in order to show that these things have their history, their reasons for being the way they are, their effects on what follows from them and that the starting point is not a (natural) given but a (cultural) construct, usually blind to itself.

The point of critique is to make visible those blind spots in order to open a system to change. Not to replace what is with a fully formulated, ideal plan, but to open the possibility for thinking, and so acting, differently. Here at last was a way to make feminist history achieve the radical promise its advocates had offered, but—to my way of thinking at least—had not yet delivered. I spent the next several years reading and writing as much about disciplinary presuppositions as about women, seeking to expose and so intervene in "the politics of history." The results were published in *Gender and the Politics of History* (1988; 1999).

*   *   *

My time at Brown was transformational. There I began a process that has by no means ended and I acquired the resources and the stimulus to stake out a territory of my own—one beholden neither to the pressures of mainstream historians of women, nor to the conventions of the discipline of history, although both have claimed my critical attention. When I left Brown in 1985 for what seemed an irresistible offer to become a permanent faculty member at the Institute for Advanced Study, my metamorphosis was well underway, though perhaps not as apparent as it would become. I was hired for my work as a social historian; I think it's fair to say that I became more of an intellectual historian at the Institute, one for whom theory—feminist theory—was and is a primary preoccupation. Or, perhaps it is more precise to designate the object of my work as the question of difference in history: its uses, enunciations, implementations, justifications, and transformations in the construction of social and political life. Difference not just as sexual difference, but as any of those factors in human life upon which primary distinctions, hierarchies, and conflicts come to be based; factors whose grounding in nature, culture, religion, ethnicity, or race needs to be interrogated rather than simply described.

Here again, the institutional location in which I worked mattered a lot. The School of Social Science, to which I was appointed, was the creation of anthropologist Clifford Geertz, who envisioned it as a place where disciplinary orthodoxies would be challenged. As he conceived it, the School was to be "a thorn in the side of the main direction of things." That's a good way of describing critique—though Cliff's notion of it was more philosophical and less explicitly political than mine. Those differences mattered less, however, than the ethos of critical thinking itself: the interrogation of prevailing disciplinary norms, the questioning of the value of scientific models for thinking about human social relations, the insistence on interpretation as both the object of inquiry and the method of the inquirer. The rich resources and open space of the Institute—physical and intellectual—encourage and reward exploratory and innovative thinking. And the interdisciplinary composition of the faculty and members, as those who come for a year with fellowship support are called, of the School of Social Science brought new perspectives into view.

New perspectives might be the theme of my twenty-some years at the Institute. In addition to engaging with philosophers, literary scholars, and all manner of social scientists, I began to explore themes and theories I had once either underestimated or ignored. Some of this was the influence of members—such as Judith Butler, Drucilla Cornell, and Wendy Brown. Their work took critique to new arenas: sexuality, the law, political philosophy. The growing interest in sexuality studies and queer theory, as well the use these scholars and others made of psychoanalysis, turned my attention to Freud and Lacan, whom I read in seminars I gave at Rutgers with amazingly smart graduate students. In my essay "Gender: A Useful Category of Historical Analysis" (1986), I had minimized the importance of psychoanalysis for historical work, but now I began to rethink that too-hasty dismissal. This coincided with my own decision to seek psychotherapy, which I did with an analyst of the "old school."

It did not always work well to pursue theory while undergoing psychoanalysis, but there were some advantages. Among them, I learned that theory only went so far for explaining the highly individualized formations of the psyche and that the best insights one gained did not come from the application of diagnostic labels. Rather, they came from astute attention to language, from the interpretive readings of dreams, stories, and fantasies in the context of a particular life experience. Of course, these interpretations were theory-driven, in the sense that they were based on an understanding of the workings of the unconscious, of operations such as displacement and condensation, imagination and symbolic representation, and of the importance of sex and sexual difference as a dilemma for the identification of subjects. This kind of psychoanalytic reading—which posited the assumption of masculinity and femininity as an ongoing problem rather than an accepted social assignment—gave greater flexibility to the notion of gender I had tried to articulate. While my attempt to make gender a *question* for historical investigation has too often been read as a set of methodological prescriptions, psychoanalysis's theorizing of sexual difference insists on interrogation—at both the individual and collective levels. It offers a way of reading gender, the social and political policing of sexual boundaries, as an attempt to negotiate the anxieties attached to sexual difference—a difference that is known, but whose meanings and effects are never clear. Gender is the always failed attempt, in particular historical contexts, to fully secure those meanings; politics at once creates and depends on these meanings to produce its vision of social order. Conflicting visions of social order and so also of gender are the stuff of politics.

My own psychoanalysis had a different kind of effect—a calming one— on the psychic underpinnings of my attraction to critique. Earlier in these pages I described the psychodynamics of this critique as "a critical refusal to accept the rules (the terms of identity) set by someone (or some group) I nonetheless care about, indeed whose aims I share and whose approval and affection I also seek." I attribute this to a complex Oedipal formation and, for many years, it was driven by anger. The desire to be accepted by those whose premises I was challenging, their failure even to be willing to think about the contradictions or limitations I saw, their inevitable refusal to accept the critique—to see that it was offered affectionately, aimed at improvement, not rejection—had anger as its cause and effect. The loss of that anger did not diminish either the force or attraction of critique; if anything, it made the intellectual aspects clearer and the experience more pleasurable.

* * *

Critique doesn't work without theory, although there are many theoretical positions one can take. I think this is what distinguishes the history I most like from that which informs, but doesn't enlighten or excite me. And there's lots of "faux theory" around these days—people who make big gestures to Foucault, Freud, or for that matter Marx, and end up doing conventional descriptive narratives of ideas, events, or movements. The recuperative power of the discipline relies on the ambition of its young

practitioners—I've watched it claim students of great promise and tor-
ture the most creative students I know. These latter haven't succumbed
and they are, I think, paradoxically, the future hope of the discipline. For,
as Adorno long ago pointed out, critique, or what he called "open thinking," "points beyond itself."

Or to turn to Foucault again and, with him, to the link between critical
thinking and politics:

> I don't think we should oppose critique and transformation, critique as "ideal"
> and transformation as "real." A critique does not consist in saying that things
> aren't as they should be. It consists in seeing on what types of evidence, collo-
> quialisms, and inherited modes of thought rest the practices that we take for
> granted.... There is always a bit of thought even in the most stupid of institu-
> tions, there is always thought even in mute habits. Critique consists in flushing
> out this thought and in trying to change it.... In these conditions, critique (rad-
> ical critique) is absolutely indispensable for all transformation.

*   *   *

My recent writing takes up Foucault's challenge, working critique through
the retelling of the histories of French feminism and of two recent legal
enactments in France. These books are about feminism (*Only Paradoxes
to Offer: French Feminists and the Rights of Man* [1996] and *Parité: Sexual
Equality and the Crisis of French Universalism* [2005]) and about republican objections to Islamic headscarves (*The Politics of the Veil* [2007]).
Although written as histories, the three are also a sustained critical examination of the effects of the French doctrine of universalism. By refusing
the standard story which extols universalism as *the* accomplishment of the
French Revolution, I intervene in an ongoing conversation about the limits
and meanings of French national identity. My most recent project, written
as the Wellek lectures for the University of California, Irvine, will become a
book on academic freedom—a history of the concept in the United States
and an analysis of its applications. This is my way of taking part in a contemporary struggle—at once political and intellectual—about the future
direction of the university. Then I will turn my attention to a book of essays on the value of psychoanalysis for historians, especially on the uses
of the concept of fantasy for our interpretive readings. This is a critical
intervention in the way we think about the practice of history.

What comes after that remains to be seen; my choice of topics will depend on what political/conceptual problems draw my interest, what useful contributions I might make. What I do know is that my passion for critique, and the ongoing need for it, are inexhaustible. A good reason— even with time seeming to run out—to keep writing critical history.

DWIGHT T. PITCAITHLEY

Taking the Long Way from Euterpe to Clio

I am a public historian. I have been a public historian for thirty years. I didn't intend to become a public historian. In fact, public history did not really exist when I first became interested in history. Over time, however, it has provided me with much satisfaction, including a thirty-year career in the National Park Service, the last ten years spent as its chief historian. During those years I have gathered my share of awards and honors, but the beginnings of my tale offer no hint of a successful career in history or, quite frankly, a successful career in anything.

I was a poor student throughout my public school years, having no interest in either pleasing my parents or teachers with good grades or in being intellectually challenged. I would not fault my teachers, for my perception at the time was that it was not socially acceptable to excel scholastically. I was, however, a dedicated reader, mostly of fiction, and that probably allowed me to get by—albeit without distinction.

As I thought about writing this essay, I ordered, with great trepidation, my transcript from Carlsbad High School in Carlsbad, New Mexico, where I was born near the end of the Second World War. It is painfully revealing. I escaped high school with a cumulative grade point average of 2.44 and that level of achievement was attained despite earning a D in social studies and a D in history. In the seventh grade I became a drummer. By the time I graduated from high school, I was invited to join the United States High School Band of America. Sponsored by the Lions Club International, the band attended the Lions Club international conference in Nice, France, that summer of 1962 and then toured Europe for two weeks. It seemed natural to major in music—to follow Euterpe, music's muse, upon entering college even though I had no passion for the subject. Indeed, being a music major is quite demanding, requiring many hours of study and practice outside the classroom. My lack of real interest in music, or any other subject, caught up with me at the end of my second year when Eastern New Mexico University placed me on academic suspension due to a dramatically descending academic performance, which culminated in a 1.091 grade point average for the final semester.

My short-lived college career, however, was not a complete failure. Over the previous two years, I had become a certified life saving and water safety instructor, placed first in the intramural mile run, and developed a life-long love for the music of Giacomo Puccini while playing in the orchestra for the university's production of his opera *Tosca*. Moreover, I had spent my summers working as a seasonal employee of the National Park Service picking up litter and cleaning toilets 750 feet underground at Carlsbad Caverns National Park. At that time, I viewed the National Park Service as a summer employer, not a career choice. During my two years at Eastern New Mexico University, I had taken no history courses with the exception of the history of music for which I received a less than stellar grade. All in all, it was not an auspicious academic beginning.

The military draft was alive and well during the summer of 1964, so my chances of being called up for military service, since I had lost my student deferment, were high. Although my father and his brother had served honorably in the United States Army during the Second World War, I had no interest in joining up. Wanting to have some choice in the matter, however, and in the belief I was out-smarting the local draft board, I enlisted in the United States Marine Corps one month before the 1964 Gulf of Tonkin, the incident that drew the country into its decade-long misadventure in Vietnam. Much to my father's chagrin, I didn't inform the Marine Corps of my musical abilities and so became a radio operator for a 105-mm artillery battery first in California and then Hawaii.

By the spring of 1966, I found myself, along with the Fifth Marine Division, landing on the beaches of Chu Lai, Vietnam. I spent the next six months encamped on a hill just north of Chu Lai accompanying squad- and platoon-sized patrols into the surrounding countryside as a forward observer. In August 1966, three companies of the battalion (including mine) were moved by helicopter northwest of Chu Lai to participate in a large sweep east to the South China Sea. On August 10, during a heavy rain-storm, we were ambushed by two battalions of North Vietnamese regulars. Along with five or six others in the headquarters group, I was wounded by shrapnel from a 60-mm mortar. Those of us who were wounded were taken by helicopter first to a field hospital at Tam Ky and then to the larger naval hospital at Da Nang. After an operation in Japan, I returned to California for a year of recovery in and out of the naval hospital in San Diego.

Returning to college in the fall of 1967, I still had no idea what I wanted to study. Eastern New Mexico University had graciously reinstated me with the stipulation that I make 2.5 "on each enrollment until all defi-ciencies are removed." With a cumulative grade point average well below that, it was clear I had many deficiencies to remove. While enrolled in general requirement courses that first semester, my future wife suggested I take a battery of university-administered aptitude tests to discover what latent intellectual skills I might have. Since I had no clear idea for a major, I agreed and over a three-week period took numerous tests designed to reveal some hidden talent. At the appointed hour, I arrived at the dean's office to discover my life's work. I remember, with great clarity, his analy-sis of the tests. He pronounced with authority: "I think you had better go back into the Marine Corps, because you don't have what it takes to go to college!"

Fortunately, I took his words as a challenge and became determined to master the art of being a student. About that same time, still without a declared major, I decided that history might be an interesting course of study. While working on college algebra problems one day in a rented room, I glanced at my lone bookshelf and realized that there were more history books than any other kind. William Manchester's *The Death of a President* and Bernard Fall's *Hell in a Very Small Place: The Siege of Dien Bien Phu* and *Ho Chi Minh on Revolution: Selected Writings, 1920–66* were books I had purchased and read during my last year in the Marine Corps. I had also taken full advantage of my long hospital stay in San Diego by absorbing William J. Lederer and Eugene Burdick's *The Ugly American*, *A Nation of Sheep*, and their fine novel *Sarkhan* on Vietnam. The next se-mester I signed up for two survey history courses and surprised myself by doing well in both of them.

My interest in Vietnam stemmed from a need to understand the war I had just experienced. I had gone to Vietnam convinced that the United States was in the right and, as a result, that the war would not last long.

Upon my return, I began reading books on the war to understand this country's foreign policy and how the war contributed to the country's national security. David Halberstam's *The Making of a Quagmire*, William Lederer's *Our Own Worst Enemy*, and Colonel William Corson's *The Betrayal*, provided a perspective on the war quite different from that offered by the Marine Corps or the Johnson administration. Combining my experiences in Vietnam with the larger context for the war offered by these writers, I developed a different understanding of the United States' military and political efforts in Southeast Asia and concluded by the summer of 1968 that the reasons for initiating and continuing the war were deeply flawed.

As it turned out, Eastern New Mexico University had an excellent history department during those years. Forrest Walker, a former student of Gilbert Fite at the University of Oklahoma, Bernard Halperin, and Robert Matheny (who later became president of the university) were all gifted and inspiring teachers. They encouraged me to continue in history, although I remained undecided about what to do with a degree in history once I had it.

I considered getting a teaching degree, but several education courses convinced me otherwise. Education courses (at least the ones I took) focused on theories and philosophies of education and seemed devoid of any intellectual substance. As a result, I ended up with a master's degree with an emphasis in western history. Without a teaching certificate, however, my options were limited. With the encouragement of my wife, I applied for the doctoral program in history at Texas Tech University, where I embarked on a study of the history of the western United States. Texas Tech had a strong western history program with Seymour V. (Ike) Connor, Earnest Wallace, and David Vigness. Connor, a Walter Prescott Webb student at the University of Texas, became my principal advisor.

The New Social History of the late 1960s and 1970s was becoming fashionable at this time in colleges and universities around the country (although it was not emphasized at Texas Tech), but western history remained unaffected. So, my classmates and I focused on the movement of the frontier across the western landscape. Thinking back, I believe I gravitated toward western history to understand the southeast corner of New Mexico in which I was raised. Carlsbad, after all, was only fifty years old when I was born. It was not far removed from its "frontier" period, yet what I knew about the town did not match Frederick Jackson Turner's or Webb's model of western history.

Carlsbad, New Mexico, in the 1950s was a farming, ranching, and potash mining community that also drew significant income from the tourism industry because of the proximity of Carlsbad Caverns National Park. It was also a typically western town that owed much of its existence and prosperity, not to the rugged individualism of hardy pioneers, but to the largess of the federal government. The original 1890s system of dams and canals that allowed farming to occur along the Pecos River in that corner of the Great American Desert quickly failed and was given over to the Bureau of Reclamation, which rebuilt it and then allowed the local farmers to buy out the government's interest over the next several decades. In 1923, President Calvin Coolidge signed legislation creating Carlsbad Cave National Monument, which brought even more federal funds to Carlsbad, and during the Second World War the federal government constructed a large military base on the south edge of town. Thus my hometown resembled none of the towns I was studying in graduate school. While not in the strict sense a company town, Carlsbad had been dependent on federal monies from its founding and, as a result, became a reasonably prosperous community during the postwar years.

The avowed purpose of the graduate history program at Texas Tech University, as we were regularly reminded, was to produce history teachers for small colleges and universities in Texas. As I continued to progress through the program, I thought that was a worthy, if not very exciting, goal. Then, quite unexpectedly, an opportunity presented itself that changed my outlook about the discipline of history and its career possibilities. During my third year, Ike Connor and James Kitchen, a professor of park administration, were awarded a contract from the National Park Service's regional office in Santa Fe, New Mexico, to produce an inventory of old buildings and farmsteads in a developing national park in Arkansas. That park, Buffalo National River, in the heart of the Arkansas Ozarks, had been established by Congress in 1972. By virtue of an executive order signed by Richard Nixon a year earlier, all federal land-managing agencies were required to survey their land and determine which buildings might qualify for listing in the National Register of Historic Places, the country's index of historic buildings worthy of preservation. So the National Park Service was implementing the executive order well in advance of any planning for new roads, parking lots, or visitor facilities. Because of my seasonal work at Carlsbad Caverns, Connor offered the contract to me. I readily accepted because I had never been to Arkansas, the salary was more than I was getting as a teaching assistant, and the project offered a very different way of using the research skills I had developed.

I spent the summer of 1974 driving thousands of miles on dirt roads up and down the 136-mile-long Buffalo River valley photographing old buildings, interviewing owners and former owners and neighbors, and undertaking research in deed records in county courthouses. Exploring that section of northwest Arkansas gave me an appreciation for the history and geography of a specific place. It encouraged me to think about how local history could be constructed within a national narrative, and how the residents of a place embrace their past in a manner that transcends academic history.

As I had not yet decided on a dissertation topic, Connor suggested that I look around in the Ozarks for a suitable subject. In addition to my National Park Service labors, I visited local libraries and wondered how my inventory of buildings could be crafted into a dissertation. It turned out that while histories of the surrounding counties existed—mostly antiquarian productions from the 1950s and 1960s—there was no regional history to provide a historical context for local narratives. Producing a social and cultural history of the Buffalo River corner of the Ozark Mountains was geographically distant from my studies of the traditional American West, but served well as a study of the American frontier.

My inventory of Buffalo River buildings seemed to be satisfactory to the National Park Service; and with its submission to Santa Fe, I could concentrate on writing the dissertation. Several research trips to the Arkansas Historical Commission in Little Rock and the University of Arkansas archives in Fayetteville allowed me to craft a very traditional narrative of the Buffalo River watershed. It offered no radical interpretations of the region's history and, looking back, clung too closely to folklorist Vance Randolph's view of the Ozarks as a backward and isolated region inhabited by culturally deprived subsistence farmers. It did, however, allow me to receive a doctorate of philosophy in history and had the added value of providing the National Park Service a reliable history that served park managers for several decades. But then what? An exceptionally large number of history doctorates also graduated in 1976 all looking for teaching jobs. I unsuccessfully applied for several positions before arranging part-time work to get through the summer. Then serendipity again came to call when I received an offer from the Santa Fe regional office of the National Park Service for a four-month temporary position.

The National Park Service coordinator for the Buffalo River project had been regional historian Richard Sellars. Following graduation, I contacted him and inquired about job possibilities. He remembered the Arkansas inventory and, thinking well of it, extended the offer of temporary employment. Suddenly, I was employed as a historian although not where I had anticipated—not at a small college, but within a large federal agency. I had passed all the academic requirements for a doctorate in history, but had I, indeed, become a historian? Except for the Buffalo River inventory, printed by Texas Tech University, and two book reviews, I had not published anything. And to complicate my career trajectory, I was employed in a most nontraditional environment—at least by 1976 standards. While I was very pleased to have the Ph.D. in hand, I remained unsure what my future as a historian might be.

I continued to believe that the "normal" path for a historian with my training was to teach in a small college. Other career paths simply did not seem realistic or possible; certainly not a career in public history. Indeed, the term "public history" had only just been coined by Robert Kelley of the University of California, Santa Barbara, in 1975 with the first class of public history students starting there in the fall of the following year. Without any other options, I determined to learn what I could from the National Park Service and then attempt to find a "real" job as a historian in academia. To that end, Sellars turned out to be a refreshingly creative mentor. He encouraged me to find small research projects preparing National Register nominations for historic sites within southwestern national parks. I prepared documentation reports for the Butterfield Stage route through the Guadalupe Mountains in west Texas, Civilian Conservation Corps log cabins on the Buffalo River, an early nineteenth-century tourist complex in Canyon de Chelly in northeast Arizona, a post–Civil War fort at Fort Union National Monument, and bat guano mining remains in the back country of Carlsbad Caverns National Park.

This last project awakened me to one of the dramatic differences between research in archives and research in the National Park Service. To document the guano mining equipment left behind when the market dropped out of the guano fertilizer business, I had to descend into Ogle Cave. Knowing I had done a bit of spelunking during my summers at Carlsbad Caverns, Sellars asked me if I wanted to check out the mining artifacts in this particular cave. I quickly said yes. It was then that Sellars informed me that the only way into the cave was via a one hundred and eighty-foot vertical drop. This was taking the investigation of history to a new level. Over the next few weeks, the region's scientist, Milford Fletcher, taught me the basics of rappelling and, on the scheduled day, I successfully completed the descent and very necessary ascent.

While I never developed the National Register nomination for Ogle Cave, my experience there, and the other research I did for historic places in the Southwest broadened my sense of the importance of local history and reminded me that nationally significant events occur in local places. Those research projects also gave me an appreciation for the various ways one could approach the methodology of history. Having been traditionally trained to pursue historical research in libraries and archives, I was forced to recognize that historians could find research material almost anywhere. While later I would come to admire how the study of material culture could inform our understanding of the past, the Santa Fe projects began to shape my understanding of how objects, landscapes, and buildings individually and collectively could be subjects of historical inquiry.

For the next three years I used all the historical skills I had acquired in graduate school, yet was not in a tenure-track position, which remained a nagging concern. Nevertheless, when the position of regional historian became available in Boston for the seven-state North Atlantic Region, I decided that for better or worse I would eschew an academic career and cast my professional lot with the National Park Service.

Unfortunately, as I was coming to realize, there were few formal connections in those days between the National Park Service and the rest of the academic profession. The prevailing view within the agency was that history in the National Park Service was different from that pursued in colleges and universities and that academic historians had little interest in the Park Service and its historic properties. At the same time, the general view among academics was that history as practiced by the National Park Service bordered on the antiquarian and did not merit the interest or attention of true scholars. While a small number of Park Service historians attended historical conferences, few attempted to publish their research in journals or university presses; they relied, instead, on the Government Printing Office to print their work. Since the GPO is a printing office, not a peer-reviewed press, its offerings (while containing some excellent publications) have been thought of as "gray literature" largely marginal to mainstream scholarly work. At the time, the Government Printing Office printed officially sponsored National Park Service research in batches seldom exceeding one hundred, so even high-quality studies rarely worked their way into accepted historical literature. Since Park Service historians were not encouraged to publish in professional journals and prior to 1996 could not publish with academic presses, there were few scholarly exchanges between them and their academic colleagues during this period. It is no wonder that each so misunderstood the other.

The other peculiarity of the National Park Service during the 1970s and 1980s was that historians worked almost wholly within the sphere of cultural resource management and seldom ventured into the area of historic site interpretation. Since historians were trained to interpret the past, I thought it strange that there seemed little communication between park interpreters and historians in parks and regional offices, not to mention the Washington office. As I began to think about my role as a historian in Boston, I came to understand that the fundamental work of the National Park Service began with preserving places but of necessity resulted in telling stories to the visiting public about those places. Preservation was not an end in itself but a springboard for educating the public about the values inherent in Ellis Island or the home of Franklin and Eleanor Roosevelt or the Seneca Falls, New York, site of the 1848 women's rights convention. Thus, I reasoned, if I were to function as a historian in the public realm, my primary role should be not as a writer of National Register nomination forms or historic structure reports but as a creator of interpretive programs for the public—substantive interpretive programs based on current historical scholarship.

Around the same time, near the end of the 1970s, the idea of public history was taking form with the organization in 1979 of the National Council on Public History in California and the creation of public history programs in a handful of universities around the country. Suddenly, academically trained historians who were interested in exploring history beyond the classroom had an organization and a forum for discussing common issues and problems. Having never encountered the idea of public history during my graduate studies, I was encouraged by the growing number of colleagues who understood, and even embraced, the engagement of history with the public.

My sense of how National Park Service historians and academic historians might profitably work with one another evolved during the restoration of the Statue of Liberty. During the early 1980s, Congress created the Statue of Liberty Ellis Island Centennial Commission and its fund-raising counterpart, the Statue of Liberty–Ellis Island Foundation, to restore and reinterpret those national monuments. Shortly thereafter, F. Ross Holland, director of restoration and preservation for the Foundation, and

Heather Huyck of the National Park Service's Division of Interpretation organized a meeting of prominent historians who specialized in immigration and ethnic history. The idea behind the meeting was to ensure that the new exhibits and films scheduled for the Statue of Liberty and the expansive museum planned for Ellis Island would be informed by the best current scholarship on immigration.

The 1983 gathering of historians resulted in a standing committee that advised the Commission on the development of interpretive media from proposed exhibits to the film being developed for Liberty Island and Ellis Island. Chaired by Rudolph Vecoli of the University of Minnesota, the History Committee of the Statue of Liberty–Ellis Island Commission met on a regular basis for the next eight years to review exhibit and film scripts. To my knowledge, this committee was the first in the history of the National Park Service to bring together a large group of scholars to ensure the intellectual quality of Park Service interpretive products. As regional historian in the National Park Service office in charge of the restoration project, I became an ex-officio member of the committee.

The initial gatherings of this group with interpretive planners from the National Park Service demonstrated the vast gulf between history as understood and interpreted by the Park Service and history as understood by scholars. While the latter grappled with primary materials to analyze and examine the past within large historical contexts and evolving historiographical interpretations, the National Park Service traditionally focused on describing an event or a site associated with the life of a historically significant figure. Conflicting interpretations by historians or, worse, conflicts in the historical record were noticeably absent from National Park Service exhibits and publications. The agency had over the past fifty years told one-dimensional stories that were solidly anchored in the "consensus" school of historical interpretation. It sought the most middle-of-the-road, conservative (not to mention, safe) approach to developing interpretive programs and exhibits and publications that collectively gave no hint of the vibrant conversations historians had within the many fields of historical inquiry, especially that of immigration and ethnic history. In short, they provided basic descriptive information but did not encourage the visiting public to think deeply about the American past or to connect past events to present social or political circumstances.

A telling exchange between National Park Service interpreters and the foundation scholars illustrated this point. One interpretive planner asked, with all seriousness, whether the Park Service should adopt the "melting pot" or the "salad bowl" interpretation of American immigration. The answer, that it would be interesting if the Park Service presented both as examples of how historians have, over time, explored the subject, left the planner more puzzled than informed. There was simply nothing in his experience in planning exhibits for the Park Service that encouraged him to consider presenting differing historical interpretive concepts to the public.

A case could be made then—and to a certain extent can be made today—that the New Social History that became popular among historians during the 1960s and 1970s had not become incorporated in any significant way into National Park Service interpretive planning efforts. A multifaceted approach to understanding the past, an approach that included stories of women and different races and social classes, as well as different historical perspectives, would not be integrated, to the extent that is has been, into formal Park Service planning procedures for another two decades. The National Park Service had, and still has, difficulty presenting a complicated past to the visiting public.

The meetings of the Statue of Liberty–Ellis Island History Committee not only revealed how much the National Park Service had detached itself from the academic world, but provided me much food for thought on the role the Park Service should play in educating visitors about American history. Ongoing scholarly research on topics relevant to national parks was largely absent from conversations within the agency when it developed interpretive programs and media. At the same time, those committee meetings revealed a strong desire on the part of the members working with the National Park Service to develop interpretive exhibits that encouraged the public to think more deeply about the Statue of Liberty and Ellis Island and their place in American history. Indeed, they embraced the intellectual challenge of converting their research from one-dimensional text-based productions into three-dimensional museum exhibits. I became convinced that there were various roles for historical scholars within the National Park Service and that by joining forces with recognized scholars, the Park Service could more comfortably address "controversial" or contentious historical subjects.

During these gatherings, I also began gradually to reconceptualize the fundamental purpose of the National Park Service. While the preservation of special places was at the core of the Park Service's congressionally mandated mission, preservation is not an end in itself. The stories that were being developed for Ellis Island's interpretive program suggested that the National Park Service had a major role to play in educating the

American public. If park-based interpretive presentations were anchored in current scholarship, then those programs naturally served as an extension of the monographs, books, and articles being generated by the Ellis Island committee members. The primary purpose of the National Park Service, I reasoned, was to combine the presence of place with insightful historical explanations of the events that occurred there. This expansion of the Service's educational mission could create opportunities for stronger and more productive relationships between scholars and park interpreters. Moreover, it had the potential to change the Park Service's attitude toward its interpretive programs from one that considered them "informative," but educational in the most complex meaning of the word.

My thinking about the importance of presenting a more complex—and more honest—history to the public at historic sites became clearer yet again when the History Division in the Washington Office decided to eliminate its library and began sending its research reports on various parks to the appropriate regional offices. By mistake, I received a report on Lincoln's birthplace cabin in Hodgenville, Kentucky. Although I had heard that the little log cabin enshrined in a magnificent 1911 marble "tomb" designed by John Russell Pope may not have been the original, I did not become aware of the extent of the cabin's strange history until I read the 1949 report by the Abraham Lincoln Birthplace National Historic Site's historian Benjamin Davis.

In brief, Davis argued that the log cabin placed within Pope's memorial building in 1911 could be documented only to 1895. Its history prior to then was clouded in mystery. I became intrigued by Davis's reinterpretation of the cabin story and decided to examine the provenance of the cabin for myself. After several years and several research trips to Kentucky, I produced a paper and slide presentation that confirmed Davis's argument and tried to suggest how the twisted tale of the cabin could be made acceptable to a public that considered the birthplace a genuine American shrine.

The truth about the cabin is complex and fascinating. The small cabin presented as the birthplace of Abraham Lincoln did not come to the public's attention until 1895. Hoping to attract large numbers of Civil War veterans who were holding a Grand Army of the Republic reunion in Louisville that year, Alfred Dennett, a New York–based businessman, acquired a two-story cabin and had the best of its logs reassembled on the former Thomas Lincoln farm. Dennett later moved the cabin to Nashville (where he displayed it next to the alleged birthplace of Jefferson Davis) and New York City before the logs eventually returned to Louisville. Somewhere along the way, the logs of the Lincoln and Davis cabins became so intermingled that the owners could not tell the Lincoln logs from the Davis logs. In 1911, the best of the logs were trucked down to Hodgenville and installed in the recently completed memorial building. It seems, however, that Pope thought the cabin too large for the interior space of his monumental structure. Undeterred, he reduced the cabin in size two feet in length and several more feet in width. Since 1911, this miniaturized cabin, which quite possibly contains logs from Jefferson's Davis birthplace, has been on display in a shrine-like setting in central Kentucky.

The National Park Service, troubled by the revelation that the cabin did not witness the birth of President Lincoln, opted to obfuscate. Beginning in 1950, the agency referred to the cabin as the traditional birthplace cabin hoping no respectful visitor would inquire about its true origins. Bothered by this less-than-truthful approach to presenting the cabin, I lobbied the park to come clean. After all, the strange story of the Lincoln logs had much to say about the art of shrine making at the turn of the twentieth century and, ultimately, about that generation's reverence for the martyred president. Current interpretation of the Lincoln birthplace correctly identifies it as a symbolic cabin and openly informs the visitor of its less-than-authentic origins. Indeed, the development of places after they are officially proclaimed historic often says more about the attitudes and perceptions of the preservers than it does about the historic figures or events being preserved.

As I worked my way through the interpretive "problem" of the Lincoln cabin, I realized that all parks, cultural as well as natural, were created by a political process that makes interpretive choices and that the public had a right to understand how those choices affected the places they were visiting. By this time in my career I had been involved in a large number of Park Service gatherings where preservation issues needed to be decided. What is the appropriate date of preservation? Should the site be preserved, restored, or reconstructed? Should the interior be left vacant or refurnished? Should the existing furnishings be maintained or should furnishings of an earlier date be presented? I had also read a number of Park Service–generated administrative histories, which present the history of specific historic sites as they have developed under the administration of the National Park Service. These histories are invaluable for understanding the preservation and interpretive decisions made by past managers. While the story of the Lincoln cabin may be among the most strange, it is not the only historic site managed by the National Park Service whose origins are different from what the visiting public expects.

George Washington's birthplace, Wakefield, Virginia, possesses an equally interesting history. Reconstructed by the Wakefield National Memorial Association for the bicentennial of Washington's birth in 1932, the small brick building was immediately transferred to the National Park Service following the dedication ceremonies. The interpretive problem for the National Park Service was that very little evidence existed for the birthplace; what evidence the Memorial Association thought it had was blatantly ignored because it wanted to build a house fitting for a president. It is an impressive structure, one in which Washington should have been born, but unfortunately was built completely out of whole cloth and on the wrong site. The Park Service has struggled with the interpretation of Washington's birthplace for the last seventy-five years. While studying both of these supposedly venerable places, I developed a sense that in many instances the preservation history of a historic site was often as interesting as the history that prompted preservation in the first place. By not honestly presenting this second layer of history to the visiting and often adoring public, the National Park Service was both misleading these pilgrims and missing an opportunity to inform them of the vagaries inherent in historic research and preservation.

As I struggled with park planning and historic preservation issues in Boston and later in Washington, D.C., when I became regional chief of cultural resources of the National Capital Region in 1989, I continued to ponder the role historians should play in the National Park Service. Specifically, I questioned whether they were being used to their fullest potential since for the most part, they worked in the field of historic preservation rather than in historical interpretation. They conducted studies of specific buildings and events and turned that research into historic structures reports and historic resource studies, but seldom were they involved in translating that research into park brochures or films or exhibits. The Park Service's Harpers Ferry Design Center, for example, where most park interpretive products are designed, has no resident historian on staff. While working on numerous Cultural Resources Management projects between 1979 and 1995 in Boston and Washington I became increasingly concerned that the park-visiting public was receiving much less than it deserved in the area of historical interpretation.

Beginning in 1995, however, I was able to implement some of my thoughts on the preservation of significant places and the role of historians in interpreting them. A year earlier, Edwin Cole Bearss, the revered Civil War historian and chief historian of the National Park Service, retired after almost fourteen years in that position, and Roger G. Kennedy, then director of the Park Service, initiated a search for his successor. During the search for a new chief historian, and concerned that the interpretation of history in the parks was not as scholastically based as he would have liked, Kennedy enlisted the assistance of James Oliver Horton. A professor of history and American studies, Horton was brought into the Washington office on a temporary, nine-month position to advise the director on the state of historical interpretation and education. Throughout late 1994 and early 1995, Horton and I traveled widely, spoke to a large number of park interpreters and historians, and met with superintendents and planners on specific interpretive issues.

Working with Horton afforded me further time to explore the role history had played in the interpretation of historic sites and how the Park Service ought to think about the discipline of history. Extended conversations with Horton and Kennedy, the only historian to have run the National Park Service, reminded me of how exciting historical pursuits can be and, by contrast, how isolated most National Park Service historians and interpreters were from the main currents of academic inquiry and excellence. Invigorated by those exchanges, I submitted an application for the chief historian's position and in March of 1995 was appointed to succeed the incomparable Bearss.

As a historian with extensive experience in the public sector, Kennedy brought a fresh perspective to the work of the National Park Service. He challenged the agency to think of itself as an educational institution and convened a working group to develop a white paper on the subject. Coming from the Smithsonian Institution where research and education worked hand-in-hand to craft historical exhibits, Kennedy throughout his tenure as director (1993–97) pushed Park Service managers to think more critically about their work as educators. Working for and with Kennedy was both invigorating and daunting. Unlike other directors I had known, he was always thinking about the Park Service not in the next year, but in the next decade, always promoting it as an educational institution, always pushing it to advance not by small, but by giant, steps. If the Smithsonian museum that Kennedy had previously directed was widely acknowledged as an education institution, why, he asked, should the Park Service not be considered in the same way?

At about the same time, the National Park Service's interpretive program was undergoing a refreshing revolution under the leadership of Corky Mayo, the new chief of interpretation. Mayo and a talented group of Park Service interpreters reorganized and strengthened the Park Service's interpretive training requirements. Under his direction, the new training program placed far greater emphasis on interpretive content than had been the case in the recent past. Finally, just before I became chief historian, Kennedy convened a meeting of historians and anthropologists from inside and outside the Park Service to discuss the future of history and archeology in the National Park Service. This gathering in early 1994 produced a report that served as a blueprint for the incorporation of current and continuing historical and archeological scholarship into Park Service management and interpretive programs

One of the items recommended in that report was the creation of cooperative agreements between the National Park Service and leading history organizations. This led to a formal agreement between the Park Service and the Organization of American Historians in October 1994. By 1995 the National Park Service was taking a number of steps toward professionalizing the practice of history throughout the agency.

Changing direction for established bureaucracies is difficult, but the Park Service was definitely headed in a new direction. Supported by Kennedy and working within an environment of change and intellectual vitality, I refocused the efforts of the History Program over the next decade in three areas: nurturing relationships between the National Park Service and the rest of the academic profession, encouraging the incorporation of current historical scholarship into interpretive programs and media, and inserting historical perspectives into all areas of park management, planning, research, and interpretation. As I began to implement a new direction for the discipline of history in the National Park Service, I encountered the final and most important element in my evolution as a historian—the section of the 1995 *National Standards for History* titled, "Significance of History for the Educated Citizen." The much-maligned standards that grew out of a National Endowment for the Humanities directive from then Director Lynn Cheney were roundly and unfairly criticized by the political right for being insufficiently "patriotic." The "Significance" section of the standards, however, passed almost unnoticed and yet directly spoke to the need for history education in a democracy. Gary B. Nash and Charlotte Crabtree, codirectors of the project, eloquently argued for a strong national history education program. Without historical knowledge and inquiry, they concluded, "we cannot achieve the informed, discriminating citizenship essential to effective participation in the democratic processes of governance and the fulfillment for all our citizens of the nation's democratic ideals."

While similar arguments for the study of history had been expressed in earlier guidelines prepared in 1988 by the Bradley Commission on History in Schools and Paul Gagnon's response to them, I found the Nash-Crabtree justification for a strong history education agenda particularly compelling and timely. This simple, straightforward explanation of why the United States—as a democracy—should promote historical literacy among all its citizens regardless of age struck me as exceedingly appropriate and relevant not only for public schools but also for the National Park Service.

The Nash-Crabtree statement became the last link in the chain of historical thought I had been constructing for twenty years and helped refine my earlier thinking about scholarship, interpretation, and the role of the National Park Service in American society. The result was a philosophy of education for the History Program. First, the importance of historical literacy in a participatory democracy such as ours is critical to all citizens and should not be structured only for the young. Second, if the goal of history education in this country is to develop a historically literate society, historians—academic as well as public—should seek to engage the public in conversations about the past. Third, historic sites are formally preserved not simply to prevent their destruction, but because they have stories to tell and we have things to learn from those stories. Fourth, because the interpretive component of historic sites should be perceived as part of this nation's educational system, historians should be involved at every step in developing interpretive programs and media.

This way of thinking about the responsibility of historians shaped both my perceptions of the discipline itself and the role of history throughout the National Park Service. Historical interpretation at historic sites should not simply be about providing historical understanding—as important as that is. It should be about encouraging civic reflection and responsibility by making connections between past and present. Making connections between Pearl Harbor and the Japanese internment camp at Manzanar, for example, encourages thoughts about war and constitutional rights. Making connections between Appomattox Court House and Brown vs. Board of Education National Historic Site in Topeka, Kansas, leads to thinking through time and about the implications in our own time of past decisions. Historic sites do not exist in isolation from each other, but are related in time, historic time. Park Service interpreters have an obligation to convey to visitors the threads of understandings scholars have followed among historic sites, and between historic sites and scholarly studies. When done well, each supports and enriches the other, and our society benefits.

The degree to which the National Park Service viewed historic places in isolation and declined to offer a broad understanding can be found in its interpretation of Civil War battlefields. Indeed, saying something meaningful about the American Civil War, its causes and its consequences, was something the National Park Service had consciously avoided over the sixty years it had managed Civil War battlefields. Franklin Roosevelt transferred the Civil War national battlefield parks from the War Department to the National Park Service in 1933. From then until the late 1990s, the Park Service had avoided saying anything about the causes of the war in any of its exhibits, films, or publications. The closest it came to explaining the causes appeared in the park brochure for Fort Sumter. "On December 20, 1860," it began, "after decades of sectional conflict, the people of South Carolina" voted to secede from the Union. Inquiring readers might want to know what the National Park Service meant by the phrase "after decades of sectional conflict," but they would not find the answer in any interpretive material generated by the agency. The Park Service had informally determined that the causes of the Civil War, especially the role of slavery, were simply not to be part of battlefield interpretive fare because they were too "controversial."

Fortunately, a new generation of battlefield superintendents decided in 1998 that the story of the battles simply did not make sense without an understanding of the causes of the war. At a meeting in Nashville, National Park Service battlefield superintendents agreed that almost 150 years after Appomattox it was time to start incorporating the causes of the war into battlefield interpretations. As word of the decision became known, Civil War buffs throughout the country quickly voiced their objections. Over the next year or so, my office received approximately 2,500 letters, the vast majority critical of the National Park Service. The war was not fought over the institution of slavery, the letters charged; slavery, they said, didn't enter the war until Lincoln's Emancipation Proclamation of 1863. The agency was accused of "hijacking" history, of slandering and demonizing the South, and of dishonoring the men, North and South, who fought and died on the battlefields managed by the National Park Service.

All of these arguments were based on a fear that the National Park Service was going to both abandon the traditional military interpretation of the battlefields and judge the South and slave owners. Civil War periodicals, the Sons of Confederate Veterans, and Civil War Roundtables generated a flood of protest to force the National Park Service to back away from its decision to introduce the causes of the war—and slavery—into its military history programs. The correspondence, including many from members of Congress, ended up on my desk.

The public reaction to the superintendents' decision required me, as chief historian, to become the spokesperson for the National Park Service on this contentious subject. Responding to accusatory correspondence forced me to learn more about the Civil War and led me to view each response as an educational opportunity. I became an avid student of the war and its causes, and I became a better public historian. The controversy prompted the National Park Service to implement the philosophy embedded in the Nash-Crabtree justification for a robust history education system. The Park Service response to the public's concerns was designed to take nineteenth-century history directly to the public, to explain to a largely hostile audience why a conversation about slavery and the coming of the war was historically justified, appropriate for a federal agency, and beneficial to our society. The National Park Service, through its new exhibits and publications, had the opportunity to broaden the perceptions of millions of park visitors annually regarding the causes and consequences of the war. Instead of shying away from controversy, the National Park Service embraced it with the complete support of Kennedy's successor as director, Robert G. Stanton, the first African American director of the agency.

Without question, these were the most challenging and intellectually stimulating years of my Park Service career. The public's response to the Park Service's embrace of its educational responsibilities regarding the Civil War required me to balance my roles as a scholar and an employee of the federal government. Many of the letters we received were addressed to United States senators and congressmen and women who passed them along to the National Park Service. While I did not believe that any member of Congress would suggest that the Service retreat from its decision to interpret the causes of the war, I was well aware that our responses must be respectful, direct, and historically based. Angry letters could not be addressed with angry responses. My job was to answer each as directly and as professionally as possible without any hint of emotion even when the writers attacked me personally.

Many of those protesting the superintendents' decision reflected on their own military experience to bolster their claim that the National Park Service was dishonoring their ancestors by addressing the issue of slavery as a cause of the war. The presumption on their part, it seemed, was that those responsible for the change in direction had not served in the military and hence could not understand the "insult" to Civil War descendants the Service was formulating. Once this pattern began to take shape in the letters that made their way to my desk, I began including a bit of personal history in my responses. Interestingly enough, the fact that the chief historian of the National Park Service was a Marine Corps veteran and the recipient of a Purple Heart had a moderating effect on some my correspondents. That knowledge seemed to reduce the distance between the federal agency and those who felt aggrieved. Additionally, I started to wear my Purple Heart lapel pin when I addressed Civil War audiences. It certainly didn't change any minds about what the Park Service was doing, but it did tend to reduce the hostility in a room and create a more civil environment during discussions and debates.

In crafting our responses, we learned valuable lessons that lie at the core of the delicate art of public history. The public, we discovered, did not share our understanding of how history is constructed, how historians go about their craft. Most of our correspondents made a clean distinction between history and the interpretation of history. History, in their minds, was a collection of facts, that is, truth, while interpretation involved playing fast and loose with the facts and resulted in fabricated truth or "politically correct" history. It became very clear to us, in other words, that historical interpretation, as historians understand and use the term, is a very misunderstood concept on the part of the public and, ultimately, considered suspect. So our initial attempts to quote James McPherson or Eric Foner on the coming of the war were met with comments that they were merely "Yankee" historians and didn't understand Southern history. We quickly adjusted and cited Ed Ayers, William Davis, and William Cooper, all again to no avail. These scholars were "scalawag" historians who pandered to the "political correctness" found among northern historians. Interpretation to our audience was no different from opinion, and one person's opinion was as good as another's.

Attempts to explain how historians go about their work fell largely on deaf ears. We made better progress when we resorted to using primary sources of evidence such as declarations of secession, speeches of leading Southern politicians, and the letters and speeches of secession commissioners. Committed neo-Confederates had trouble discounting Alexander Stephens's Cornerstone speech or Mississippi's declaration of secession. The National Park Service found that using these sources of historical evidence also proved useful in exhibits and publications. The above mentioned "after decades of sectional conflict" park brochure from Fort Sumter has since been revised to include quotations from South Carolina's declaration of secession. Likewise the new Civil War interpretive center at Corinth, Mississippi, has placed the full text of Mississippi's declaration of secession at the center of its exhibit on the coming of the war. Using primary source evidence helped alter the public's perception of the historian's work as mere opinion.

Interestingly enough, during my thirty years with the National Park Service, I can recall only two incidents (during the late 1990s and just after President George Bush's election) when politics intruded into the realm of historical interpretation. The first arose when a congressman visited Women's Rights National Historical Park in Seneca Falls, New York, and objected to an interpretive panel that cast Ronald Reagan's environmental record in an unfavorable light. The congressman's letter of protest to the Secretary of the Interior landed on my desk along with a request to fix the problem. After reviewing the text, I concluded that while not technically incorrect, the panel was not as prudent as it might have been in assessing President Reagan's environmental legacy. I quickly organized a small committee of scholars and through a series of conversations conducted via e-mail, developed an alternative exhibit text that was both historically sound and politically viable. The suggested language was approved by the department and installed at Seneca Falls.

The second occasion involved two congressmen who complained about the interpretive film at the Lincoln Memorial. The film, to their thinking, contained too much footage of liberal protestors in front of the memorial and not enough of conservative protestors. Specifically, they wanted footage inserted of anti-abortion and anti-gay protestors to counter existing footage of pro-choice and gay rights demonstrators in front of the memorial. The congressmen's demands were heard by the then director of the National Park Service and secretary of the interior who agreed to look into the matter and make the suggested changes. Unfortunately, for the congressmen, director, and secretary, demonstrators for conservative issues such as anti-abortion and anti-gay protestors usually protest at the eastern end of the National Mall near the Supreme Court building. As a result, no footage exists of the desired protestors in front of the Lincoln

Memorial. The National Park Service ultimately determined that the historical accuracy of the film would be undermined with the addition of footage taken elsewhere on the Mall. The film continues to be shown in the lower level of the Lincoln Memorial.

Conversing with the public about the troubled landscape of the Civil War has unquestionably made me a better historian because the public asks different questions from my fellow academics, questions that are meaningful and relevant to their lives, questions that make me think differently about what I know about the past and how I put the pieces together. Even when passions rise and the topic turns to immigration reform, the legacy of the Vietnam War, or the causes of the Civil War, I believe historians should be at the center of civic conversations even when the conversation threatens to turn contentious. Having a conversation with members of the public who do not agree with one's interpretation of the past is, after all, far less difficult than running a marathon, being in combat, or, I can only imagine, giving birth. It is also immensely gratifying to shape interpretive programs that offer the visiting public a way of thinking about the past that challenges presumed historical truths and provides narratives that encourage them to think more deeply and critically about the past and how it influences today's society.

In my case, having become a historian means that I have not only become proficient and published in the fields of the American West, historic preservation, and the Civil War, but that I have sought ways to encourage a broader public understanding of history and its importance to our society. My becoming a historian, thus, has been a journey of shifting perceptions of what historians do and how they function in our society. Becoming a historian is, for me at least, best represented not by a threshold that is crossed but by a continuing process of acquiring skills and knowledge, of examining beliefs and assessing conclusions, and of responding to, and influencing, the needs of our discipline. Quite by chance, I became a public historian. By choice, I decided that remaining a public historian was how I could best contribute to the discipline of history and the public's understanding of its history. At this point in my career, I am convinced that my early decision to leave Euterpe for Clio's embrace was a choice that has served me well.

LINDA GORDON

History Constructs a Historian

I consider myself still in the process of becoming a historian. When I look back at my earlier work, I often wince at its lack of subtlety, even as I marvel at how much the scholarship in my field has advanced. So what follows does not focus exclusively on my education and early years in the profession; the essay here has no completion, none of the maturity that should be the outcome of a *bildungsroman*. I have tried instead to mark some of the influences on that continuing process, influences that stemmed more from larger world events than from teachers and other intellectuals. There is a circularity here: the kind of historian I am today determines how I see the history of my becoming a historian.

* * *

Everyone's life is imbedded in historical events, often major ones, but many children are allowed—or even encouraged—to remain oblivious to them. Especially when events are, as they so often are, painful, unjust, and horrendous. Lack of oblivion to history was an early-appearing constant in my life.

My father, Bill Gordon, once Wolf Gordonovich, came to the United States in adolescence with only his older brother for escort. Their father, Yisroel, died while their mother, Liebe, was pregnant with her youngest,

Avram, or Abe. They came from a tiny *shtetl*, Shumsk, located approximately twenty miles (twenty-eight versts) south of Vilna (today Vilnius, Lithuania). I knew about Shumsk from earliest memory. Although less than a village in terms of numbers of permanent residents, once a week on Wednesdays it had a market and on those days the village was teeming. Peasants from surrounding villages, merchants of every description, would come to buy.

The widow, Liebe, my grandmother, supported her family by selling cigarettes, bread she baked, and *schnitt*—small dry goods. She frequently bartered her goods for food. She owned a wool-combing machine, inside her tiny house, which she rented to peasants. At sheep-shearing times they brought raw wool and frequently spent the night in the house until they completed their work. My father remembered it well: it had a huge drum in the center and belts with steel teeth; raw wool would be placed on a belt, combed by brushes, enter first the large drum and then a smaller drum where it was wound.

Around Shumsk, Polish-Jewish relations were peaceful, customary. But there were occasional pogroms, for Shumsk was located on a main road of travel from Vilna to Minsk, and as the First World War developed, that road was used by marching and pillaging armies. Liebe remarried, but this second husband was then drafted, leaving the family unprotected. So her relatives moved Liebe and her family to Shchedrin, a larger but less accessible village, located about eighteen miles from the nearest railroad station and about thirty miles from the provincial town of Bobruisk in White Russia. Shchedrin was unusual in that here the Jews farmed, which was generally forbidden in Czarist Russia. But a pogrom reached even here, and a unit of irregular (volunteer) Polish cavalry, probably followers of Józef Piłsudski entered the village as they advanced against the Russians.* In addition to the usual pillage and beatings, the Poles set up a public gibbet (a hanging structure) in the town square and issued an ultimatum to the village elders: they must provide specified amounts of gold and other precious items or randomly chosen Jews would be hanged. The young Wolf remembered the Poles bursting into the house, searching for valuables, breaking furniture, and leaving everything in shambles. Most frightening, they found, or claimed to find, a bullet in the house, and accused the family of harboring weapons. Somehow the family emerged unharmed.

---

* Józef Piłsudski was a Polish nationalist leader, later dictator of Poland, who led the Polish campaign against the Russian Bolshevik revolution.

Returning to Shumsk in 1918 at age ten, Wolf then experienced the hardest years of all. Hunger and starvation were widespread. It was not uncommon for men to walk thirty or forty miles with a sack of wheat or other grain on their backs, only to be waylaid by other starving men and come home empty handed. Liebe's husband's return from the war did not diminish the hardships. She baked bread of 10 percent wheat or rye flour, the balance consisting of cheaper vegetables. Even potatoes were a luxury. Frequently there was not enough to eat.

So in 1920 Liebe sent her two older sons, twelve-year-old Wolf and fourteen-year-old Yisroel, to America, to their father's youngest brother Nathan who had immigrated to Cleveland. She kept Abe with her, no doubt thinking him too young to be away from his mother, but also not wanting to be childless herself. A distant relative, a "Dr." Unterman, who was traveling to Warsaw and back on business, was enlisted to bring the boys to the United States and entrusted with the money for their passage. The boys were to go by train from Vilna to Warsaw, and my father believed the train was one of the very last to get through before the Red Army seized Vilna from the Polish army and sealed it off. The boys had been instructed to find Unterman through the offices of the *Forwärts*, the Yiddish language newspaper, but when they arrived they learned that he had stopped there but had left without a forwarding address or any message. (The family concluded that he had taken the money and run.) The boys were stranded. Yisroel found a sympathetic rabbi who got them admitted to an orphanage, run by the Warsaw *Kehilah*, until travel arrangements could be worked out. Meanwhile the Red Army had severed communications with Poland, so they had no way of communicating with their family. After three months at the orphanage, HIAS (the Hebrew Immigrant Aid Society) provided them tickets to Danzig (now Gdansk), where they stayed in a refugee camp with hundreds of other stranded immigrants on a small island across the Vistula.

There they remained for another three months, without funds. And in Danzig there was not the help available in a large Jewish community like that of Warsaw. There was a bread shortage and strict rationing, so the resourceful Yisroel found a way to participate in the black market. Using forged ration cards, they bought bread, smuggled it under loose-fitting clothing into the barracks where the other immigrants were housed, and sold it for the then exorbitant price of ten marks a loaf. They made the trips in rowboat they rented for fifty pfennigs a trip. Finally, in December 1920, they sailed from Danzig on a Danish ship, Oskar II, which stopped in Copenhagen, Oslo, then known as Christiana, and finally New York. There Wolf was renamed William, called Bill, Yisroel renamed Irwin, and Gordonovich became Gordon. They were sent to Cleveland.

At this point my father's stories became vague and fragmented. He didn't like to talk about his life in Cleveland. So I shift to what my father learned only later. In 1939 the Germany army moved across Poland. (I was named after his parents: Irene for Yisroel, Linda for Liebe.) In *shtetls* such as Shumsk they rounded up the Jews, forced them to dig trenches, and then machine-gunned them into the trenches. My uncle Abe, then a twenty-four-year-old medical student in Prague, was sent to concentration camp Dachau. As a physician he somehow survived, and I learned never to ask how, and starting in 1945 my father began a search to find him and bring him to the United States, which he finally achieved in 1947.

My immigrant parents had both arrived long enough before Nazis came to power that they registered the genocide only gradually. I do not remember a moment when they discovered it, and I know that my father had hopes of his mother's escape until a postwar refugee described to him the fate of Shumsk.

So as a young child I understood, perhaps unconsciously, that my own life was produced by the contingencies of history, the lucky escapes. This lesson, I now think, shaped my interests as I became a historian. It made me quick to see individual lives as produced by large-scale political-economic forces and to formulate large-scale generalizations–too quick, one of my college history professors thought, and without enough regard for the cases that do not fit the generalization. Over years of school and research and writing, I had to learn to hold back that propensity to identify patterns prematurely, before completing the research.

*   *   *

My route to academia was also paved by luck—of place and of time. I didn't know it at the time: growing up in the 1950s, I would never have considered myself fortunate. My family moved to Portland, Oregon. Both my parents worked, earning a modest income, as a social worker (my father) and a day-care-center teacher (my mother). I got a poor high school education. At Cleveland High my U.S. history teacher's pedagogical technique was to have the students take turns reading aloud from the textbook day after day. (The highlight of the course, one we looked forward to because the teacher did it year after year and everyone knew about it, was when he asked for several repeat readings of the paragraph about Irish immigration. He was Irish.) McCarthyist culture dominated the school, enforcing social conformity and middle-class snobbery toward working-class students. I could never fix my hair right, and my parents both disdained and could not afford the Pendleton plaid skirts and cashmere sweaters that the popular girls wore. I could not seem to pick up the social styles of these girls, and had no high school friends.

But hailing from Oregon got me accepted at elite colleges looking to draw nationwide student bodies. High school boredom made me fascinated by Reed College, close to our house. I was attracted to the unconventional look of the students and a sense that it would not be uncool to be "smart" there. But I wanted to leave home and feared that Reed might expect me to live with my parents as a commuter student. Neither I nor my parents knew much about the array of college possibilities and I chose Swarthmore on the illusion that it was like Reed. I realized later that I would never have been accepted at Swarthmore if I had come from New York because it had a Jewish quota thinly disguised as a New York quota. At least this is widely believed—I have never seen the evidence on this matter.

Then my second piece of good luck, symbolized by *Sputnik*. The cold war that lay behind the conformist teenage culture of the time also produced competition with the Soviet Union. Its educational system and development of scientific expertise seemed particularly challenging to U.S. power, and thus stimulated investment in U.S. education through scholarship programs. I got one of the first National Merit Scholarships and could use it at any school that accepted me. It paid for the entire cost of my tuition, room, and board. Later, my dissertation research was funded by another cold-war program—a National Defense Education Act fellowship. Had I been just five years older, I would have had difficulty paying for college education. Choosing Swarthmore was also lucky, but I did not know this right away. The preparation and skills of the other Swarthmore students intimidated me when I first arrived. I received poor grades my first semester, and the dean placed me on academic warning. One of my worst grades was in a required history class, Western Civ, taught by Mary Albertson. There is an ironic story here: Albertson was one of the small number of outstanding women historians educated in the Progressive era who managed to get academic jobs. Born in 1895, she published her dissertation as *London Merchants and Their Landed Property during the Reigns of the Yorkists* (Philadelphia, printed by the John C. Winston Company, in 1932), but apparently nothing after that. Years later I came to understand them as my forebears and shiver at how their careers were stunted by discrimination. When I began to study women in 1969, I had forgotten all about Mary Albertson and thought that my cohort was inventing a women's history for the first time. But at Swarthmore, Albertson was my nemesis. I found her course foggy and dull, and something in me refused the kind of memorization of fragments of unaffiliated facts that appeared necessary for me to pass the course. Four years later, I ran into her in the mailroom just as I received an acceptance from Yale graduate school, so I told her, excitedly, my news. She responded, "Congratulations. This is indeed a surprise."

And this was the only woman professor I ever had. Now I can offer a social-historical explanation for Albertson's personality, teaching style, and attitude toward college girls. But as a freshman in her class, I assumed that she epitomized what the study of history was like.

By contrast I developed a relationship with a woman adjunct who taught Russian language—a common position for women, allowed to teach only the language, not the (sophisticated) literature courses. She was an intellectual of the first rank with an extraordinary range of experience and knowledge, but the Swarthmore faculty ignored and disdained her. Her intellectual sophistication and cosmopolitanism drew me like a magnet. I felt I understood her: her life was shaped by world-historical events, like my father's but at a more conscious and activist level. This feeling came from youthful arrogance of course. I now know that she also produced her life herself, individually, and that chance events also contributed.

Olga Abramovna Lang was born in 1898 to a Russian Jewish socialist family in Ekaterinoslav (a large industrial city, now called Dnepropetrovsk, in eastern Ukraine). She studied Russian and European history and literature at the elite Women's University in Petrograd and at Moscow University. She became active first in the Socialist Revolutionary Party before and during the 1917 revolutions, then worked for the Central Council of Trade Unions. For a time she was the personal and political partner of Menshevik leader Feodor Dan. Later she married a German Leftist; moving to Berlin in 1927, she became the German correspondent covering labor and politics for the Soviet labor journal *Trud*. A participant-observer, she interviewed workers and attended strike meetings and conventions. At some point she joined the German Communist Party. In 1932, a collection of her "sketches" was published in Moscow as *Images of German Workers*. As Hitler came to power, Lang married again, this time to the historian Karl August Wittfogel, soon to be renowned for his study *Oriental Despotism*.

Lang and Wittfogel were key members of the Left intelligentsia of Berlin. Harassment and outright attacks on Communists escalated, and when their own apartment was raided, they went into hiding. Later that year, Wittfogel was arrested while trying to leave the country and sent to a prison camp. Lang devoted herself to campaigning for his release over the next eight months, even, with her strongly accented German, appealing in person to SS officials at Gestapo headquarters. Her efforts finally succeeded, and the couple fled first to England, then China.* To know her was to learn firsthand about the great events I studied in my history courses. Her sense of history, rather than Albertson's, first drew me to the discipline.

In China, Lang reinvented herself as a China scholar. She learned to speak and write the language and began to study Chinese family and gender. (I was completely uninterested in gender at the time.) Her book, *Chinese Family and Society* (1946), was for many years a definitive work on the subject. When Japan invaded China in 1937, she came to the United States. Her skills, if not her erudition, were valued by the armed forces during the Second World War, when she worked for the Army Specialized Training Program. She also helped compile and edit a dictionary of spoken Russian. After the war, she worked for the newly formed United Nations and as an interpreter and researcher at the Nuremberg trials. In 1951, she enrolled in graduate school at Columbia and received a Ph.D. in Chinese and Japanese.†

She always kept an apartment in New York, on 110th Street, and I visited her there several times. Her death in 1992 went unnoticed by Swarthmore—and by me. I still feel sad and guilty that I knew so little of her life, undervalued her as an intellectual, and remained oblivious to the discrimination she encountered at Swarthmore and elsewhere. I owe her much. I was not an outstanding student of the language, but I couldn't get enough of her experience of history. Another piece of luck: she recognized my intellectual seriousness and critical perspective on the world and talked with

---

* Wittfogel later renounced communism. In 1951 testimony before a McCarthy-era House Subcommittee on Internal Security, he named Lang—by then his ex-wife—along with several of his former friends and colleagues.

† She became an expert on Pa Chin, an anarchist writer influential among Chinese students in the 1930s and 1940s. Her dissertation was published as *Pa Chin and His Writing: Chinese Youth Between the Two Revolutions* (1967). At Swarthmore, however, Lang never taught Chinese, as the College offered no Asian languages at the time. After retiring from Swarthmore, she returned to Columbia as an adjunct associate professor of Russian. She continued her research on Chinese-Russian cultural relations and remained there until 1985.

me of serious matters, such as Stalinism, fascism and Russian literature. She could recite hours and hours of Russian poetry and I can still recite a few verses of Pushkin myself.

* * *

After my first-year experience with Albertson, I had no thought of more history courses until I heard other students praise French historian Paul Beik. I took his course on the Russian revolution and became a history major instantly. He demonstrated historical thought as a critical intellectual discipline, analyzing and interpreting historical structures and processes. I now think that my work in his courses and seminars formed the ground for everything I have done since. He introduced us to the great French social historians François-Alphonse Aulard, Albert Mathiez, and Georges Lefebvre, the passionate anti-Stalinist historian Isaac Deutscher, and anti-nationalists such as Hajo Holborn. Beik showed us how to think about history not as narrative but as structural analysis; not driven only by leaders but also by social and economic developments; not as a matter of empirical objectivity but as interpretation; not only as national but also as global. Above all he encouraged his students to understand what was at stake in matters such as the French Revolution and British imperialism, how they shaped our lives ever after. In other words, Beik's approach fit my existing orientation, garnered from my father and Olga Lang, while introducing me to rigor as well as imagination. When I later read the British Marxist historians E. P. Thompson and Eric Hobsbawm, I understood them in this tradition.

A master teacher, unfailingly generous, Paul Beik turned many students into history majors and quite a few into historians. When one of my books won a prize from the American Historical Association, I could nominate a favorite teacher for the distinguished teacher award and put together a big dossier on Beik. Unfortunately the prize went to someone else, someone much less deserving, I thought.

Beik was my favorite, but Swarthmore was rich with fine teachers. Lawrence Lafore's honors history seminars sparkled, Monroe Beardsley's aesthetics seminar (philosophy was my minor) provided a best-practices induction into rigorous and morally engaged thinking, Michael Scriven's philosophy of science course drew students into the actual practice of making precise philosophical statements. But the geographic range of the history I learned was small. The only course on the history of non-Europeans offered was called British Empire. After my lousy first semester I became a good student, for two reasons: fine teachers make fine students; and I learned to study. I did not know how to do this when I arrived at college, because I breezed through high school without much work. I had a great deal of intellectual arrogance, partly a compensation I developed for my social failures. After my first college semester, I registered that at Swarthmore everyone, no matter how smart, had to study. I learned to do it and to love it.

Wonderful as the faculty was, most of my education at Swarthmore came from other students—and this owed a great deal to the college's structure and culture, the honors program foremost. Students with a good GPA could opt for this program junior and senior year: instead of four courses we did two intensive weekly seminars at a time, ungraded, typically writing a paper a week that was distributed and read by all seminar members. Thus each student did only eight seminars in her last two years, but what we lost in breadth we gained in depth. Often seminars were as small as six, often they met in the evening and continued until the instructor shut us up. We took ourselves undeservedly seriously and in many ways behaved like grad students, making scathing critiques of fine books and generalizing on the basis of very little knowledge. So while Swarthmore showed us the excitement of intellectual life, it also reinforced my tendency toward grand generalization. I was never required to write a research paper at Swarthmore. But we worked like hell.

The honors program ended with high drama and agonizing tension. For the final honors exams, we had to write closed-book essays on questions set by outside examiners, and then submit to oral examination by them. After two years with no grades at all, this was frightening. Those of us who typed our exams had to bring our typewriters into the gym where dozens of typing tables lined the walls. If I remember correctly, we had three hours to answer a question. In theory, the Swarthmore faculty gave the examiners no information whatsoever about the students, so that we lost whatever leg up our participation in the seminar had given us. But the honors-seminar experience was incomparable and it has represented ever since my model of ideal learning.

At Swarthmore my social life transformed into, I think, average, but average for me was ecstatic. Swarthmore's Quaker culture blurred the class differences between me and most other students. For example, students were not allowed to have cars, so one major source of privilege disappeared. The college was big enough to have discrete crowds, of course, and mine—bohemians, intellectuals, and folkies—was big enough for me to have plenty of friends. Our social culture involved mostly group, not coupled activities. We sang folk music and talked and talked, mostly over beer in Media, Pennsylvania. (Swarthmore was and remains a dry town and we had not discovered marijuana yet.) Without cars, the only way to get to a bar was to hike—and we typically walked along the Media local train tracks at night (I don't remember even considering that this might be dangerous), which supplied a bit of exercise for my entirely sports-free life. (Physical education was required for freshmen, and I hated it. Girls in my day were not encouraged toward anything athletic, a fact that I much regret today. I was a serious dancer in my teens, strong and agile, and I know now that I could have been good at tennis or softball or track. Looking back, I resent the fact that only boys had the fun of sports.)

When the Swarthmore students slightly younger than I was began organizing protests to support the civil rights movement, my friends and I at first disdained their earnestness. We thought they were naïve. We were really latter-day beats, cultivating cynicism and alienation, and while we heartily condemned conservative ideas and policies, we were pessimistic about social change. We had reactivated an older Swarthmore group, however, the Forum for Free Speech and invited some radical speakers, such as Harry Bridges of the International Longshore and Warehouse Union. When we discovered that the cleaning staff, composed of African American women, were not allowed to enter the main building by the front door and not allowed to socialize with students in the snack bar, we organized a protest. The dean then offered me a personal lesson in the college's class assumptions. I was part of a delegation asking him to change that policy and when we presented our case in his office, he turned to me and asked, "Linda, what door does the maid use in your home?" (My family, of course, had no maid.) By my senior year, the "youngsters" had won us over and several of my crowd were picketing Woolworths in Chester, Pennsylvania, in solidarity with civil rights sit-ins in the South.

Once again my trajectory was determined by my historical position: I was just a few years too old to become part of the giant student movement that coalesced around opposition to the Vietnam War. From college I went immediately to grad school and here too I did not recognize my good luck until well afterward. I was not accepted at first by Yale's history department.

But someone in the graduate school, seeing my record, offered me admission instead to a Russian studies master's program, created as a cold-war initiative. Looking back years later, when I realized how very few history grad students were female, I suspected sex discrimination in this strange admissions practice, since scholars considered area studies more light-weight than the traditional disciplines. Some of my Russian studies courses were demanding and weighty: Dostoevsky with René Wellek and Russian history with Firuz Kazemzadeh, who became my advisor. He was another of my pieces of luck. A Persian raised in the Soviet Union, he did not share in the Russian nationalism that then marked academics in that field; a member—and later a leader—in the Bahá-í faith, he was probably more sympathetic to academic women and Jews than was the norm at Yale. I learned a great deal from my fellow students, particularly my then boyfriend, the Brazilian Roberto Schwarz, now a well-known Marxist literary critic, then a graduate student in comparative literature. We met in Wellek's course on Dostoevsky and it was his brilliance that attracted me. Steeped in European Marxism and Frankfurt school thought, he saw works of literature as expressions of social and economic relations.

My first research paper was my master's thesis in Russian studies. It involved only a modest bit of research, since there were not many Russian sources available in New Haven. But it got me admission to the history graduate program. Shortly after arriving there, however, I began to lose interest. With the exception of Hajo Holborn's course on modern European diplomatic history, nothing I studied matched Swarthmore's intellectualism. Furthermore, these studies had to compete for my attention with the far more important and vivid civil rights movement. In my first Yale years, 1961–63, the Yale law school was a center of civil rights and civil liberties discourse, the students influenced by Professor Thomas Emerson; some quite brilliant law students, Eleanor Holmes (now Eleanor Holmes Norton) and John Ely became friends of mine. So after two years I dropped out of graduate school, restless but without a clear alternative. I did not intend to return and planned to seek another career.

This was the first of two steps off the academic path, but both times I returned. Numerous brilliant students of my generation dropped out more definitively, taking working-class jobs or living on very low-paid jobs for social movements. I might have done likewise, or found a different professional path, had I been lucky and confident enough to find such a path. But I think now that I was too economically insecure to try something that did not provide a reliable paycheck.

From Yale I went to Washington, D.C., took a civil service exam, learned that a girl with a master's and my lack of confidence could get a clerical job, and volunteered in the Washington office of the militant civil rights organization, Student Nonviolent Coordinating Committee. The bravery, drama, and moral passion of civil rights gripped me like no previous experience. Although I did not know it at the time, civil rights was pregnant with the other great social movements of the period—antiwar, women's liberation, gay liberation—and taught me and thousands of others how to think about power and domination. Ultimately, the civil rights movement and its intellectuals influenced my historical thinking more than graduate school did, because it taught me how to ferret out and analyze power in relationships that had been ideologized as natural; to see how domination worked socially and politically, how exploitation worked economically, how subordination worked culturally. Equally important, the movement showed me the complexities of power, and acquiescence and resistance to power—how race could not be disentangled from other scales of hierarchy, how those on top and those below calculate their options, how neither the top nor the bottom are homogeneous. Many years later these understandings were illustrated and further developed by one of my favorite books, one I frequently teach, Charles Payne's *I've Got the Light of Freedom*, still one of the great books on a social movement.

But while the civil rights movement was emotionally and intellectually gripping, I remained committed to that regular paycheck. Since I couldn't get a decent job, and couldn't imagine a job I could get that I would like, I returned in absentia to graduate school to work on my dissertation. (Note: my recommitment to academia, a decision for which I am most grateful today, was the result of a failure.) In 1967 I set out to do research in the Soviet Union on my sixteenth-century topic—the origins and early battles of the Ukrainian (Zaporogian) Cossacks. These groups of brigands, influenced by the Crimean Tatars, were a product of the intersection between peasants fleeing serfdom and an ungoverned frontier which neither nobility nor state yet controlled. But when I arrived in the USSR, I could not get access to archives I needed. I had imagined that by writing about the sixteenth century, I would escape cold-war politics, but in the USSR nothing was exempt. Imagining my whole academic career a bust, I retreated to London where I lived for a year and a half—my second dropping out. There, after getting over my anger and frustration, I found sources for my dissertation in the British Museum and the Polish Library, and traveled for other research to Warsaw and Cracow.

I worked on my dissertation desultorily, but my main interest once again was a social movement. As an American, I felt obliged to join an anti–Vietnam War group. As an American in England, I was astounded by a class system more naked than I was accustomed to. And as an American Leftist in England, I was taken aback to find a British Left rooted among working class people rather than elite college students. I read E. P. Thompson and Eric Hobsbawm, and their influence, along with that of friends, turned my dissertation into a more social and analytic work than it could have been previously. In learning to think about class I was connecting with my parents' experience in yet another way: growing up as a Jew in Portland, I had felt sharply the difference between our family and the affluent Jews I met in Sunday school.

There were no women in my dissertation. While I was living in London, pioneer feminist theorist Juliet Mitchell began teaching a course on women at a Left "open university," and when I saw the notice of this, I thought, what an odd and trivial topic.

*   *   *

I returned from England to take a job teaching at the University of Massachusetts, Boston—a job I got by letter from England with no interview. The end of the 1960s saw the continuing expansion of universities, also a cold-war phenomenon, and jobs were easy to get. (I know this is galling for younger academics to hear, but the fact is essential to a realistic evaluation of the accomplishments of my generation: we had it easy.) Then the women's liberation movement came along and I was an instant convert. The first time an articulate feminist spoke to me I knew immediately that everything she was saying was not only right, but so obvious that to this day I remain bewildered by how blatant were the things I didn't notice. This gave me great respect for the blinding force of ideology when it becomes hegemonic and is taken to be common sense.

Still, the women's movement did not immediately connect with my work. I was teaching Western civilization, a course not only required of all freshmen, but one in which instructors were required to use a book of readings edited by the chair of the department. So the course seemed deadening at first. I did my best to introduce students to social history, history from the bottom-up as we called it then, and to the idea that not everything published was necessarily true—an important first step in teaching still today. Rebelling against the Europeanist required curriculum, three of us young faculty, all influenced by the New Left, organized an alternative introductory course, which we taught as a team, on modern revolutions. (In retrospect I see how European history continued to undergird our approach.) Two extraordinary colleagues, David Hunt and Peter Weiler, a French and a British historian, and I taught as a team. We started with the French revolution and ended with the anticolonial struggles of Vietnam and the Portuguese colonies in Africa. We took turns lecturing and taught discussion classes individually. We cared passionately about what we taught but our political bias was probably less than that of the Western-civ curriculum.

It was not long before it occurred to several young feminist scholars around Boston that there could be a history of women. We formed a group to search out this untold history. At one time or another the group included Mari Jo Buhle, Ellen DuBois, Maurine Greenwald, Linda Hunt, Priscilla Long Irons, Elizabeth Pleck, Ann Popkin, Susan Reverby, Lillian Robinson, Rochelle Ziegler Ruthchild, Kathryn Kish Sklar, Sharon Strom, Meredith Tax, Lise Vogel and me. I was stunned to find in Harvard's Widener Library a few extremely smart women's history books written thirty or forty years previously—notably Alice Clark's *Working Life of Women in the Seventeenth Century*—that were entirely unknown to contemporary historians; and I mean unknown—the check-out slips on the inside back cover had last been stamped in the 1930s. (That discovery has haunted me. Is it possible that good history books will once again be buried?) These few books suggested new research paths—and the Schlesinger Library at Radcliffe was waiting for us. Established in 1943 by Elizabeth Schlesinger, mother of Arthur Schlesinger, Jr., it was created by first-wave feminists when their movement was at a low point; it was stubbornly maintained until second-wave feminism and the scholarship it created made it a major research library and archive.

Though guided to some extent by the few earlier scholars, my generation of women's historians was mostly on its own. The development of the field of women's history was a collective project, taking place simultaneously in several locations. Its collectivity escalated both our confidence and our excitement about what we were doing and finding. Our Boston group first focused on male social theorists theorizing about women, and we saw that this theorizing was about gender, because we registered that we were dealing with a socially constructed binary—that is, there could be no female without male. I think of the founding intellectual insights of feminism as twofold: distinguishing gender from sex,* and breaking through the distinction between the personal and the political. Both of these premises are historical and so it seems in some way inevitable that the movement gave rise to a new history. As to gender, we learned not to accept any particular behavior as essentially male or female, not to take any sex difference as a given or as transhistorical. We learned that the repressive upbringing we had experienced in the 1950s was in large part a legacy of Victorian culture and therefore quintessentially modern rather than "traditional." Such insights would have been less momentous had they not been combined with the second idea that, as women's liberation groups put it, "the personal is political." The history-writing consequences of this can be seen in some ways as a development of "history from the bottom up." If the subordinated are to be subjects, historians needed to stretch the boundaries of what they considered significant.

It was an added thrill to study something about which no history had been written before. For me it started with birth control; for others it was shopping, domestic service, sexuality, friendship. So I left Russian history: I had been miserable in the Soviet Union, not only because I was refused access to sources but also because of the society's lack of freedom; and I now perceived the pleasures of doing research at home. (Yet another piece of luck: my minor field at Yale was twentieth-century U.S. history.) This process shifted my historical preoccupations considerably. Once focused on patterns of world-historical political economy, I began to love research, and particularly the detective quality of research. I had tasted that in my dissertation research, found the pleasures of search and discovery. To this day I'm often at my happiest in an archive or any room with documents and a table to lay them on. I am usually studying matters of deep concern to me, but the satisfactions of research come no matter what the topic. The process became passionate now that it was closer to home, in all the meanings of home: in my place, in my time, about my experience.

Meanwhile, I had the luck not to worry about tenure—because there were always other jobs, I thought, and because the excitement of helping to develop a new field tended to block out my personal anxiety. So despite my

* In the early 1970s, this distinction seemed fundamental and relatively fixed. In the thirty years since then, the distinction has become fuzzy again, for several reasons: because sex is no longer so fixed and scholars must now think of anatomical and physiological sex as a continuum rather than a binary; and because we now know that some of what 1970s feminists conceived as social/cultural traits may well have physical, biochemical bases.

department's lack of enthusiasm (to say the least), I invented a course on women's history in 1970. It was a feeble thing at first, mainly built around intellectuals and their views of women—from the classical, the Christian, the liberal, the Marxist, and the Freudian traditions. Yet the students found it riveting and helped the syllabus grow. Goddard College opened an adult master's program in Cambridge, and I taught a course there in 1970 that was more accurately a cooperative seminar.

By no means all the fruits of my first women's history ventures were welcome. To my surprise, because I knew how solid my research was, I could not get an academic publisher for my birth-control book. I have to fill in the context here: I had no help. I had had no mentor in grad school. I had been treated with benign neglect at Yale—that is, no one insulted me but no one took me seriously either. My Yale professors offered no help in getting my dissertation published. When I began to apply for postdoc fellowships, I had no one to write even a vaguely positive recommendation for me. Only later did I come to understand that while I was on my own in graduate school, many of the men in my cohort were being encouraged, groomed, and promoted. In those days, it was customary that a manuscript arrived at a publisher on the basis of a recommendation from a senior scholar, and I had no one to do this for me. Instead, I found a literary agent, Charlotte Sheedy, herself a feminist who was willing to take chances on (and accept only puny profits from) women's historians; she represented several fine historians of my generation. She got me a contract with Grossman, a subsidiary of Viking Press, which was similar to Knopf in its reputation for publishing serious nonfiction. To the degree my book gradually made an impact, this was a result of academic failure, not a choice to speak to a larger public.

This lesson, that the academy would not respect my work, stayed with me for a long time. After publication, *Woman's Body, Woman's Right: A Social History of Birth Control in America* was savaged in academic reviews that ignored both the book's arguments and evidence and condemned the whole undertaking, that is, connecting the widespread prohibitions on birth control with male supremacy, nationalism, and economic exploitation. The academic reviews were so egregious that none other than Elizabeth Fox Genovese—who ended her life opposed to women's reproductive rights—wrote a review of the reviews, pointing out that they were exclusively ideological and did not consider the substance of the book at all. (The book was treated with a bit more respect in its few nonacademic reviews.) The bruising reviews brought home to me how strong was the resistance among scholars to the new women edging their way into the universities and the new topics they brought in. I pretended to have expected the bad reviews but in fact they hurt. Still, I had luck once again: I was awarded tenure just *before* the book was published so there were no reviews yet.

Up to this point, the lessons confirmed my characteristically New Left hostility to the elitism and timidity of the universities. I imagined myself a revolutionary soldier, writing in the service of the women's movement, an idea I soon discovered was naive to say the least. To my dismay, the book was criticized by some birth control advocates and feminists. In the research, I found complexity, multiple axes of conflict—it would be academically fashionable today to call it "intersectionality." I argued that the case for controlling reproduction had historically been made on mixed and often mutually contradictory grounds, both democratic and antidemocratic, individualist and anti-individualist, feminist and antifeminist. Birth-control advocates traveled along with Malthusianism and neo-Malthusianism; with communal societies, including those with authoritarian leaders in which women were stripped of agency; with population control programs brought to the colonies as a means of social control; with eugenics aimed at protecting superior races; and with the cold-war suburban, consumerist family. It seemed to me that birth control had no essential political character but was rather a sexual technology that could have different meanings and consequences in different contexts. But some in the feminist and advocacy communities did not want to hear this. They wanted a story both simpler and simply celebratory. My next book, about the historical politics of family violence, caught similar flak from a few domestic violence advocates who charged that by identifying characteristics that made women particularly vulnerable or resistant to being victimized, I was presenting a victim-blaming argument.

As if it were not uncomfortable enough to be criticized by advocates of causes I support, my birth control arguments were used by unscrupulous antiabortion, antifeminist zealots. As the religious Right used *Roe v Wade* to bring birth control to the center of American politics, they used my discussion of eugenics cynically to prove that, for example, Margaret Sanger and the campaign for birth control constituted a racist conspiracy. (I think you can find this material still on the web if you look.) Of course they are using my evidence in an entirely fraudulent manner. Nevertheless, their appropriation of my work confirmed the view of the Planned Parenthood establishment that I should not have been washing birth control's dirty linen in plain sight.

From these surprises I learned a few things. For example, that the academy can change. In the 1970s much of the history profession remained an old-boys' club, defending its own work and work culture against the threats of barbarians. With so few critical thinkers in the faculties, students against the Vietnam War were standing up in lecture halls, challenging professors whose lectures on U.S. foreign policy sounded like State Department press releases. The history profession today is unrecognizable from the perspective of 1970. The radicals of the 1970s are the senior statesmen now. These changes happened because of our 1960s and 1970s anger, even including some of its occasional macho posturing. Forty years later, most critical scholars are not denouncing but defending university traditions, even those we once opposed, like tenure. In part we are like union members resisting employers who seek to drive down the cost of labor by recruiting casual workers with no benefits and job security, although most academics do this without the benefit of a union. In some respects we are simply defending our privileges. But we also see that higher educational institutions provide increasingly rare space for freedom of speech and freedom of assembly against cries of disloyalty or even treason, space for sanity and thoughtfulness and citizenship.

I also learned, correspondingly, that the relation between a scholar and the causes she supports is unlikely to be a perfect fit. It must be a restrained, cautious, complex, even tense relation. My whole career was made possible by a social movement—in my case, primarily feminism but more broadly, the New Left. The social movement gave us not only access to jobs. It also gave us our topics and particularly our questions. But the fact that we take our questions from movements does not mean that we get our answers there. We can ask questions as citizens, concerned to make our world better, but we have to answer as scholars, guarding against wishful thinking, refusing to glide lightly over the failings of those on our side. We do not serve causes best by telling social movements what they want to hear or writing the propaganda they want to put out; the scholar necessarily must risk coming up with unwanted, un-PC findings.

*   *   *

It seemed obvious that reproduction control was a major factor in opening a broad range of possibilities for women, but I did not realize when I began where the research would take me. (This has ever since been one of my great pleasures in research—the thrill of following clues to unexpected

intersections.) One history of birth control existed before mine, but it was
a technological history, tracing contraceptive methods.* I thought of birth
control as encompassing not only all attempts to control reproduction but
also their meanings. Its practice in some contexts could threaten to un-
dermine male and priestly supremacy, national population aspirations, or
sexual repression. In others it could help develop orderly, functional societies or even utopias. Birth control had no fixed social meaning. At the
same time the study was radical in that it dragged a subject matter widely
defined as personal, private, even off-color, into public historical consideration. The issues at stake with respect to birth control were as fundamental to modes of governance, individual and social rights, morality and
society as were the better-known nineteenth-century reforms and revolutions, such as universal manhood suffrage and freedom of the press. At
the same time birth control is a matter of bodies, especially but not exclusively female bodies. It expresses the human drive for physical pleasure,
women's physical vulnerability to male sexual demands and, not less im-
portantly, the drive to transcend bodies, particularly as regards pregnan-
cies and childbirths.

When I was writing the book, I rather uncritically assumed that sup-
pression of birth control was over. I was writing a *history*. It seemed so
obvious in the early 1970s that industrial and postindustrial society and
culture demanded the separation of sex from reproduction; that small
families and individualist and consumerist practices inevitably led to an
insuppressible demand for personal control over reproduction. I was right
about those observations but naive about the power of American conservatism to mobilize religious and familial fears of women's and sexual freedom, even though other aspects of the conservative program—notably,
support for an ever-expanding market—created the very phenomena it
wanted to stop. As I write this, the birth-control controversies seem endless. What began as a fight about abortion clearly now extends to contraception and varieties of sexual activity. The fact that this early book
of mine went through two revisions—one published in 1990, another in
2002 under a new title because it was so extensively revised—is actually a
negative sign of the power of the backlash against reproductive freedom,
sexual honesty, and the secular state.

From my birth-control research I came to understand that social policy in the United States is typically debated without historical perspective.

* Norman Hines, *Medical History of Contraception* (New York: Gamut Press, 1963).

In trying to add that perspective, I found myself becoming a historian of social policy. I never intended this and was not trained for it, with the result that my research strategies were sometimes flawed. When I decided to study the history of family violence—child abuse, child neglect, child sexual abuse, and "wife-beating"—I devised a local study based on social work case records. Historians had rarely used case records before this, I had no idea how laborious a task it would be, and ultimately I spent twelve years on the project. Never having done quantitative work before, I created a coding system with too many variables. Since real cases and real families are always complicated, I could not get from them the quantifiable correlations and patterns I had expected and wasted time and money and the efforts of some wonderful research assistants. Probably as little as 10 percent of my analyses derived from the quantitative work. To my ear, the qualitative evidence rang louder, though it required listening closely to hear the agency clients' understandings of their own problems, as filtered through the caseworkers' ears. It required trying to understand the often contradictory actions of the clients as evidence of their own strategies; the caseworkers' accommodations to their job description, instructions, and family values on the one hand, and their responses to clients on the other hand. These close readings of case records showed, more than the quantitative analyses could have done, the power relations within families and how they intersected with the class, gender, religious, and ethnic power relations imbedded in client/caseworker interactions.

Still, reading those hundreds of case records brought home a good lesson: the limitations of social-control analysis. Argued in relation to child-welfare by historian Anthony Platt, and in a theoretical vein by sociologist Stanley Cohen, social-control analysis helped explain how complex societies retained legitimacy and consent while reproducing orders of hierarchy. The New Left and feminism needed and used this analysis to explain, for example, how racial and gender ideologies and formations work. But when considered as a totalizing picture of organized institutional socialization, the theory weighted the controllers too heavily and neglected the agency of their subjects. Family-violence clients, both victims and perpetrators, tried to manipulate social workers in their own interests. They usually lost the contest but they educated some social workers in the process.

I turned to the history of welfare because of what I learned about family violence. Despite the best efforts of child-protection agencies in educating and punishing abusers, the single most effective tool against family violence was the simplest: giving money to needy parents and children. This finding has never been challenged but it has been obscured.*

Writing about welfare was demoralizing. I had been critical of the New Deal and the 1960s War on Poverty for not doing nearly enough to reduce inequality; by the time I finished that book, the 1930s and the 1960s looked wonderful. So my work since then derives, I have to admit, not only from interest in exploring narrative but also from escapism—escape from contemporary politics, from the National Archives, from a national canvas and an impersonal voice.

* * *

My father's life then intruded again into my understandings of history. This time, though, his experience confirmed where my own intellectual journey was taking me, while earlier it was my education that confirmed my dad's experience. After completing my family-violence book, I interviewed him rather formally so as to ghostwrite a brief autobiography of his early life. In one of our conversations, he told me something I had not heard before: that his stepfather had been abusive. He did not want me to write it that bluntly so we agreed on a text more authentic to his typically careful, understated, historicized voice:

> I believe it was shortly after our return to Shumsk that my stepfather returned from the army. Soon afterwards, my elder brother entered a *yeshiva* in Vilna and I became the eldest son at home. This contributed to my bad relationship with my stepfather. He was very rigid—even my grandmother yelled at him—and my mother was very passive. He insisted that I accompany him on his long, hateful trips on foot to neighboring villages, to barter items of merchandise for food. I was often away for two days at a time. I do not understand why he

---

* As family violence was "rediscovered" in the 1960s, a democratic impulse led advocates to insist that family violence occurred "across all classes." This accurate but misleading emphasis obscured the fact that family violence was and remains highly correlated with poverty, unemployment, other forms of relative deprivation and the stresses they create. There is a popular and journalistic tendency to imagine high stress as a problem of people in leadership positions with many responsibilities. In fact stress is far more common among the poor who worry about money, health, children's safety, dangerous neighborhoods. Many comparative scholarly studies have by now shown that the weakness of the American welfare state is a major contributor to poverty, crime, poor educational attainment, infant mortality, teenage pregnancy, poor health and other social problems. Nevertheless, in 1996 Congress passed a Clinton administration bill repealing ADC. So much for the influence of scholars.

insisted that I come; I was never given the reason. Perhaps he wanted company or he may have felt safer from molestation having a child of nine along; perhaps he needed help carrying. In any event, it was a bitter experience for me, trudging long distances trying to keep up with an adult pace.... my mother could not or did not side with me, but yielded to her husband's demands.... She sent her two older boys away because she could not protect them, and because she had to protect her second marriage.

This new information confirmed my family-violence findings. The stresses of poverty, unemployment, insecurity, ill health, heavy drinking, social isolation, generational conflict lay behind much family violence, but there were always personal factors too. Darlene Clark Hine found the same thing with respect to African American women moving northward on their own in the "Great Migration": many were fleeing domestic abuse as well as seeking higher wages and escape from racism. In other words, personal stories contribute to large structural developments. This is an understanding that I would previously have accepted in theory but had not been moved to explore. Now I found it fascinating and I soon turned to narrative and microhistory in an effort to explore the interactions of great and small.

I had also observed how often Americans debate policy issues through discussing soap opera–style crimes and legal conflicts—witness O. J. Simpson, Anita Hill, Elián Gonzalez. So I set about looking for a story to tell. I set several criteria it had to meet: it had to involve racial formations other than the black-white binary; it had to include a significant gender angle; it had to have complexity; it had to be a story that mattered. I considered a Hollywood scandal and a child murder in Madison, Wisconsin. I found the one I chose in Carey McWilliams's book *North from Mexico* (1948) and it became *The Great Arizona Orphan Abduction* (1999).

That book was made possible by the University of Wisconsin–Madison, where I had taken a job in 1984. It was a big change: teaching graduate students, using a world-class library, working in a much larger university, living in a much smaller city. We moved so that my husband and I could live in the same city and our daughter could have a full-time father—he had been commuting from Cambridge to teach at Hampshire College. Gerda Lerner had initiated a graduate program in women's history at UW and got the department to agree, though by no means unanimously, to hire a second faculty member in the field. Teaching became more demanding as I soon had many graduate students, all the more demanding because

the students were so good. By 1984 women's and gender history had become strong enough that superb students were attracted by the quality of
the scholarship in the field and the confidence that they could get jobs.
They were right: eighteen University of Wisconsin students completed
Ph.D.'s under my direction and they all have good jobs, many of them
becoming pioneers in the field in their schools. Moreover, in these years
the UW history department had no U.S. labor historian or historian interested in social movements, so I ended up directing and serving on committees of students working in those fields as well. So I was working much
harder at teaching. But the university also provided at the time superb
opportunities for research support and research leaves, so that while one
is never on leave from graduate students, I had many semesters free of
other teaching obligations. In 1993 the university awarded me its highest
honor, a Vilas Research Professorship that allowed me to spend every
other semester on full-time research, without teaching classes. This gift of
time was invaluable, and I will be forever grateful to UW for it.

The orphan story, like many narratives, was a microhistory, and I originally planned to write the book as a continuous narrative, as much like a
novel as possible. But I could not do it and the struggle over *how* to tell
the story showed me something of how hard it would be to write a real
novel. The organizational problems were daunting. The story contains si-
multaneous happenings at the same time at different places; if I inserted
all the context into the narrative it became cumbersome and hard to follow. My structural-analysis taste clicked in and I felt it imperative to explain context. Soon it was clear that there was more context than story.
If I tried to follow the rule, tell the readers what they need to know just
when they need to know it, the result was fragmentation—little driplets of
information about, say, mining, scattered in many places. Once I decided
to alternate action scenes with topical chapters, I still had to figure out
which of the latter should go with which of the former. I surrounded myself with lists of individuals who needed to be introduced and of continuity
problems, for example, before telling about incident 3, I had to introduce
not only incidents 1 and 2 but also contextual factors a, b, and c. These
organizational issues are also content issues. The order of the book rep-
resents an argument. The environment and the human use of it seemed
to me primary. Only slightly less primary was the human labor needed
to exploit the major environmental resource—copper ore—and how they
did the work. These came first because I was convinced that mining and
those who controlled it were the major constructors of social relations in

Clifton, Morenci, and their environs. I brought in Catholic religious leaders next, because they played such a big part in the events, though I did
not see popular religiosity as a driving force. Then the family and community lives of the townsfolk—first the majority, mineworkers and their
families, mainly Mexican American, focusing on the women who organized family and community lives. Then the minority middle and upper
class, the Anglos. Then two chapters on the legacy of immediate history,
the class/race conflict in the strike a year earlier, then the history and culture of vigilantism.

There were detours I chose not to follow. There is a legal history story
to be told, concerning precedents before the judicial decisions in this case
and the influence of this case on future legal developments regarding child
custody and the "best interest of the child" principle in adjudicating custody. But I decided that this would take readers too far afield. The major
omission, of course, was the later history of the orphans. I learned early on
that I should not inquire into their history: at the time of the events the
most common practice was not to tell adopted children of their origins,
and to let them believe, when possible, that they were the biological children of their parents. Were I to try to trace the orphans and their descendants, I might well be revealing family secrets that the family members
themselves did not know, which would create an unjustified and unethical
intervention. Besides, I felt that the Aristotelian unity of time, place, and
action gave the story greater power.

*   *   *

Some historians, I have observed, choose a question or subject or region
and continue to study it more and more deeply, or from ever different
perspectives. Such patience and discipline are not my nature, evidently.
I am restless. And I love most the digging kind of research, the almost
giddy feeling of discovery I get from identifying facts and relationships
and patterns previously unknown—or unknown to historians. There is an
occupational hazard in this kind of research and in microhistory in general: that no one else cares or should care. Mapping individual stories and
homes in old Clifton thrilled me but I had to remind myself that this project
was not, say, George Chauncey's *Gay New York*—of those who would read
my book, few if any had that degree of interest in old Clifton.

My latest project, a biography of photographer Dorothea Lange, is another sort of microhistory, in the sense that an individual is usually by

definition "micro" in relation to the sweep of history. Its organization presents problems similar to previous ones: how to create a narrative that carries the reader along while providing the context and demonstrating the historical significance. But in other respects I am finding this work considerably different. Lange is "famous," unlike anyone in *The Great Arizona Orphan Abduction*. Some readers will care about the minutiae of her life. A great deal has been written about Lange but I cannot let my hesitance to repeat what's already been published interfere with telling a whole story, a whole life. So I have less of the pleasure of discovery and more of the challenge of synthesis. I'm still figuring it out.

DAVID A. HOLLINGER

Church People and Others

When I was a child in Idaho, I learned that human beings were divided into groups. There were church people, who were good, and not-church people, who were bad. Within the ranks of the church people, there were more refined distinctions. Mormons, Catholics, and Pentecostals went to the wrong churches. Methodists, Presbyterians, Brethren, Mennonites, Lutherans, Quakers, and Congregationalists were prominent among those who went to the right churches. I did not know that it was possible to divide people up into groups on any basis other than what churches they went to, or whether they went to church at all, unless they were Japanese or German. I knew about the Japanese as a separate group because my parents told me how dreadful it was that Americans of Japanese ancestry had been taken from their homes and put into camps during the Second World War. I assumed this had been done by not-church people, but later found out that it was more complicated. I knew about the Germans because when my mother sent relief packages to her cousins in Germany right after the war, I discovered that having German ancestors was an important part of me, and that because of my father's German heritage from a migration much earlier than my mother's, our family was Pennsylvania Dutch even though we did not live anywhere near Pennsylvania and had no ancestors from Holland. Most Germans in Germany were not church people, my mother explained, and that is why there had been a war, but her cousins most definitely went to a Lutheran church. I did not meet a black person until I moved away from Idaho, and I did not realize that Jews were a contemporary presence, rather than merely a group that flourished in Biblical times, until I was in the seventh grade in California and met a boy named Stan Swerdloff who went to church on Saturdays but who was not a Seventh Day Adventist.

I also knew about Indians, and that's how I got started as a historian. Or, more precisely, it was in reading about the Nez Perce Indians after moving away from Idaho that I became interested in becoming a historian. But once I really got going as a historian, some years later, what most engaged me was a tension between cosmopolitan and provincial impulses that assign significance—or deny it—to distinctions between human beings based on race, ethnicity, religion, location, and nationality.

Our family had moved to California by the time I started reading about the Nez Perce, but we often went back to Idaho to visit an aunt and I retained a strong Idaho identity as a teenager. I was fourteen when I first decided I wanted to be a historian, and the decision was marked by my purchase of *War Chief Joseph*, by Helen Addison Howard and Dan McGrath. This was the first book I bought with my own money, earned by mowing lawns. I had read a library copy, but loved it so much I was determined to have a copy of my own. When this biography of the great Nez Perce chief arrived in that summer of 1955 by mail-order from the Caxton Printers in Caldwell, Idaho, I felt a personal connection to the writing of history that I had not felt in reading library books, or even the few history books owned by my parents. The following spring, I had mowed enough lawns to buy Bruce Catton's three-volume history of the Army of the Potomac.

Why the Nez Perce and the Civil War? I was approaching history through specific local settings that were meaningful to me. The Idaho with which I identified was the land of the Nez Perce Indians, and thus the story of the Nez Perce was "ancient history": the part of the past that came before "we" did—the European-derived settlers who, I was often told, had simply stolen Idaho from the Indians. The American Civil War was also "local" for me because my father had grown up on a farm just north of the Gettysburg battlefield, and the stories he and his siblings told of life in Gettysburg evoked for me a past larger than Idaho's, yet equally accessible to me personally.

My father and my aunts and uncles were present in 1913 at the fiftieth anniversary of the battle of Gettysburg. Their recollections of the Confederate and Union veterans I had heard long before I first saw the film of the aged Blues and Grays shaking hands on Ken Burns's PBS documentary. At fourteen I thrilled to Catton's account of Gettysburg in *Glory Road*, and even more to "Toward the Dunker Church" in *Mr. Lincoln's Army*—still affecting as I read it again more than fifty years later because there Catton's description of the battle of Antietam centered on a tiny church in which my own great-grandfather may have preached before the war. No ancestor of mine had fought in the Civil War (as German Baptist Brethren, or "Dunkers," and Mennonites, they refused military service on scriptural grounds). But the notion that the two greatest battles of the nation-defining struggle over slavery had taken place partly on ground that the Hollingers had owned or on which they had worshiped gave me a connection to Catton's books akin to that felt by descendants of the soldiers.

My attraction at the age of fourteen to a career as a historian was not quite a desire to celebrate my own ancestors, or even to find fault with them. Chief Joseph and Gettysburg were most important as local points of access to a more general engagement with the ways in which contemporary life had been shaped by previous events. Why did I experience this engagement at age fourteen, rather than some other?

I fell into history largely because it seemed the most accessible to me of all learned endeavors at a time when I was in the process of deciding that I'd like to be a professor of one kind or another. In a moment, I'll talk about why I was attracted to academia in general. But history was appealing in part because I could pick up widely praised works of history and absorb them with pleasure and understanding. Catton's *Stillness at Appomattox* was just then being hailed as a masterpiece, although not so much by professionals, I later learned, as by lay audiences and journalists. I was less comfortable with what samplings I managed of other fields, of whose character I understood even less than I understood history. Theology and philosophy, to both of which I felt attracted, were less welcoming, at least as I encountered them. The analytic vocabulary in both cases was too technical for me. And neither of these subjects was taught in junior high school. Science and math were taught, but neither grabbed my attention so firmly as did the fields I later learned to call the humanities and social sciences. English literature I knew only as novels and poems and plays, not as criticism. I was engaged by what was called "social studies," but even the best teachers of that amorphous subject did not put me in contact with sociology, economics, and political science the way an eighth grade history course seemed to put me in touch with what historians did.

Only geography seemed remotely as accessible as history, but I never heard about individual geographers by name the way I heard about Arnold Toynbee and Will Durant, and, of course, Bruce Catton. I loved *National Geographic*, and in later years defended it against critics unable to forgive its bourgeois ethos and its too-often patronizing view of societies beyond the North Atlantic West. This magazine opened up countless worlds for me, symbolized by the wonderful maps, dozens of which I still own. The journey from the local to the global has to start somewhere, and for many of us growing up in the 1950s *National Geographic* was not a bad starting point. But *National Geographic* did not translate geography into the terms of a vocation, unless it might be that of explorers like Admiral Richard Byrd. I did try to imagine what it would be like to be a writer or editor for that magazine, but the prevailing popular culture and the junior high schools of the day did not encourage me to see geography as a career. They did enable me to see history in that way.

Am I suggesting that I went for history because it appeared to be easy? Yes. History was one learned pursuit that I thought I understood well enough to see myself in it. That was the key. By why was I, at fourteen, so inclined to say, "I'd like to become a college professor," whenever I was asked what I wanted to do when I grew up? That was more complicated, psychologically and culturally. I am not certain that I understand it even now. But I do know one thing for sure: a powerful factor was the deep respect both my parents had for learning.

My father had earned his high school diploma at the age of thirty-three, having gone to night school for three years while working forty-hour weeks as a shoe salesman at a Sears store in Chicago. He came there to begin the education he needed to become a minister. He later worked his way through college, too, painting houses, and even through a theological seminary, although by the time I reached adolescence he had left the ministry and was earning a living again as a self-employed house painter. My father, who never put any pressure on me to pursue any particular calling, said little, then or later, about this huge change in his life. Yet as an early teen I was puzzled and privately disturbed by the obvious gap between how he spent every working day and the education he had struggled to attain and of which he remained proud. He remained active in the church, and did some guest preaching. One of my uncles, who also painted houses for a living, had no schooling beyond the eighth grade. Another uncle, who had completed high school, was a school custodian. My mother, who had been a high school home economics teacher before she stopped working outside the home when I was born, was much more direct in encouraging me to read and to stretch myself intellectually. I sensed that she wanted me to make a life in which education would be put to good use. Both of my parents spoke with reverence about great scholars and great universities.

"He's got a Ph.D.," my father used to remark of this or that visiting speaker at church, or, more often, of someone who appeared on the TV shows of Alastair Cooke (*Omnibus*) and David Garroway (*Wide Wide World*) that we watched every Sunday afternoon. I absorbed my parents' awe for people with doctorates. I later came to see my parents' respect for learning as part of a secularization process. They inherited a feel for the value of Biblical learning, but they had come to believe that all truth was sacred. My parents never gave up the religious faith, away from which I gradually drifted, but I understood even as a teenager that Biblical scholarship and other kinds of learning were somehow part of a single intellectual piece. By pursuing learning, I would be carrying on a family tradition of sorts, even though the many preachers in my father's "Pennsylvania Dutch" ancestry had all been farmers with very little schooling. They were "called" to the ministry by their congregational peers in classic Anabaptist fashion, but continued to live as farmers. My father had been part of a generation that sought to modernize the Brethren ministry.

Yet academia was remote. One aunt whom I rarely saw approached it late in life, earning her masters at age fifty-eight. She taught education at Gettysburg College and was the only one of my father's siblings to remain in Pennsylvania and to leave the Brethren (she married a Presbyterian). She contributed to the mystique of elite higher education by repeatedly telling us, during occasional visits to the West Coast, the story of once having seen the great scholar Owen Lattimore standing outside the library at Johns Hopkins. "He was smoking a cigarette during a break from his research," she invariably said, as if the mere sighting of such an important academic in an informal moment was a moving experience.

The closest I came to viewing the academic life during my high school years was meeting some faculty members at our local denominational institution, La Verne College. Those people, whom my parents and I met in church, usually got their Ph.D.s at mid-career. "He's working on his Ph.D. at USC," it was said of one La Verne professor after another. I got the impression that the Ph.D. was an enormous undertaking, achieved fairly late

in life, and that to teach at USC, like Frank C. Baxter, the English professor whose local program, *Shakespeare on TV,* I watched every week, was
the pinnacle of academic achievement.

Given the apparent difficulties of getting into academia, I needed a
path to it that I could reasonably hope to actually travel. History, being
uniquely accessible, was that path, and choosing it happened simultaneously with my starting to tell people that I expected to become "a college
professor." It is ironic that my idol, Bruce Catton, was not a college professor, did not have a Ph.D., and dropped out of Oberlin College without
even completing his bachelor's. I did not know this at the time, of course,
and I associated Catton with all that talk about having a Ph.D. Moreover,
what I thought historians did had little relation to the more realistic conception to which I was later introduced. Indeed, it may be misleading for
me to claim that I had decided at the age of fourteen to be a historian.
What I eventually became was rather different from the practice exemplified so wonderfully by Bruce Catton.

The latter meant telling stories about the past and making sure that the
documentary record supported the stories. This conception stayed with
me through my high school years, when I wrote term papers on the Nez
Perce. I had no grasp whatsoever of the hermeneutic problem. Like most
high school students and most readers of Bruce Catton's books, I assumed
a single and permanent historical truth that was there to be discovered.
Indeed, had I any inkling of the challenges of historical interpretation as
I later faced them, I cannot imagine having started down the historian's
path. I suppose I might have eventually gotten there from some other domain, but I was able to hold fast throughout high school to my ambition of
becoming a historian because I had very little idea what it really involved.
One might say that I became a historian because I did not know what I
was doing.

During my senior year in high school teachers encouraged me to consider a career in law or business, but I shied away from both. Our family
knew intimately not a single lawyer or businessman. I had the impression
that colleges and universities were more rationally stable and ethically
sound settings than courtrooms and corporations, less subject to the abuses
of charismatic authority. I would not have used this phrase then, but my
suspicions had developed in high school in response to television and
film portrayals of lawyers and businessmen, who seemed to get ahead—in
terms of money and status—by manipulating people with sheer force of
personality. My parents' greatest living hero was the self-effacing mission-

ary doctor, Albert Schweitzer, and they were never comfortable with profit-making, rather than merely life-sustaining endeavors.

My concern about charismatic authority was accentuated by discussions of religion with other high school students. Many of the latter were evangelical Protestants, deferring to an emotional preaching style violently at odds with the plainer style of the Brethren and Mennonite tradition. The families of these young people generally took Billy Graham as their hero, and I remember being shocked that youths who went to church every Sunday, and were good at quoting scripture, had never heard of Schweitzer. My mother had been raised in the Church of the Nazarene, and had fled that denomination's florid alter calls to join the more reserved Brethren. She warned me against the revivalist sensibilities of some of my high school friends. Although I was not considering the ministry as a vocation, my contacts with Southern Baptists moved me further from anything associated with charisma and the playing on the emotions of one's fellows. Hence I finished high school with a renewed resolve to become a professor of history, a job I associated with reason, fair-mindedness, and lack of avarice. It was a secular vocation of which church people of my kind could approve.

College changed my understanding of what it meant to be a historian, but not much. As a history major at La Verne College, which I entered in 1959, I found the study of facts comforting. I was good at memorizing details, and did much better on multiple-choice tests than on the essay examinations, which required a facility for abstraction and a capacity to mobilize facts in support of an argument. Nevertheless, while at La Verne I did encounter two understandings of what historians did that were, for me, "post-Catton." Both sustained my vocational choice while expanding my horizons, yet continued to protect me, so to speak, from what I would encounter in graduate school. One of these understandings was embodied in the work of Arnold Toynbee. The other was the Amherst Pamphlets.

I actually read only snippets of Toynbee's prodigious *A Study of History*, but at La Verne I often heard it said that Toynbee addressed the *meaning* of history. *All* history. Toynbee generalized; he had a "theory" of history. He had apparently discovered the dynamics by which entire civilizations rose and fell on the basis of the same kind of detailed evidence that Catton used to explain General Grant's military success in Virginia. I had been accustomed to thinking of the historian's calling as a modest and manageable one, but Toynbee, or I should say the image of Toynbee, made me wonder if history might be a successor-subject to theology and philosophy. I had yet to hear of Vico, nor did I have a sense of the claims that the ostensibly particularizing study of history might make on the domains of the generalizing social sciences. The buzz about Toynbee gave me a hint of a grander dimension of historical study. I was intimidated by this, and also attracted to it. Perhaps the path I had chosen had more possibilities than I supposed? Above all, what I heard said about Toynbee got me brooding about "meaning." Catton had implied something of what the Civil War "meant," but he never said it explicitly; rather Catton left me with the impression that the meaning of events was transparent in their accurate description.

This impression was challenged more directly by the Amherst Pamphlets. Popular with the history professors at La Verne, these practical, 100-page, double-columned paperback anthologies of prominent scholarly writings on major questions introduced me to the idea that responsible scholars could offer conflicting interpretations of historical events. The basic character of episodes like the American Revolution and Jacksonian Democracy could be contested. Properly called "Problems in American Civilization," these pamphlets were known popularly by the name of Amherst College because its American Studies faculty designed them for the D. C. Heath publishing company.

The Amherst Pamphlets encouraged students to evaluate conflicting interpretations, usually presented in the form of two easily summarized alternatives. *The New Deal: Revolution or Evolution?* is the title of one I still own. The mood was well put in the introduction to another I have kept on my shelves all these years, *Reconstruction in the South*: "The reader will have to determine," declared Edwin C. Rozwenc, "whether the Reconstruction of the South must be judged to have been primarily 'a blackout of honest government' resulting from political rule by ignorant Negroes and villainous white carpetbaggers and scalawags, or whether the story of Reconstruction should be written in terms of 'quietly constructive' political and social achievements." Reexamining this pamphlet now, what I find most striking is not the antiquated construction of the issues and the heavy tilt toward what we now recognize as a deeply racist interpretation of Reconstruction (Rozwenc described the excerpt from W. E. B. Du Bois as written with "racial feeling" but said nothing of the sort about the several white supremacist writers he anthologized, including Woodrow Wilson). Rather, what hits me now is that there were two sides—and only two—to every story, or at least to most of the stories historians tell. This made it easier to deal with conflicting interpretations: historians debated questions in straightforward terms, and, like a courtroom jury, decided them either one way, or the other. That simplified the matter of "meaning": an event meant one thing, or it meant another.

One nonacademic experience at La Verne affected my later choices as a historian. During the fall of 1960 while driving through Oklahoma with seven other La Verne students, one of whom was black, I saw with my own eyes racial segregation in public accommodations. Our group was returning from a national meeting of Brethren youth leaders in Ohio. Our Volkswagen microbus broke down on Highway 66 near the town of Vinita, Oklahoma, where, while the vehicle was being repaired, we found we could not eat or sleep in the same facility. We were not "freedom riders." We had neither the political sophistication nor the personal courage to undertake such a project. We were simply Californians caught by surprise. During the two or three days it took to repair the vehicle we could sleep and eat together only in the homes of members of the nearest Church of the Brethren, in Bartlesville. Eventually, having been immersed in a racially segregated society for several days, one of our hosts, a beautiful young mother of two children in whose home I stayed, explained to me with great patience that we young Californians would approve of segregation if we lived in the South and saw "how the Negroes actually live, you know, the dirt and all." We resumed our journey on Highway 66 back to La Verne. On the way, we tried a pancake house in Amarillo, Texas, but were again turned away.

The experience of segregation marked all of us in ways that did not always register immediately. One of the travelers, my closest friend at La Verne, transferred the very next year to historically black Howard University, partly because he wanted to engage the parts of the world we encountered in the South. I did not see him again for another forty years, but at our reunion he and I immediately began talking about that incident and the ways in which it had changed each of us. We both remembered seeing our fellow student weeping disconsolately, and were glad we cannot remember what we said to her, because neither of us could imagine that it was up to the occasion. That so tame an incident could mark us white students so vividly is no doubt a sign of how insulated we were from major features of the society in which we lived. But my own engagement with the history of the black-white color line dates from that experience.

I felt increasingly isolated at La Verne during my four years there. My three closest friends—two others, in addition to the one Howard-bound—left after the sophomore year for other colleges. Almost none

of the remaining students shared my academic ambitions. I spent more
and more time in the library exploring what my friends regarded as obscure periodicals. I was befriended there by the campus's handful of foreign students, some of whom saw me reading *The Manchester Guardian
Weekly* and were pleased to learn that I cared about what was going on in
Africa and India. I regularly read essays and reviews in *Partisan Review*
and *Hudson Review*. As editor of the campus newspaper, I imitated the
Hudson's enthusiastic reviews of foreign films. These movies I saw in the
neighboring town of Claremont, site of a number of colleges, including
Pomona College, that were much closer to the academic mainstream than
La Verne. To Claremont's Village Theater I took several uncomprehend-
ing dates. "What was that about," the girl would ask about *Virgin Spring,*
or *L'Avventura* or *La Dolce vita*. Not that I was so wise about Bergman,
Antonioni, and Fellini. I just wished that others I knew were as engaged
by their movies as I was.

My difficulty in finding college friends, male or female, who were interested in the same issues I was renewed my determination to go forward
in academia. I appreciated the personal qualities of many people I got to
know at La Verne, but I was looking for a different kind of intellectual
community. I felt I belonged somewhere else, but I was not sure where.
History was the strongest undergraduate major at La Verne, reinforcing
my vocational choice. I joined the American Historical Association and
what was then the Mississippi Valley Historical Association (later the Organization of American Historians). Professional journals, along with the
Hudson Review, which I liked so much I became a paid subscriber to it,
now came directly to my dormitory room. My friends were amused, but
they put up with my peculiarities. They knew I was headed for someplace
really different from La Verne, and they wished me well.

That someplace turned out to be Berkeley. Shortly after arriving in the
fall of 1963, I was immersed in a practice built around the making of arguments. That historians were mostly in the business of making arguments
was implicit in some of my previous experience, especially through the
Amherst Pamphlets, but I had not fully absorbed it. The other graduate
students, in and out of class, talked about assessing so-and-so's argument
about this or that, or about how they were making this or that argument
in a paper they were writing. Most people who become historians probably get that from the start, and thus know what they are doing when they
decide to go into history. It was more like being a lawyer than I had re-

alized. For me the insight, however elementary, came late, and I could quickly see that nearly all of the other graduate students I came to know that first year were a lot better at making arguments than I was.

I decided to specialize in colonial American diplomatic and constitutional history because in those fields, it seemed to me, arguments were easier to make without having to know much about social theory and other modern discourses of which I was so much more ignorant than were the other students. Wrong again. Even in those ostensibly less theoretically entangled subfields, I was out of my depth. My first research paper, based on a reading of the *Archives of Maryland* from 1634 to 1670, was close to a disaster. I studied all the documents and reported what seemed to be their most important content, but could not figure out what they meant, except in the most literal of terms. What was my argument? What assumptions about human behavior enabled one to explain the actions of magistrates? The instructor, Winthrop D. Jordan, then teaching his first graduate seminar at Berkeley, was terribly generous, but also made abundantly clear in both written and oral comments that I did not know what I was doing.

Finding my way as a historian that first year at Berkeley was made more difficult by the distractions of culture shock. The transition from La Verne to Berkeley was not easy for me. In making friends with other graduate students, I soon learned to shut up about my own background because the graduates of Columbia and Harvard were stunned when I told the truth, and implied that I was from a distant and exotic country. One emblem for the culture gap was the practice of moderate social drinking, which was altogether new to me. La Verne banned the consumption of alcohol out of deference to the Brethren tradition (I Corinthians, 6:19, to the effect that the body is the temple of the holy spirit, which was understood to ban smoking, too). Before arriving at Berkeley I had never been at a social event, even a dinner in a private home, at which wine was served. I had never met an atheist or a communist, and had met so few Jews that I had trouble distinguishing them from persons of Italian extraction.

Toward the end of that year a graduate student from New York rather awkwardly asked me (this was while drinking coffee in the Mediterranean Café on Telegraph Avenue, then a favorite hangout for humanities graduate students), "If you don't mind a personal question, I'd like to know what it feels like for someone like you to be a member of a minority group." I had no idea what he was talking about. Then he, incredulous, explained that he knew me to be an Anglo-Saxon Protestant, and that most of the graduate students in our circle were Jewish. I had not yet learned how to read the signs, nor to assign to them the socially prescribed significance.

Yet amid these striking novelties, that first year at Berkeley was as thrilling for me as it was unsettling. I met people who really did share my intellectual interests. I felt I was in the right place, however challenging and numerous were the changes I had to make in myself in order to function in that new environment. Many of my new acquaintances from New York and New England and San Francisco were humane and responsive as well as intellectually acute. Some others, however, made me feel like a hick. I can see why meeting someone like me tested whatever generosity of spirit they possessed: I *was* a hick by their standards! At the time I was too willing to accept their standards and to take their superciliousness as something I deserved. It took me too many years to realize that most of the people who treated me as a hick had their own problems to deal with—hidden from me by their superior social skills—the working out of which entailed being condescending toward me.

The following year was easier for me personally, and was enlivened by the career-transforming experience of reading the works of Perry Miller. Here was a really different kind of history: intellectual history, and directed at the history of theological and philosophical ideas, yet it was more rigorously argumentative than what I had been reading in diplomatic and constitutional history, to say nothing of Bruce Catton, or even most of what appeared in the Amherst Pamphlets. It was also literary in the finest sense: Miller was a compelling and even commanding writer, and by then I had realized that very few works by professional historians of the United States reached the prose standard attained by the better works in European and Asian history. Had I read Miller earlier, I probably would not have been prepared to appreciate his work. But I encountered Miller at just the right time. More than a year of professional immersion had prepared me to understand and appreciate something so very different from what I had previously understood history to be. Intellectual interests of my own that I not yet found a way to explore suddenly came into play. It was a bracing, integrating experience. The immediate setting was the graduate seminar on colonial America taught by another then-junior professor, Robert L. Middlekauff. He assigned not only both volumes of *The New England Mind*, but also *Jonathan Edwards* and several of the essays in *Errand into the Wilderness*. Week after week of that fall of 1964, I alternated

between Puritan theology and the Free Speech Movement. Both proved
to be exciting.

I invoke the Free Speech Movement in relation to becoming a historian because at the time, generated by issues in free expression closely
connected to the civil rights movement and by quarrels over the role of
universities in society, it invigorated interaction among Berkeley graduate
students. I was quickly absorbed into a larger, more interactive community. Conversations about contemporary political affairs and about whatever we were reading in our classes or were teaching to undergraduates as
teaching assistants somehow got connected in one long, informal seminar
that lasted all day and well into many nights. My social integration into
a community of intellectually ambitious and politically engaged graduate
students meant that I was no longer "bowling alone," to borrow Robert
Putnam's popular figure of speech. I found every aspect of life lived to a
higher degree of intensity just as Putnam argues that interactive behavior
in one domain can promote it in other domains as well. Discussions about
the professional merged with conversations about the political. Yet lines
could be drawn. Middlekauff's sympathy for the Free Speech Movement
was undisguised, but my friends and I admired his professionalism and
when we went to his classroom in Haviland Hall, we knew we were there
to talk about Puritanism, and we did. The moral intensity of the Free
Speech Movement and of the seventeenth-century Puritans and of Miller
himself all spun into one another, without getting in each other's way.

Miller's *The New England Mind* did more than any other work to reveal to me the promise of intellectual history as a specific kind of scholarship. The essays collected in his *Errand into the Wilderness* did more
than any other writings to provide me with a sense of what it meant to
write an analytic essay on a historical question. Richard Hofstadter performed the latter service for most historians of my generation who were
attracted to the analytical essay as a genre, but despite my respect for
Hofstadter's work, especially his *American Political Tradition*, I found
Miller to be a more ambitious writer and more capable of achieving em-
pathic identification with historical actors different from oneself. Miller,
an atheist, showed great appreciation for the hold of religious ideas on
previous generations, while Hofstadter seemed less able to get out of his
own generational and ethno-religious skin. Once I focused on writing analytic essays, I found the form more challenging and satisfying than the
sort of narrative history Catton had led me to emulate. I never lost my

appreciation for good narrative history, but part of Miller's impact on me was to convert me to the analytic essay as my favored genre. To this day, most of what I write takes that form. Finally, I knew what I was doing methodologically, at least as judged from the perspective of the historian I eventually became.

Figuring out what I was doing substantively, rather that methodologically, came about through reading scholarly books and essays about China. This may seem odd, since I as a specialist in United States history have never worked in the field of Chinese history, never even took a course in it, and cannot read a word of Chinese. Graduate students in Asian history, whom I probably would not have gotten to know without the cross-field connections created by the Free Speech Movement (and its successor, the antiwar movement), often talked about one of their professors, the esteemed sinologist, Joseph R. Levenson. "If you are going to be an intellectual historian, you've got to read Levenson," they would say.

Immediately after passing my U.S. history orals in the spring of 1966 I read all three volumes of *Confucian China and Its Modern Fate*. I was captivated by the vast scope of the enterprise, and, subversive as this may be of an authentically sinological focus, I was captivated even more by Levenson's use of Western European categories to interpret Chinese history. He was constantly citing European and American philosophers and writers, and representing aspects of the Chinese past in their terms. I was enthralled by his conclusion to volume 3 that the Confucian bureaucracy's aestheticism and antispecialized amateur ideal had rendered China incapable of defending its culture against the scientific-rationalist-specialized energies of the West: Confucianists never "had to fight Jonathan Swift's battle of the books, for the ancient against the modern," because "when the issue arose in China it was post-Confucian, forced in China because it had come to the test in Europe first, and Swift had lost."

I was also attracted to Levenson's combination of abstraction (he meditated on the difference between "*historical* significance" and "historical *significance*") and playfulness. He was not afraid to have fun, even if some readers suspected that levity took precedent over *Wissenschaft*. He loved language, as Miller did, but Levenson let himself go in ways that the more austere Miller did not. At the end of his imposing trilogy, having written a conclusion to his third volume, he added, characteristically, this note to the reader: "Having concluded roundly, let us conclude squarely with a concluding conclusion." He then brought all three volumes to a close. Levenson wrote "musically," it was often said. No wonder a book of essays dedicated to his memory was entitled *The Mozartian Historian*. Levenson's books, chapters, pages, and paragraphs were all subject to a certain architectural design. I could understand readily why some China specialists found Levenson's approach insufficiently empirical, but I was reading these volumes less for their truth-value than for their conceptualization and style. Beyond all that, however, I discovered something else in Levenson that was altogether unexpected and that proved to be much more important.

Levenson was interested in the world-historical dynamic of provincialism and cosmopolitanism, and more specifically in the ways historical actors dealt with the threats and opportunities presented by a traditional community's contact with modern formations of larger scale, if not global in scope. This was true of *Confucian China and Its Modern Fate*, but more explicitly in the work he did immediately thereafter, including the posthumously published *Revolution and Cosmopolitanism: The Western Stage and the Chinese Stages*. It was Levenson who first engaged me with the tension between cosmopolitanism and provincialism, and with the questions of identity, peoplehood, and nationality that have dominated my work. It was also Levenson's obvious projection onto China of some of the dilemmas of Jewish identity in the West that propelled some of my investigations of the history of Jewish intellectuals in the United States. Nothing of Levenson's did more to shape me intellectually than an article of 1967 entitled "The Province, the Nation, and the World: The Problem of Chinese Identity." This essay helped me formulate for United States history the chief questions on which I have worked for more than forty years.

Ostensibly about China, this remarkable essay is, like so much of what Levenson wrote, a meditation on the effect of modernization on localities in Europe and the United States as well as China. Laced with references to Trotsky, Freud, Emerson, Blake, Levi-Strauss, Allen Tate, Henry James, Marx, Hume, Dickens, Lawrence, Proust, Ortega y Gasset, Yeats, Michelet, and a variety of Chinese thinkers of whom I had never heard, this essay amounted to a magnet drawn through the canon of world literature and philosophy charged with picking up bits of discursive metal defined by provincialism or cosmopolitanism. For me, it was a de-facto anthology of shorthand references to aspects of history about which I wanted to learn more. "Yeats, like Tagore with his cosmopolitan culture," runs a typical sentence, "was as far from a lost Bengal or Connemara as any faceless victim of standardized mass society." Someone with a better education than I had might have been less dazzled by Levenson's learning.

But as with Miller, Levenson came at the right time for me. I was ready to go in directions I did not recognize until I saw them in Levenson's work.

Why was I so engaged with the tension between provincialism and cosmopolitanism? No doubt being from Idaho and the Brethren, surrounded with Ivy League graduates and others from backgrounds very different from my own, usually more broadly educated, had something to do with it. I understood what it meant to be provincial. Nobody else I knew in graduate school had grown up with the view of human groups I summarized at the start of this essay. I also understood—without, I hope, judging provincials, in Idaho and elsewhere, too ungenerously for being what history had made of them—what it meant to try for a more capacious life, one that embraced more of human possibility. "Variousness and possibility" was the theme of another work I was reading in 1967, Lionel Trilling's *Liberal Imagination*. I was especially affected by the essay on *The Princess Casamassima*, in which Trilling connects James's hero in that novel, Hyacinth Robinson, to the "Young Man from the Provinces," equipped with "poverty, pride, and intelligence" as a standard character in modern literature. Such a young man "stands outside life and seeks to enter," wrote Trilling, and seeks entry usually by going to the metropole. Of course I thought of my father, penniless and alone, hitchhiking to Chicago during the depression summer of 1933 from Saskatchewan, where, after departing Gettysburg, he had tried to make a living as a wheat farmer. And I thought of myself more fortunate than my father, yet also recognizable as a variation on the type.

In 1967 I switched from the intellectual history of the eighteenth century to that of the twentieth; largely because it was about the twentieth century that I thought I had the most to learn, and potentially the most to contribute to the study of provincialism and cosmopolitanism. Henry F. May, the director of my dissertation, was wonderfully kind in putting up with a period of indecision, during which I dropped a dissertation topic on John Locke in America, in which May had been vitally interested, and took up instead, the career of the Jewish cosmopolitan philosopher of science, Morris R. Cohen. By then, I knew what I was doing. Perhaps for the first time? At least I felt that I was making an informed decision between viable alternatives, rather than being pushed and pulled by circumstance, and ending up with position achieved largely by default.

The China connection thus amounts to a hauling of coal to Newcastle. Levenson's sensitivity to the dynamics of provincialism and cosmopolitanism in the North Atlantic West, especially as those dynamics affected

Jews in relation to the Enlightenment, framed his study of Chinese history. Yet it was in reading Levenson on China that I came to recognize the questions about the United States that most engaged me. And so it happened: a son of Idaho and of a small Anabaptist sect, having been inspired by a Harvard atheist's studies of New England Puritanism, found his career-defining preoccupations when connections made through a political movement brought him into contact with the work of an orthodox Jew addressing the cultural dynamics of the modernization process through a meditation on Confucian China's encounter with communism.

Was there a more efficient way for me to get from Idaho and La Verne to Morris Cohen, Jewish intellectuals, and the tension between cosmopolitanism and provincialism in American culture? No doubt there was. Perhaps this turn in my life, which I make so much of here, is simply another instance of my not knowing what I was doing? I don't think so. Rather, I take it an example of how an individual makes his or her decisions on the basis of an inventory of possibilities that happen to be at hand. You play, as they say, the cards you are dealt. Levenson was one of the best cards I was ever dealt. I never met Levenson, who died in 1969 in an accidental drowning in the Russian River at the age of forty-nine. I was still in Berkeley that spring, finishing up my dissertation. I went to his funeral.

During the years after Levenson's death, when China specialists warned me more and more often of Levenson's peculiar "take" on China, Levenson's example ended up presenting me with yet another gift: a profound cautionary tale. Levenson seems to have weakened his interpretation of Chinese history by projecting too much of himself into his subject. I wanted my own pursuit of the cosmopolitanism-provincialism dynamic to be heuristically informed by my own experience, but not captured by it. Would my ambivalence toward the provinces known to me, and my attractions to many varieties of cosmopolitanism, prevent me from seeing and proclaiming the most warrantable of the truths embedded in my objects of study? Whatever the answer to this question, the frequency with which I have interrogated myself in its terms is another way in which Levenson's writings affect me to this day.

My Levenson-inspired self-interrogation has been keyed by Idaho and the Brethren. My trajectory away from what a great antiprovincial called "the idiocy of rural life" has made it too easy for me, I have reminded myself repeatedly through the decades, to treat in too frosty a fashion worlds of the sort from which I myself had come. Having found the cultures of my upbringing too confining, there was a danger that my appreciation for the cultures of my adulthood would blind me to the needs many people have for tightly bounded communities and to the dignity that can attend on a provincial life. I have also been aware of the possibility that I would blind myself to the particular virtues of the kind of Protestantism with which my life began. This self-interrogation has affected most of what I have written, especially *In the American Province* (1985), *Postethnic America* (1995), and *Cosmopolitanism and Solidarity* (2006).

But the very attraction to cosmopolitanism and the self-interrogation about it that defines so much of the historian I became is deeply embedded in my Brethren past. I want to elaborate a bit more on that past. Most important was a formidable universalist strain in Christianity that came to me through the Brethren.

The German Baptist Brethren were anything but universalist. This sect was ethnically defined for two hundred years before its name became Church of the Brethren in 1908. The Brethren remained a largely descent-defined denomination in fact long after it ceased to be so in name. During the years of my upbringing, however, Brethren leaders were in a decidedly ecumenical phase. I was exposed to a certain selection of Brethren themes, focusing on service and inclusion. This was the agenda of the educated elite of the Church, especially the editors of denominational periodicals and the professors at the denominational colleges and seminary. These leaders wanted to make the Brethren more like the Methodists, that is, to walk humbly in the Lord but to do so in a more modern manner, less suspicious of the world. The old Brethren tradition had been highly sectarian. The celebration of Christmas was too worldly (the view of my grandfather). Women were to be excommunicated ("churched" was the Brethren term) for not wearing the proper bonnet (the fate of my aunt who married a Presbyterian and became a professor at Gettysburg College).

In this new ecumenical context, universalist sentiments flourished. Galatians 3:28 taught that in Christ there is no Greek or Jew, no male nor female, no slave nor free. The second chapter of Acts advanced this universalist vision at its most radical and dramatic, presenting the reader with a mythic moment when the curse of Babel was revoked and all the tribes of the earth could understand each other as they spoke the gospel with cloven tongues of fire. In church in Idaho and later in California, we used to sing "In Christ there is no East or West, In Him no South or North; But one great fellowship of love, throughout the whole wide earth" (Hymn 362 in *The Brethren Hymnal*, 1943 edition). I soon learned to take this extravagant idealism for what it was, the enunciation of an ideal rather than the summary of a practice, but the ideal was presented to me with sufficient vigor that I know it had something to do with my engagements as a historian.

The work of another Berkeley professor of Levenson's generation, with whom I did not study, led me to conclude that I should engage the cosmopolitanism-provincialism problematic through the cultural functions of science and the ways in which science was defined by public moralists. It was also in 1967 that I first read Thomas S. Khun's *The Structure of Scientific Revolutions*. Kuhn had left Berkeley by then, but the memory of him was still vivid in Dwinelle Hall and every "with-it" graduate student had read his great book. The issues to which Kuhn introduced me led me to choose, as the topic of my dissertation, the career of a philosopher known for his defense of science as a foundation for culture.

Kuhn led me not only to Morris Cohen, but also to a sharpening of the methodological principles I had derived from Perry Miller. Kuhn's account of the dynamics of scientific communities spoke to the dynamics of other kinds of discursive communities in much the same way that Levenson's account of Chinese history spoke to other cases of the tension between provincialism and cosmopolitanism. During the next several decades I would repeatedly cite the methodological good sense embedded within Kuhn's understanding of how science works. But Kuhn's legacy in the Berkeley of my graduate years consisted also in the contribution he made to the department's remarkable focus on intellectual history.

Berkeley in the 1960s was truly an extraordinary place to do intellectual history. At the time I did not recognize this distinction. Of the Berkeley historians I have already mentioned, Kuhn, Levenson, and May were primarily intellectual historians, but Jordan and Middlekauff, too, were then doing important work in intellectual history. I served as a research assistant for Jordan's *White over Black: White Attitudes toward Negroes in America, 1550–1812.* May's lecture course on the intellectual history of the United States since 1865 has always been a model for my own, and has affected the character of the source book, dedicated to him, that I have coedited in many editions with Charles Capper, another Berkeley Ph.D. from that era. But there were many more intellectual historians, including William J. Bouwsma, the Renaissance and Reformation specialist, in whose historiography seminar I wrote what would become my first published article (on Perry Miller). I did not study with Carl Schorske, Samuel

Haber, Hunter Dupree, Nicholas Riasanovsky, Adrienne Koch, George Stocking, or Martin Malia, but I invoke their names here to mark the department's exceptionally strong representation of intellectual history during the time that I was deciding just what kind of historian I wanted to be.

I was lucky to have been at Berkeley when I was. Indeed, so much of what I have narrated here seems to me a story of luck, mostly good. I am breaking off this account in the late 1960s because by then the basic foundation of the historian I became had been established, mostly by the remarkable people with whom I came into direct or indirect contact as a graduate student at Berkeley. Nearly all of these Berkeley people, as it happened, were not church people, including Joan Heifetz Hollinger, whom I married in 1967. But the good luck goes back even prior to Berkeley, back to the church people. From my parents and their religious culture I derived a set of basic resources that served me remarkably well as I proceeded to a life very different from the ones they had led. Long after I left the ranks of church people, my favorite scripture remained Amos 9:7, in which those who think their group superior to others are urged to cool it: "Are you not like the Ethiopians to me, O people of Israel?" I was lucky enough, also, to go through the state of California's junior high and high schools at a time when these schools actually delivered— magnificently!—on the promise of public education.

Perhaps the luckiest thing of all was simply to have been part of a small enough generational cohort to enable me to gain admission to a place like Berkeley on the basis of my unimpressive qualifications. Having served now on the admissions committee of the same department that admitted me, I know full well that I would not be accepted at Berkeley now. An irony of my career is that nearly all of the graduate students I now teach at Berkeley are better than I was at their stage, yet here I am, one of their professors. I hope they have a streak of luck as good as I have had, but I fear that many of them will not. There are not enough jobs now. And this brings me to another instance of generational good luck.

When I went on the job market in the fall of 1968, I told my doctoral mentor, Henry May, that I did not want him to nominate me for any job south of the Mason-Dixon line or in the cities of New York and Chicago. The brass of it now seems incredible. Was this yet another case of my not knowing what I was doing? In terms of taste and tact, probably yes. But cognitively, I acted on the valid understanding that there were plenty of jobs. I wrote in a matter-of-fact way, simply registering a set of preferences as to where I did and did not want to live. The job market was so flush that it did not occur to me that I would not get a job, and a good one. Some of us were able to develop full careers as historians because the institutional support was there to enable us not only to get started, but to stay with it, and to act upon whatever intellectual ambitions we had developed as graduate students. Talent and enterprise? Of course they play a role. But those of us who became historians under the fortunate circumstances of the 1960s should never forget how much luck had to do with it.

MAUREEN MURPHY NUTTING

Choices

My education as a historian began in Manhattan. It has continued across this country and beyond, under the tutelage of men and women from many walks of life. They have given me opportunities to learn history and to learn about myself, and to make choices about what to study in history and what to do in crafting my life. My varied experiences and the elements of my life as a history teacher, activist, wife, and mother have made me the historian I am; they cannot be separated. Nor would I want them to be.

I grew up in Washington Heights, a few blocks north and east of the George Washington Bridge. I thrived on 182nd Street between Audubon and Amsterdam Avenues, where I played with dozens of Irish Americans and Polish Americans (Catholics) and Greeks and Jews (both Orthodox). We sometimes engaged in religious wars and ethnic drubbings but generally set aside those differences when skating or playing stickball, stoopball, or hopscotch. Oddly enough, headgear united us. The Catholic girls' school beanies were not unlike the Jewish boys' yarmulkes, and thanks to our rivalries many of these trademark head coverings decorated the light poles on St. Nicholas Avenue.

But sudden change came to my section of the Heights in the early 1950s, when Puerto Ricans and African Americans from North Carolina began moving in. By the time I started fourth grade, most of our white neighbors had fled to the suburbs. The Murphys stayed.

When these new families moved in, absentee landlords converted many of the neighborhood's brownstones to single room weekly rentals, which housed one family to a room. By the mid-1950s, the very few white families who had not moved out were living in a multiracial, multiethnic world, and the Murphys' basement had become *the* Puerto Rican community center in the Heights. Every day, children came for English and religious instruction, arts and crafts, and cocoa and cookies. Their parents stopped by to select everything from coats to cereal and whatever else had been donated. Within a short time, our young black neighbors were also coming. So were Cuban children and their parents.

The genius behind this operation was Ivan Illich, a Ph.D. in history from the University of Salzburg and then a young parish priest at the Church of the Incarnation in the Heights. Illich provided the setup and strategy and my mother single-handedly managed the day-to-day operations until Illich recruited four young Austrian women to help her. Before arriving in the Heights they had been working in refugee camps built on the Austrian border for Hungarians who had escaped the repression in their homeland.

Illich began this project shortly after my mother, a thorn in many a side, challenged him as we rode to Gate of Heaven Cemetery to bury a neighbor. Why, she asked him as he sat captive with her in the car, was he so busy talking about gospel values and not doing anything in the neighborhood? When he told her he had no place to do this work and that it should be done in homes, not in church buildings, she told him that our basement was available. He came, and she recruited the children and their parents. In 1962, the city condemned our block for a new public intermediate school, and my family moved to the Bronx; until that time, long after Illich left for a new post in Puerto Rico, our home was a home away from home for hundreds of neighbors.

The transformation of my home profoundly affected me. My new companions taught me street Spanish and introduced me to their food and traditions. On a personal level they taught me about living with poverty, hunger, neglect, and marginalization, and to be grateful for what I had. Illich's small corps of volunteers demonstrated that unmarried women could transform their own lives and those of others. And Father Illich and my parents made it clear that all of us were equal in the eyes of God and should be equal in the eyes of each other. The activities and noise levels at home also forced me to find quiet time and space for myself in the New York Public Library branch on West 178th Street, where I spent hours reading and doing homework every week.

This Heights project primed Illich for his subsequent assignment as Vice Rector of the Catholic University of Ponce and, later, as founding director of the Center for Documentation in Guadalajara, Mexico, where he trained priests, sisters, and lay men and women volunteers for Latin American missions. His efforts in our basement not only set the course for his later projects, but also influenced his writings on work, education, economic development. He criticized First World involvement in Third World communities, and reprimanded wealthy governments and organizations that dealt with the Third World without finding any common ground with Third World people. The project also instilled in me a deep, abiding interest in the Latin American community that has manifested itself in my teaching and research in Latin American history and in my willingness to accept Illich's implicit challenge to do something worthwhile with my life, preferably in service to people who have less than I do.

My parents sent a similar message. With limited resources and little schooling, my mother, a full-time housewife, and my father, a bus driver, were odd agents of social change. Both had emigrated on their own from Ireland in the 1920s, my father at sixteen and my mother at fifteen. My father, Patrick Murphy, was the ninth of fourteen children and as he would often tell us, a proud graduate of the college of hard knocks. He and my mother were adamant that my brother and I secure the education they never had but valued so much. Paddy had finished the fourth book in the National School in Castleisland, County Kerry, and then had worked in his father's fields before joining an older teenage brother in Manhattan and finding work as a streetcar conductor. My mother, Marie Clarke, had attended a convent school in County Sligo until she was thirteen. When she arrived in New York, she was taken directly to an estate in Greenwich, Connecticut, where she worked as a live-in girl until marrying Paddy at twenty-three. They met in New York a few months before that at a party where he was the only stranger playing Twenty-five, an Irish card game. Knowing that the other players were not Irish speakers, she began reading their cards to him in Gaelic to catch his attention. It worked; he won their hands that night and hers in April 1935.

Neither of my parents ever went to school again, but my father read most New York newspapers every day on his 42nd Street cross-town bus. He also read the Bible and the Catholic press. A union man, he quoted Leo XIII on social justice, listened faithfully to radio commentator Gabriel Heatter, and watched the evening news after we got a television set.

He routinely counseled the young Irish fellows who rode with him daily to their jobs on the Circle Line boats. For Paddy, faith, family, and social justice were seamlessly integrated. So the chaotic community center in our home made sense to him—and he fully supported it.

My dad had a formidable memory. At the drop of a hat, he could list world capitals, major river systems, and mountain ranges, name past and present world leaders, and give content-rich, entertaining, and accurate accounts of Brian Borou, Daniel O'Connell, and Irish history from the days of the Four Masters to the times of the Troubles. He would quote poetry and sing Irish songs for hours on end without skipping a word; he insisted on correct spelling and memorization; and he often said that one who mixed languages showed the signs of a weak mind. Yet we had very few books in our home: a well-thumbed Douay-Rheims Bible, a copy of *Moore's Irish Melodies*, and one of *Gulliver's Travels*, and, a portent of things to come for me, *Reminiscences: The Autobiography of Julia Ward Howe*. I read these books often and habitually borrowed more from the library.

With poor vision and very little time to spare, my mother didn't read much. But she set high expectations for us and underscored my father's commitments to self-discipline and hard work. A strict disciplinarian, she enforced house rules and put up with little nonsense. For our Irish Catholic family, Sunday Mass attendance and daily prayer at home were mandatory, and parochial school was the only educational option, so my brother and I attended St. Elizabeth's grammar school in the Heights. The Holy Child Sisters who taught us echoed my father's love of history, geography, and poetry. They introduced me to maps, mathematics, new books, and new people—Laura Ingalls Wilder, Harriet Tubman, Thomas Jefferson, Mark Twain, Henry Wadsworth Longfellow, and Winston Churchill among them. They also encouraged seventh and eighth grade girls to work in the school library, and so I did. In school and public libraries, I found ideas and images that took me beyond myself and far beyond my neighborhood. Our parish choir director, Edward O'Donnell, also gave me a precious gift in the form of an introduction to Gregorian chant when I joined the Schola Cantorum in fifth grade. From then through eighth grade, I sang Kyries, Glorias, Sanctuses, and the Proper of the Mass every week under his direction. I still sing these medieval chants often at Seattle's St. James Cathedral.

After eighth grade, and two years after my brother John had left the Heights to attend a Carmelite high school, founded by a cousin, in Massachusetts, I enrolled in the Academy of Mount Saint Ursula in the Bronx,

New York State's oldest Catholic high school for girls. The Ursulines of
the Roman Union, the oldest teaching order of women in the Catholic
Church, ran the Mount and they took teaching and learning seriously.
Many of my contemporaries were obsessed with sex, drugs, and rock and
roll and were intent on challenging authority; I had no time or energy
for those pursuits, since I was inundated with homework and bound by
rules. In an environment steeped in religious and ethical values, I was
constantly reminded of the importance of academic integrity, personal
responsibility, and order. And did we ever have rules! We could wear
lipstick and clear nail polish, but no other cosmetics. Our uniforms were
to be clean and pressed, blue Oxfords and loafers shined, and blue velvet
berets and white gloves ready to wear for all special school events. For being out of uniform or untidy, one earned a demerit. Two demerits earned
a detention—a full Saturday of supervised school dusting. Two detentions
brought on suspension, and suspensions led to expulsions. Enforcement
was fast, even-handed, and ubiquitous, so we knew that creases, missing
buttons, eye shadow, and runs in stockings brought on suffering.

We also watched these task mistresses dispense support, encouragement, and praise fairly, and we looked forward to earning subject medals
and gold satin bows for academic honors, which we proudly wore on the lap-
els of our blue wool blazers. We Mounties, as we were termed, were called
to succeed and serve—and to ignore the common culture. Without varsity
sports, proms, yearbooks or other activities the nuns deemed diversions
from scholarly pursuits, we wrote papers, translated Cicero and Molière,
worked logic problems, performed classical pieces and plays, volunteered
regularly in the community, and set our sights on college.

But how could one do all this homework in a house that was seething
with activity? I found my haven just one station beyond my regular stop
on the A train—in the Cloisters, a world away from the mayhem of Manhattan and the Murphy household. There, I could sit on the low wall of the
Chapter House from Notre-Dame-de Pontraut and work on my French
or math or biology until closing time. There I could take breaks and wan-
der through the Cuxa Cloister and marvel over the exquisite detail of the
Unicorn and Five Worthies tapestries or read a page from the *Hours of
Jeanne d'Évreux*. The art displayed in the Cloisters gave context to the
Gregorian chants I sang, and the galleries became integral to the life of
my mind and a refuge from my other worlds. This was *my* museum.

In many ways, Mount teachers introduced me to the magic of teaching and learning history and tying the past to the present time and place.

I recall Mrs. Muriel Koepfler telling us how it felt one day in Yankee Stadium—just blocks south of us—when she and her father watched from their bench as Babe Ruth came up, pointed his bat "out there" and hit the home run that made baseball history. I remember Mother Mary Ellen Smith earnestly explaining the importance of the Bill of Rights and entreating us to make sure that those rights were protected in the future. History classes at the Mount were alive with debate and discussion, heavy in workload, and oh so much fun. Religion classes also were intriguing in those heady days of the early 1960s, while bishops meeting in Rome for the Second Vatican Council voted to revise and replace many of the Catholic customs, teachings, and traditions that their predecessors had last examined and embraced at the Council of Trent in the mid-1500s. To make sense of what was changing in the present, we needed to understand the past—and so our religion classes were rife with history as well.

As a very selective school that drew students from across the Bronx, Manhattan, Queens, and Westchester, the Mount also introduced me to issues of class. The parents of many of the girls were American born, college-educated, and affluent. Some of these girls made palpably clear that they lived in a different world from those who came from the Heights and similar neighborhoods, despite the fact that in school we wore the same uniform and shared common classes. Being in their world at school and another at home taught me much about their lives and values and about the importance of understanding how and why class distinctions are developed and maintained.

The nuns did not discriminate on the basis of race, class, or ethnicity; for them, academics and character were the measure of a young woman, and they were determined to cultivate our minds and convert the spirits of those who needed conversion. To this end the Ursulines offered a robust curriculum. They even provided us with role models in two strong women saints, Ursula, the apocryphal leader of thousands of virgin martyrs, and Angela Merici, founder of the Ursulines, the first order whose express mission was to educate girls. Under the nuns' direction, I applied myself and did well. By senior year, I considered attending the College of New Rochelle, their school, but then applied to Fordham University. If Fordham was the best Catholic university for men in New York, then it was the best place for me.

Fortuitously, after 122 years of teaching men in the Bronx, the Jesuits at Fordham had voted in 1963 to admit the first class of undergraduate women to their Rose Hill campus in the Bronx. In the fall of 1964, after securing a few scholarships, I joined the charter class of Thomas More College, Fordham's new coordinate college for women. We were given our own dean, Father John Donohue, S.J., and during our freshman year we followed a separate core curriculum before joining the men in most of our sophomore classes. The 213 young women in our group got to know each other quickly. In a short time we had surveyed the campus and calculated that the odds of landing a date were fifteen to one. I must admit that my first semester focused on dating my quota of fifteen and not on history.

But it didn't mean that I had lost interest in history. By the time I started Fordham, I had identified three major interest areas—American history, American politics, and literature. My high school history instructors had been particularly engaging, lively, and articulate, and they made two points very clear: historical issues are complex, and historical characters share our own humanity. My English teachers had introduced me to many Western writers, and I thoroughly enjoyed reading the novels, essays, and poetry they assigned and recommended. Though I had never studied political science, I enjoyed political debate and discussion and declared that major when applying. However, before taking a single course in political science, I changed my major to history when James Finlay, S.J., took over as chairman of the political science department. Although I was awed by Finlay (who would eventually become a good friend and mentor and later Fordham's president), I decided it was time to ditch my first major because Findlay's Irish mother was my mother's good friend, and I wanted to ensure that their relationship didn't complicate my education.

Since I consulted with no one about this I did not realize that one needed to submit signed forms to make this change. But after several months my dean caught on to what I had done; he then gently counseled me about giving more serious thought to one's choice of majors. Memories of that conversation dissuaded me from switching again the following year, this time from history to English. The deadline for doing so coincided with the arrival of a vicious snowstorm. After looking out over the growing drifts across the campus and calculating that changing a major would require me to secure four signatures in four different buildings, I decided it wasn't worth the effort. Very few scholars of any standing would have said at that point that I had the makings of a good historian.

The change from high school to college was both dramatic and traumatic and the combination of a full load of courses and a part-time job off campus was wearing. My first-semester grades forced me to reassess my priorities and cut back on my social life, and I settled into more serious pursuits my second semester. But not all was lost that first semester. Maurice O'Connell, my history professor freshman year, was an engaging, and congenial Irish scholar, not to mention a relative of Daniel O'Connell, Ireland's liberator and one of my father's heroes. I looked forward to his Western civilization lectures, where he wove historical narratives as seamlessly as the creators of the medieval tapestries. In doing so, he allowed us to mentally situate ourselves in the past for a few hours every week. Inspired by O'Connell, I began reading whatever he recommended. The material was rich, but the more I studied modern Western civilization, the more I realized that it raised little passion in me.

In my sophomore year, two historians—an assistant professor and a senior scholar—challenged me as never before and introduced me to serious research and writing in history. Robert F. Jones, who taught colonial and early American national history, and Jeremiah O'Sullivan, a medievalist, were inspired teachers who brought these eras to life in their lectures and research assignments. O'Sullivan could get his students to mourn the destruction of Cluny and celebrate the coronation of Charlemagne; he introduced us to journals and manuscripts that deepened our interest in the medieval world. His lectures gave new dimensions to the art I viewed at the Cloisters and chants I sang at Mass, and piqued my interest in studying the intersections of history and culture. An academic who had worked with the displaced populations of Europe after the Second World War, he also taught us more about respect and compassion for others than any other professor who taught me before or since.

Jones, who became my advisor and who ran his classes with tough love and wicked humor, made the American colonial and early national years resonate with life and intrigue. His lectures got me to grasp the importance of understanding economic issues and policies in history and accepting heroes in history with their warts as well as their wisdom. While Jones and Sullivan reiterated my father's example by demonstrating the importance of integrating the life of the mind with faith, reason, and service, the only two women who taught me in college, Simone Retailleau (French literature) and Ruth Hawkins (American politics), convinced me that women had just as much talent and the right to teach college classes as men did. Thanks to the direction of these and other remarkable teachers, I embraced the life of the mind by my third semester in college. I also became a fixture in the university library, planted six days of the week at the same sturdy oak table within the stacks, a stained glass window to my right, a narrow walkway and railing to my left, and history journals before and behind me. When I wasn't reading my assigned works or writing papers or studying, I was reading those journals.

Time in the library was my time, and it was my precious time, as I had to balance it with work and home life. A dayhop at a largely residential university, and a working student where most students had all their time for studying and socializing, I earned my keep doing chores at home about a mile from campus and held down two other jobs as well. I continued my high school job at a charity thrift shop on East 77th Street through college. And starting with my sophomore year, I also tutored in Fordham's Running Start program, where I was the first female tutor hired by Father Timothy Healy, S.J., an English professor who then directed the program and later served as president of both Georgetown University and the New York Public Library. The Running Start students and I made a good match. They were bright, active, underprivileged, and eager—like those who had frequented my home in the Heights—and they lacked the skills they needed to get into and thrive in college. As I drilled them in grammar, vocabulary, and math, they taught me to value even more my education and to work harder to improve my own academic skills.

Early in sophomore year I became acquainted with Father Joseph Fitzpatrick, S.J, a sociologist of Latin America and a quiet yet forceful advocate for social justice. He teamed up with my old friend Illich (by then situated in Cuernavaca, Mexico) to involve Fordham students in what he called the Fordham University Mexico Project. One of the first to join, I served as project secretary and a fundraiser and began preparations for volunteer work among the field workers at El Ingenio Potrero, a sugar mill town close to Cordoba in Veracruz. After months of intensive daily language drills in Fordham's language labs and many training sessions with Father Fitzpatrick and other experts, our team of seven women and eleven men headed for Veracruz after finals in spring 1966.

In Potrero we were hosted by Father Juan Gonzales, a full-blooded Aztec and priest who dedicated his life to this sugar mill community—and who drove his Ford across unpaved, potholed roads at eighty kilometers an hour. Under the direction of Rodrigo Medellin, a young Jesuit priest committed then and now to forming *communidades de bas* among the indigenous field workers, the Fordham men built and repaired homes and footbridges, and the women either taught English or worked in the town's medical clinic under the direction of a local doctor. My clinical service introduced me to maggot-infected wounds, parasites, machete cuts, and other maladies common to field workers. Medellin introduced us to the theories and activists involved in a new social movement developing in Latin America—liberation theology. These people and my local host family, who lived in a two-room house without any floor or utilities, introduced me to their traditions and language, which had changed little since before the Spanish conquest. My summer experiences convinced me I had no future in medicine and strengthened my resolve to learn more about Latin America's past and present indigenous minorities and about the history of the Catholic Church in Latin America.

Often, while off exploring or washing clothes in the river, we were approached by local Indians who tried to sell us Indian artifacts. None of us knew that they may have been getting these from a local dig then in progress under the direction of Yale anthropologist Michael Coe at San Lorenzo, about twenty-five kilometers from us. Thirty-six years later I learned more about that dig and the local indigenous people from Coe himself, when he was the instructor and I was his student in a National Endowment for the Humanities summer institute on Mayan communities in Mexico and Guatemala.

Even the trip home from Mexico was eventful: the U.S. airlines had gone on strike, our return tickets from Texas were useless, and my traveling companion, Lorraine Archibald, and I found ourselves riding for days on a Greyhound bus from Laredo to New York City. What made our trip eventful was that Lorraine was black and I was white, we were broke, and we were sitting together on a bus in the Deep South in 1966. We were harassed, threatened, sworn at, and scolded, and so we were never so happy to see anyone as my brother when our bus finally pulled into New York's Port Authority terminal. After riding day and night for the better part of a week we had learned more about race relations in the American South than we had wanted or expected, and I had the makings of a compelling first person narrative to share with future students of American history.

That fall I returned to Fordham, eager to learn more about race relations and Latin American history in my junior year. But to my dismay I soon found myself continually challenging the race theories presented by my colonial Latin American history professor. Refusing to budge after my Greyhound experiences, I challenged him in the classroom and in the papers I wrote, and I suffered the consequences. That ordeal convinced me to focus instead on U.S. history courses and to continue to read *Americas* and the *Journal of Latin American History* on my own.

Inspired by a splendid junior year tutorial in twentieth-century philosophy, where I learned from my tutorial partner, a physics major, that no two people read a book the same way, I cobbled together a senior year curriculum that combined modern American history with philosophy, and music and literature of the twentieth century. This self-styled interdisciplinary program, which also included communications and theology, proved greater than the sum of its parts. The classes integrated well, allowing me to approach the recent past in ways I hadn't imagined and to explore aspects of American culture I had never known. They also challenged me to think creatively and across disciplines about what we as Americans, and in some cases as Catholics, had become, and what we might face in the future.

Two professors who were not historians but who taught me that year influenced me profoundly. When theologian Ewart Cousins, who lived his faith as he taught it, assigned Betty Friedan's *The Feminine Mystique* in his Theology of Marriage course, he had no way of knowing how it would affect his handful of women students. Friedan's book—and Cousins—convinced me that marriage, a lifelong commitment, would and should not be an option until I knew myself better, understood what was important to me, and had determined what I would and would not be willing to negotiate in a permanent relationship. His relationship with his wife, a professor of English at Fordham, also modeled a marriage respectful of dual careers and marriage.

Marshall McLuhan, then holder of Fordham's Albert Schweitzer Chair in the Humanities, taught my communications course. While McLuhan's classes were often theatrical, eventful, and sometimes absurd, the man with the message turned into one of my major agents of change. His concept of a global village made sense to me, and his insistence that media were breaking down barriers and forging an unanticipated and wide range of connections across cultures inspired me to look at communications technology in new ways. If radio was "cool" and television was "hot," what were the possibilities for the newfangled computer? McLuhan's insistence that we keep looking into the "rear view mirror" somehow convinced me that history has real utility and reminded me that being aware and mindful of the past helps one avoid catastrophes in the future. These ideas influenced my perceptions of history in many ways, leading me later to integrate technology into my history courses, to teach U.S. and Latin American history within a global context, and to write and speak publicly about these innovations and their effects on students.

Sometime earlier in my senior year, worried about working out a reasonable plan for the future and mindful of my limits and opportunities, I applied for graduate programs in American studies, with the intention of eventually teaching history in New York City public high schools. When several graduate programs accepted me, my mother intervened. Alarmed by the changes in the Catholic Church since the Second Vatican Council and convinced that the Jesuits had "ruined" me, she threatened to disown me if I went off to an "atheistic college."

The only Catholic university I applied to was Notre Dame. In the spring of 1968, I received my first acceptance letter from the graduate school dean. In it he offered congratulations but no funding and explained that Notre Dame admitted women as part-time students. We could earn a masters degree in six years by taking classes on Saturdays and during summer school. Furious that full-time status in this program was being denied me because I was a woman, I used a lesson I had learned about effective assertiveness as a woman at Fordham. I wrote back and told him that I was already attending a Catholic men's college, and that I would only attend Notre Dame as a first class citizen, not as what I then characterized as a "suffering suffragette." His return letter made a very different offer: admission as a full-time student and full funding for the MA program. The funding permitted me to achieve my professional goals, guaranteed my financial independence, allowed me to do what I wanted to do eight hundred miles away from New York, and kept me in the good graces of the family. I accepted. Had I not, I am certain that my future would have been outside the academy. When I announced my intentions, my mother was delighted that I was going to a *real* Catholic school; little did she know that Notre Dame harbored its own subversives.

When I flew to South Bend, Indiana, that summer to arrange for off-campus housing, I discovered that many locals were unwilling to rent to Notre Dame women; some told me that no women attended Notre Dame. Others who advertised places for rent made it clear that they would not accommodate women they assumed were coming to seduce Notre Dame men. No one I contacted would even show me a place. When my graduate student host found out, he arranged for me to meet with Father Ned Joyce, a senior administrator, who assured me that something would work out; days later I learned that I could move onto the fourth floor of Lewis Hall, a campus dormitory that had been built a few years earlier for sisters enrolled at the university. I moved in the following month with the thirty-two other laywomen who had gotten equally late invitations. We quickly built what became a vital support network for our group that lasted through graduate school. This, the first of many women's networks

I would join, most of them in history, would convince me of the importance of women helping women in academia and set me up for interesting advocacy work decades later.

From the religious sisters who lived on the floors below us, I learned that women had been attending Notre Dame for decades, but since most of the female students had been sisters and sisters weren't counted as women, coeducation had conveniently been left out of the Notre Dame story. This was easy to do because women were hard to find on Notre Dame's campus, especially before Lewis Hall opened in 1965, because women had no dormitories or other designated places to meet on campus. I am now compiling the stories of many of these early Notre Dame women.

When I met with the director of the American studies program, a very genial but old-school political scientist whose political mindset was clearly different from mine, I identified history as my major field but named American literature and the sociology of American minorities as my two minor fields. I took a course in Latino/Chicano communities taught by anthropologist Arthur J. Rubel and sociologist Julian Samora that first term. There I not only learned a great deal about these communities and their past and present issues, but realized how effective faculty could be when they consciously made interdisciplinary connections through team-taught and linked courses. I also learned so much about teaching across disciplines from these two men. Samora, a new faculty member and newly minted Ph.D. (the first Mexican American in the United States to earn a Ph.D. in sociology), went on to be a leader in Chicano studies; Rubel, who never abandoned his beloved Mexicans and Mexican American communities, went on to develop a new field, medical anthropology, and mentored many scholars from the different disciplines and communities he connected. I later adopted many of their interdisciplinary teaching techniques and integrated much of the content into my own courses on American immigration and ethnic history.

Along with these two activist scholars, historians Philip Gleason and John A. Williams III, among others, encouraged my interest in disenfranchised groups and their champions. I suspect that Notre Dame was doing much more to address race discrimination than many other leading universities in the country at that time, and that Father Theodore Hesburgh, then president of Notre Dame and chair of the U.S. Civil Rights Commission, had much to do with the university's clear commitment to recruiting and supporting students of color. To be sure, the Notre Dame men certainly did not focus on women's rights in the late 1960s and early 1970s, but that's another story. To their credit, the men who taught me at Notre Dame fostered the commitment and courage I needed to develop and teach inclusive American history courses long before many members of the academy accepted or embraced the practice.

My first semester was very challenging because of a history methods course that nearly ended my graduate career. We focused on quantitative history, and we had to learn basic Fortran programming in order to work with the census data around which the course was organized. After avoiding mathematics and math applications as best I could in college, I was unprepared for the task. Thanks to the clear and patient tutoring of a gallant classmate, Patrick Owens, I survived and swore that this historian would never work with computers again. But now this historian uses them constantly. So much for graduate school resolutions.

There were three of us in the American studies master's program: one man and two women, including myself. He focused on political science, she focused on literature, and I ended up being the only woman in my history seminars. My first graduate seminar meeting in the fall of 1968 was memorable. The professor asked each of us to identify ourselves, tell what school we had come from, and say why we were taking the course. When my turn came, the professor interrupted before I could speak: "You came here because the odds were so good." I looked at him, slowly scanned the six or seven men to my right who had already identified themselves, looked back at him, and scanned the seven or eight remaining men to my left. I then looked at the professor, gave him my name, and told him that I had come from Fordham, "where the odds were better." The fellows in the class understood my situation and welcomed me warmly. And we all learned a lesson about making superficial assumptions.

As I settled into courses it quickly became clear to me that Philip Gleason was going to be a major influence in my graduate career. Gleason, who took over the American studies graduate program shortly after I arrived, had written an article, "The Melting Pot, Symbol of Fusion or Confusion?" that had been published in 1964 and made me question many of the popular metaphors for assimilation and acculturation in the United States long before I had come to Notre Dame. That first year I studied American social, intellectual, and cultural history under him, and over the years I have had the good fortune to have him as a graduate advisor, dissertation director, and good friend. Gleason was not a dynamic lecturer but he was profound. After I left his lectures, my mind swam with new ideas, so many they were hard to process. Gleason challenged me to think particularly about the intersections of race, class, religion, and ethnicity and demonstrated how these, with other factors, influence individual and community behaviors, as well as group loyalties, affinities, and alliances. He also made me think about the life and work of the historian. Gleason lived in the library, kept current with many journals, and worked indefatigably on his own research; he encouraged his students to do the same. With his wife Maureen, one of the university's librarians, he also modeled the melding of marriage, children, and career.

I was also profoundly influenced by an elder statesman who had come to Notre Dame after retiring from the University of Buffalo, Julius W. Pratt. Pratt was the quintessential courtly scholar—tall, equally elegant in stature and prose, precise, engaging, and demanding. With him, the workings of American diplomacy took on the aspects of a chess game where every move was nuanced and critical. Under his guidance, I investigated U.S. relations with Mexico's revolutionary governments during the early twentieth century and found that my interest in Latin America had not been dampened by my disappointing Fordham course. And sometime during that year, I realized that I had found my place in history. Using the tools of the historian allowed me to make better sense of both past and present than I ever could with the tools of other disciplines. Historical narratives also appealed to me enormously. Presented cleanly and crisply in the vernacular, good history writing reveals and underscores the complexities of and connections between issues, events, and individuals. Producing that narrative requires uncovering evidence, verifying sources, presenting the information as it is found, without embellishment or fabrication. It requires careful research and honest analysis. This was what I wanted to do for the rest of my life. But, I reasoned, I could do that while teaching history in secondary school.

I elected to complete my master's degree in a year and a summer and start teaching in the fall of 1969. By that winter I knew that getting a job in New York public school system would not be a problem. But I was not confident that I could teach history effectively. I didn't know what to do but my brother did.

That April, John, who was flying B-52s out of Mather Air Force Base in Sacramento, invited me to spend spring break with him in California. While visiting Carmel with him, I shared my worries over this, and he suggested that I stay on, take more courses, and ask for financial support. So on my return I called Phil Gleason, and asked for money, explained why, and assured him that if the department funded me, I would complete the history Ph.D. Gleason responded that he had no doubt that I would and directed me to get three recommendations to the fellowship committee before they met that very evening. That same night he called me back to inform me that I had been awarded the Hearst Fellowship in American History. That and subsequent fellowships allowed me to stay at Notre Dame, to focus on history, and to complete the doctorate. I haven't been shy of asking for history funding since.

My brother's military status also affected my life and my history teaching. Issued a draft notice right after graduating from Fordham, he volunteered for the Air Force, completed officer and flight training, and spent years flying sorties over Southeast Asia. While John, cousins, neighbors, and good friends were serving overseas many of my campus friends were protesting a war that most Americans detested; collectively they exposed me to the anguish on both sides and to the particular suffering of military personnel challenged by enemies on the battlefield and by war critics at home. This tempered my own behavior, taught me a great deal about listening to all sides, and inspired me later to develop a course on recent U.S. history, beginning with the Vietnam era. This course, which I regularly teach, brings together American, Vietnamese, and Cambodian civilian and military veterans of the Vietnam War and peace movements, and their children and attracts many Iraqi and Afghanistan war veterans, refugees, and critics as well. The students find in these classes a safe place to explore differing interpretations of America's recent wars, including theirs, and the course allows some to sort out their individual and collective experiences in these wars.

My first year as a full-fledged history Ph.D. student started poorly when my back was fractured in a serious bike accident on the first day of class. Somehow, I salvaged that semester, with rich courses focusing on urban and black history and a wonderful seminar on nineteenth-century American historians led by Marshall Smelser. I was assigned Hubert Howe Bancroft. Bancroft was a gatherer, a scribe, and the master of gatherers and scribes; he had an uncanny and unmatched ability to gather and assemble and put some order to the history of California and other parts of the West. In retrospect, this class was my introduction to the practice of history beyond the classroom. My work on Bancroft certainly made me question many of his methods, but it also taught me to appreciate the valuable work that has been done by historians beyond the classroom and to do such work later in my career.

Of all my teachers, Gleason's work in American ethnic and religious history was most compelling. Gleason's findings made particular sense for me because of my own experience and background. My very traditional parents attended daily Mass, recited the rosary faithfully, completed novenas and ascribed to a pre–Vatican II model of Catholicism and the supported idea that America's cold war battles had as much to do with the anti-Christ as they did with the atomic bomb. And yet, their Heights neighbors, their own immigrant status, and their participation in union work made them strong supporters of the Church's social teachings. Given a nuanced historic framework for understanding them and their positions, I could still value their faith and embrace their faith-based commitment to the Catholic community and still clearly understand how members of the same nuclear Catholic family could hold firmly to distinctly different perceptions of the same institution.

My Catholic church, unlike the church of my parents, embraced institutional change, renewal, *aggiornamento*, ecumenism, and inclusion. It encouraged women as well as men to serve and lead. It allowed me to honor past traditions and practices while effecting change; it allowed me to worship and work collaboratively with individuals whose traditions, values, and practices differed markedly from mine. At the same time, like theirs, my church challenged me not only to recognize the dignity of people from all places, races, religions, and stations but to embrace them and respect them. It still does. That mindset and commitment—and my faith—explain why I am still a committed Catholic and perhaps why I have been particularly effective as a teacher of history and advocate for history and other causes.

Like other history graduate students, I faced the challenges of getting through comprehensive exams, completing a dissertation topic, and finding a job in a history job market that started shrinking precipitously in the early 1970s. The laywomen of Lewis Hall who shared these challenges found a creative way of dealing with comprehensives. As a resident prepared for these exams, the other women prepared her meals, did her laundry, calmed her fears, and even accompanied her to the oral exam. These women of different races, religions, and nationalities, and from different disciplines, understood the importance of sustaining each other in common pursuits, and they made themselves available day and night to whoever was facing exams or dealing with an illness or crisis. Mutually supporting each other, feeding each other literally and figuratively, crying and laughing together, we ensured each other's survival in academia.

We needed each other's support, for ours was a unique situation as laywomen studying full-time in what was still then publicly presented as an all-men's school. When Notre Dame hired its first two women members of the teaching faculty, theologian Josephine Ford and historian of science Sister Suzanne Kelly in 1967, and then lifted its ban on women teaching assistants, we became the first cohort of women to work on both sides of the desk. Notre Dame did not embrace coeducation formally until September 1972.

My interest in Latin American history also grew in graduate school, and I selected Latin America as one of my doctoral fields. Fredrick B. Pike, who never taught me formally at Notre Dame but taught me a great deal informally, directed the focus of much of my reading in the field. As it turned out, my work under Pike led to my first tenure-track position in history—as a Latin Americanist at Humboldt State University.

While exploring dissertation topics, I briefly considered writing on U.S.-Mexican relations during the Mexican Revolution under Julius Pratt, who made it clear that there was much he would like me to do. But I feared that Julius, who was in his eighties, would not live as long as it would take me to complete the dissertation; as it turned out he lived for many years after that. Instead, I followed Phil Gleason's suggestion that I write a history of the Catholic Art Association. I was intrigued by the topic, especially when my preliminary research convinced me that this dissertation had many elements that connected with my own life and attitudes.

The association, founded in the arts and crafts tradition in 1937 and disbanded in 1970, united people bound by faith and the commitment to "make a cell of good living" in this world. This eclectic group of artists, craftsmen, philosophers, liturgists, art educators, and peace activists came together from their different worlds to exercise "right reason in making and doing." They sought to improve art, architecture, and art education in a Catholic Church whose rich arts legacy had suffered great losses in the transatlantic passage.

My research revealed many connections linking theorists, artists, educators, and activists who transformed art and architecture in American churches and art education in parochial schools in the years before and immediately following the Second Vatican Council. But while the association was progressive in some areas, the men who led the association generally overlooked the work done by women members. Seldom were their voices heard or accomplishments recognized. In fact, the women members ran most operations while men in leadership positions sat back, philosophized, and didn't do much else. After realizing that this pattern of behavior could be recognized in many quarters, including my church and my beloved Notre Dame, I dedicated the dissertation "To Catholic women: may they be as equal on earth as they are in heaven." Though my dedication drew the wrath of one of my committee members, my reason for it ensured that my history teaching would always include gender.

I found my first tenure-track position at Humboldt State University in Arcata, California, with assistance from the newly formed American Historical Association's Committee on Women Historians. In December 1971, while attending my first AHA annual meeting, I was invited to add my name to a job roster for women historians. I did and soon began receiving inquiries and job announcements from schools across the country. When I received an offer from Humboldt, I resigned my graduate fellowship to accept the position rather than face the possibility of unemployment in 1973; by that time, the history job market, which had flourished in the 1960s, was shutting down. I spent the next three years prepping and teaching eight different history courses and a social studies teaching methods course, all while working on the dissertation. I established a schedule that I recommend to no one: rising at four and working on the dissertation until eight, then focusing on my classes and departmental responsibilities until eleven at night.

Apart from the secretary, I was the sole woman in the history department at Humboldt State, but my former colleagues agree that I held my own with persistence and good humor. With like-minded faculty women from other disciplines, I established Humboldt's women's studies program; and on my first two attempts to propose a course on American women's history, my otherwise affable department chair, Bill Tanner, swore at me and shoved me out of his office. My persistence and pressure from others paid off on my third visit, when he approved the requests; I launched the course in the winter quarter of 1973. The following year, our program hosted a regional meeting of the fledgling Women's Studies Association.

During my Humboldt years I joined what was then called the Coordinating Committee on Women in the Historical Profession / Conference Group in Women's History and the West Coast Association of Women Historians. I routinely brought history students with me to these meetings. At one, in Santa Cruz, Karen Offen, then at least eight months pregnant and wearing a bright red sweater, made us realize that motherhood and history both could be managed with intelligence, grace, and cheerfulness. The creative ways in which she and other women in the academy balanced career and family life helped me further understand the tensions women face in balancing marriage and family with careers. It also helped me strike my own balance when I agreed to marry Ted Nutting in 1975.

I met Ted, the local Coast Guard commander, the day I arrived in Arcata, and we dated for two and a half years before he asked me to marry him. Figuring I would be "impossible to live with" while I was working on the dissertation (and he was right, as I had no time or patience for or interest in a partner until I was done), Ted waited to propose two weeks after it was approved. Two weeks later, when he was issued orders to command a ship in Hawaii, we came to an agreement on how we would manage our careers. Since he was earning more than I and could retire with twenty years' service, I would follow his career but remain as active as I could as a historian, and upon his retirement, he would follow my career. In line with that decision, I gave notice to Steve Fox, our new department chairman, that I was resigning my position at Humboldt to accompany Ted to Hawaii, and planned to continue my history career there. He understood and fully supported my job searches in Hawaii and elsewhere.

A week after I had been awarded the doctorate, I presented a paper on the women of the Catholic Art Association at a meeting of the American Society for Church History at Stanford. The criticisms were stinging: essentially, what these women did was unimportant, and what I had written contributed little to scholarship. But these comments came from a cluster of old school scholars just three weeks after I had married Ted. Had they come from a different source or at a different time in my life they might have mattered more than they did. I flew back to Humboldt State, and finished the term, and a few weeks later, moved to Hawaii with Ted. I was not bitter; nor did I second guess my critics' motives. But I got on with a new chapter of my life. Within a few weeks we had had settled into our new home on Oahu; I was pregnant, and a new member of Chaminade University's history department in Honolulu.

In following Ted's military career through many reassignments, I set my own course and crafted my own career in history. Doing so set me on the margins of several groups: I became the working mother living among full-time homemakers, the professional academic among career officers' wives, the adjunct instructor among full-timers, and, again, the only woman in a department of men. But being on these margins wasn't so new or so challenging for I had been on other margins before, at other schools and universities. What I had learned in those places was that wherever I would go, I would find individuals who were willing and able and those who were unable and/or unwilling to understand, communicate, or work out any compromise with those who existed outside their worlds. I tried to get along well and be happy in each of these worlds and in them I welcomed opportunities to break down stereotypes and foster dialogue and cooperation. This attitude coupled with discipline, tenacity, and creativity enabled me to remove barriers in many quarters and to seek and find history work everywhere, despite an appalling job market and many disappointments along the way. For years I kept a thick pile of rejection letters I received in the process of securing those positions; more discouraging than those are my recollections of the dozens of carefully written applications I submitted that never elicited any response from search committees. Then there were the interviews I will never forget: the grilling by members of a university search committee whose members didn't extend the courtesy of introducing themselves; the interviewers whose comments underscored their disinterest in me; and the interviewers who made it clear both implicitly and explicitly that my—take your choice—pregnancy, children, spouse's career—would get in the way of my doing the kind of work they expected. While they were awful experiences that hurt me tremendously at the time, they taught me what not to do when I was on the other side of a job interview, and they steeled me for dealing with other forms of adversity. As my father would say, they were "lessons well learned from the college of hard knocks." There were also those lonely years, outside the profession, when there were few to talk to about what I was reading or thinking about history.

Along the way, I made sure I took practical measures to ensure later employment. For example, before leaving California, I secured lifetime community college teaching and administrative credentials from the state. They came in handy later, when I sought employment in community colleges in Maryland and Washington.

At Chaminade University I taught history and history teaching methods to students who were far more diverse in race, age, ethnicity, and income than students I had encountered at Humboldt and Notre Dame. Many of my students were active duty military and public school social studies teachers. The soldiers, sailors, and marines made me a more flexible teacher and a better listener, while the school teachers gave me a clear sense of how what is learned in our classrooms filters down to the secondary and primary levels. All of them underscored the importance of teaching history in ways that connect the subject to students' lives and their communities.

In Hawaii, I quickly learned some other lessons. One was that ship cap-
tains' wives like me held no command authority but traditionally assumed
ships' responsibilities, particularly when the officers and crews were at sea
and their families had serious emergencies ashore. As I dealt with those
emergencies, I learned how to deal with chains of command, which prepared me to deal with bureaucracies of all kinds, including educational institutions and professional associations. I also discovered that the officers'
wives ranks were divided between those who wore their husbands' ranks
(and seldom had their own lives) and those who didn't, and were uncomfortable with the pecking order among wives and the social segregation
of officer and enlisted families. While I joined officers' wives clubs, I also
attended enlisted wives' functions, and brought both enlisted and officers'
wives together in our home, a practice followed by few and frowned upon
by many.

My unconventional behavior drew criticism from some wives, admira-
tion from others, and many inquiries from younger military couples who,
like us, were trying to balance life and work, continue careers interrupted
by transfers, and chart their own courses in life. They saw that I was situated in the military community and understood and honored military traditions, but that I also worked in academia in what many perceived as an
antimilitary profession, and that I was in many ways a second wave feminist.
They felt I understood them and many of their issues; I suggested practical
strategies for living and working in different worlds, negotiating a life between them, and coping with mixed signals and mixed loyalties. As I employed these strategies in my own life, I also changed more than a few historians' perceptions of military life, military families, and military mindsets.

Shortly after Ted was transferred to Washington, D.C., in 1977, our
second child, Andy, was born, and I stayed home with him and his older
sister Teresa. But when the American Historical Association created a
new part-time staff position for Special Assistant to the Executive Director for the Promotion of Minorities' and Women's Scholarly and Professional Interests, I applied. The job title was practically indigestible and the
challenges the position offered were tough and unique, but with my experiences as a woman teaching and learning in essentially men's worlds,
and living and working within very distinct and diverse cultures, I felt I
had many ideas and strategies to offer. I recall being interviewed by AHA
director Mack Thompson and later being grilled on the phone by the chair
of the AHA Committee on Women Historians, Joan Scott. Her questions

were focused and at the time, I felt they got to the heart of what I thought were the issues we faced as women historians.

I was thrilled when I got the job. In that position, I did critical work at a critical time for the discipline and for women and minorities within the profession. I supported the fledgling Association of Black Women Historians, helped the Gay and Lesbian Caucus in History secure status as an affiliated society of the AHA, actively promoted curricula that included minorities and women in history courses, compiled entries for the second *Directory of Women Historians*, and edited and contributed materials to the first *Survival Guide for Women (and Other) Historians*.

But I knew that this would not last, because Ted would be issued new orders and we would be moving again. At a session at the 1979 AHA annual meeting, I began a presentation on job searches in history by announcing that I would be looking for a new job in history by the end of 1980. That year Ted assumed command of a new ship, and with our three children—Steve was born that August—we moved to Tidewater, Virginia. While living there, my work was more scattered than ever before. At home I completed the second *Directory of Women Historians* and other AHA projects; I also worked occasionally for the Association for the Preservation for Virginia Antiquities and I assisted National Park Service historians during the national bicentennial celebration at Yorktown. From the APVA and NPS historians I learned much about interpreting historical sites and material culture and about the extensive and underappreciated work done by curators, interpreters, and administrators working in museums, parks, historic sites, and other public history venues.

In 1982, when Ted's new orders took our family to Seattle, family needs took precedence over history matters, and I did not actively search for a job for the next four years. However, I continued reading my history journals and the *Chronicle of Higher Education*, and generally stayed abreast of literature in my fields; being out of work never meant leaving the discipline. But when I decided to stay home, some accused me of abandoning history and others dismissed me. Still others congratulated me for finally focusing on my family and my husband's career. Intellectually, I understood these individuals had good intentions, but their messages did not sit well with me at all. If anything, they strengthened my resolve to stay current and to never patronize men or women who were facing the same struggles as I had faced, making choices similar to the ones I had made. Dealing with family responsibilities, moves, and career transitions, I learned, gave me additional professional training and improved my time and project management skills, I reasoned, and made me a more adaptable, flexible, and responsive history professional.

One of the ways I honed my history skills while staying home in Seattle was by transcribing a courtship correspondence between my husband's paternal great-grandparents. Rufus Nutting, a student from the Western Reserve College and later a minister, wrote long, richly detailed and elegant letters. The object of his affections was Margaretta Leib Hunt, a first cousin of Civil War General Henry Jackson Hunt, a grandniece of one of the University of Michigan's founding trustees, also Henry J. Hunt, and a granddaughter of another Michigan trustee, John L. Leib. Her letters are terse by comparison, but provide insights into her life and social circle. Both sets of letters, lovingly conserved by Eileen Barry Nutting, made this historian think long and hard of the intersection of family history and U.S. history. So did the birth of our fourth child, named for her grandmother Eileen.

Ted's next set of orders sent the family to Miami in 1986. After everyone had settled in, I secured a part-time position in the history department at the University of Miami teaching the U.S. history survey and immigration history. The following year, department chair Robert M. Levine and the Arts and Sciences College dean David Wilson created a full-time undergraduate teaching position in history that was mine until we moved back to Seattle.

Levine also assigned me to work with graduate teaching assistants, encouraged me to join the university's women's studies committee, and invited me to join him in a research project dealing with Cuba's response to the Holocaust. My understanding of the networks of religious orders in the United States and their outreach to different Caribbean communities in the twentieth century informed my work on how the Catholic Church in Cuba dealt with Jewish refugees in the years leading up to the *Saint Louis* affair. My findings once again validated the work these women religious did for these refugees when people from their own communities helped them little. I remembered another Holocaust survivor, Illich, and the safe haven he and my mother had provided for so many Caribbean immigrants to New York.

To the late Bob Levine I will always be deeply grateful. At a critical time, he jump-started my career by returning me to the college classroom, giving me the opportunity to do some serious archival research, and widening and deepening my understanding of Brazilian history. And because he also forced me to get over my fear and loathing of computers by requiring me to take computer classes and then use computers in my work, he prepared me to take advantage of the many new opportunities for history research and instruction. With his support and that of Michelle Aldrich, a friend and public historian with the American Association for the Advancement of Science, I embraced the technology, soon recognized its utility, and started using computer technologies and online resources to enhance my history teaching.

At Miami, for the first time in my career, I taught a significant number of Muslims; some were international students and others were the American children of Middle Eastern and South Asian immigrants. Their careful work to establish a prayer center for Muslims on campus persuaded me to develop a better understanding of Islam and its effect on past and present cultures. While living and working in Miami I also made friends with many people from Spanish-speaking communities on campus and elsewhere, and from them I heard many family histories. These accounts prompted wider reading, particularly in Cuban, Salvadoran, and Ecuadorian history and on U.S. immigration law and policy.

When we returned to Seattle in 1990, I began teaching Western civilization for the first time in my career, in addition to women's history, at Seattle University, where once again I found myself the only woman in the history department. In 1992 I joined the Seattle Community College District, spending the first four years at Seattle Central Community College before moving to North Seattle Community College, where I now teach and chair the history department.

In the community college I focus on teaching history to local students as well as students from everywhere else in the world. They are racially, linguistically, and ethnically diverse; they represent many distinct religions and cultures. They are rich and poor, young and old, smart and slow, disciplined and unruly. Many, like me, are first-generation college students. Many are immigrants or the children of immigrants. Increasing numbers are refugees and veterans of foreign wars and ethnic cleansings. Many want to learn and work hard in classes while holding down part-time and full-time jobs and handling other responsibilities; some don't work and do not care. Some come with graduate degrees; many more need tutoring in the basics of reading and writing. Most lack the social and financial resources they need to succeed.

Focusing on the skills and competencies these students need to pass my courses and prepare for upper-division work at universities and in the job force, I have used information and tactics learned throughout my professional career to develop imaginative learning projects, instructional materials, and websites to engage them in the study of history. The unsolicited feedback I get from alumni who have transferred to universities, graduated, and moved into the work force—some even into university teaching—suggests that my strategies have secured some measure of success. But I have not been without help in these endeavors.

Since earning tenure, I have been recruiting outstanding historians with graduate degrees to join my faculty, and I have mentored them in teaching. Several of these recruits are now tenured faculty members or on tenure-track in community colleges in Washington and California and four-year colleges and universities in other states. Others are working by choice as public historians. All agree that community colleges afford historians many opportunities to develop very effective college-level teaching skills and strategies, to deepen and broaden the knowledge of history they developed as doctoral students, and to work effectively and collegially with people from all walks of life.

At the same time, with a fifteen-hour teaching load and five office hours a week (common in community colleges) as well as departmental administrative and college committee work, we understand that this limits our time for doing scholarly research and writing during the school year. In my case, managing a small but very efficient history department adds to the workload but increases job satisfaction. None of this has deterred me or my colleagues from doing research and writing or attending workshops and institutes, particularly during summer breaks. In my case I have participated in many workshops, seminars and institutes and also produced articles and papers for major national history and humanities conferences.

In the community colleges, most of the courses we teach are surveys of world history, United States history, and regional history. Our college transfer students need these courses to meet college general education requirements and our local teachers and education graduate students need them to secure subject area endorsements. While teaching these courses, I have established links with colleagues in economics, anthropology, and literature. In links we teach our own courses but assign readings and research and writing assignments that require students to integrate what they learn in both courses and thus examine how different people from different fields approach knowledge. I have also developed several coordinated studies programs with instructors from different departments. In these we team-teach a particular topic such as wars, the sea, women and men at work in the United States. Both types of interdisciplinary studies have been strongly endorsed by the Seattle Community College District, which has made interdisciplinary learning an integral part of our general education program.

In any mode, teaching history to community college students requires flexibility. Many of these students have virtually no background in history and they face many challenges, including navigating education systems they may not understand. From us they demand levels of compassion and social commitment seldom required of teachers in more elite institutions. They also require us to be creative, to do more with fewer resources than our university colleagues have, and to ensure that they master college material and produce 100- and 200-level research papers, even though many of them come with deficiencies in reading and writing. All this requires time, patience, commitment, and very hard work.

But it does not change the way I teach history, for I teach it the same way I taught history to students in the honors program at the University of Miami and to undergraduates at Notre Dame—many of them National Merit Scholars. Having learned early on that students seldom exceed above the level to which they are challenged, I set the bar high. I assign the same workloads as I would anywhere else; I require students to read what they would read in a comparable course elsewhere, to do serious research and to write substantive analytical papers, and I grade their work as I would grade other history students at other institutions. Implicit in my commitment to democratizing education is the understanding that community college history courses must be rigorous and community college students must be prepared to meet the challenges they will face in upper division courses wherever they transfer.

Teaching at a community college has not altered my identity at all. But it has altered some historians' perceptions of me; their comments suggest that I have slipped a notch. It's an unfortunate assessment I can live with. Historians are doing critical work in community colleges and many students benefit from taking lower division courses in community colleges. While these community college students pay lower tuition than they would elsewhere, they know that their professors, writing center tutors, and librarians are there to assist them every step of the way.

Community college teaching also challenges us to develop assignments that engage the students' interests so strongly that they willingly do serious work and develop the skills they need to produce solid results. One that has worked particularly well with entry-level students uses oral history.

This student research project combines family history with general U.S. history, and requires students to follow the protocols for conducting oral history interviews, library research, and online research while producing fully documented research papers. Virtually all the students have used the assignment to learn more about their families and have found that history is indeed part of their lives. Their evaluations indicate they have found it worthwhile and rewarding—even empowering—and that it was difficult, challenging and time-consuming, as a good history assignment should be.

Teaching in community colleges also offers opportunities. In the early 1990s, while preparing for a world history lecture, I studied a series of maps that traced immigration patterns worldwide in the late nineteenth and early twentieth centuries. The maps convinced me that I needed to expand my history horizons eastward. I read books colleagues recommended, and when another Coast Guard wife, Callie Daniell, told me about East West Center seminars designed to develop Asian studies awareness and curricula among faculty in two- and four-year colleges, I applied. That led to an NEH Summer Seminar on South Asia in 1994, subsequent field studies in India and China, several published articles, faculty development seminars, and revisions to our district's world history curriculum. In turn, those activities led to NEH summer seminars in Brazil and Guatemala, more research and writing, and to my return to teaching Latin American history, years after I had shelved the course after leaving Hawaii.

That institute indirectly prompted me to increase my involvement with the Community College Humanities Association. My flurry of activities in those few years also increased my visibility within history and community college circles and ultimately resulted in my election to the Council of the American Historical Association in 2000. To this governing board of the nation's oldest history guild, I brought a unique voice and perspective, for none of my council colleagues had worked in two- and four-year colleges and universities as well as in public history. In fact, my work on the staff of the American Historical Association also set me apart, since I remain the only AHA staff member ever elected to the Council. While on the AHA Council I served as councilor to the Professional Division when it rewrote the *AHA Standards on Professional Conduct*, and on the AHA Task Force on Public History, whose findings led us to recommend that the association and all academic historians address the professional interests and concerns of those practicing history beyond the academy and actively collaborate with public historians.

Since leaving the Council, I have been working as a trustee of the National History Center to promote the interests of history and historians within and beyond academia and to engage historians more widely and more effectively with the general publics we serve—government officials, the media, K–12 teachers, and the general public. These activities have increasingly required me to think in terms of learning outcomes and assessment. These buzz words in education departments and accrediting agencies alienate many professional historians and terrify the rest, but if we historians do not figure out what and how well our students are learning about the past in history classes, others who neither understand nor appreciate history will tell us how we must do this work.

At the community college level, I have been developing assessment tools and strategies that document what history faculty do and what and how well history students learn; these tools and strategies also assist faculty in their efforts to improve teaching and learning in history courses. This work has been received well by many in history and community college circles at the national and local levels, but has been either ignored or disparaged by some community college administrators and faculty who have embraced general education assessment, but have discarded history for being (they allege) obsolete, racist, and still taught the way we know it was taught fifty years ago.

For the last two years I have also been researching the history of women at Notre Dame before the university formally embraced coeducation in 1972, women overlooked in the institution's published narrative. I intend to document those many women who enrolled in the university from 1918 onwards, earned undergraduate and graduate degrees, and went on to careers in higher education, law, the arts and sciences, the Church, business, and elsewhere. By establishing our presence there and recording our histories, I aim to make more inclusive the history of the university that gave me unexpected and incredibly rich opportunities to start becoming the historian and person I aspire to be.

Notre Dame will always be important in my life. It awarded me degrees, reinforced strong personal values, and gave me the skills I needed to be an effective professional, spouse, parent, and citizen, and it did the same for my husband and two of our children. Notre Dame also issued me the parking sticker that caught the attention of alumnus Ted Nutting in California in 1972. Ted's father, Notre Dame professor Willis Nutting, had taught history there from 1936 to 1950, when he joined the faculty of the General Program of Liberal Studies, whose curriculum he helped design and develop for the next twenty-five years.

By marrying Ted, I integrated my life and my work in history in ways I could not have imagined. My dissertation had focused on a small group of do-gooders who were clearly outside of mainstream America, but that group was mainstream for the Nuttings. Ted's parents were close friends with a good number of CAA people and even collaborated with some of them on different initiatives. They corresponded with many, and spent time with some, including Dorothy Day, one of the principal people I interviewed for my history. In fact, my husband met Day long before I did; when he was a child she routinely stayed with the Nuttings whenever she visited Notre Dame or St. Mary's College. The Nuttings were Catholic activists, particularly with the Catholic Rural Life Conference, the Vernacular Society, and Cursillo. But then, so were my parents, with Illich and the Puerto Ricans in the Heights. In adding Nutting to my name, I hadn't strayed far from my center.

Had I not made other career choices, had I not married a career Coast Guard officer and had four children, I know I would have been a very different historian. I suspect I would have moved from Humboldt to a research university, published extensively, and become even more active in the field. But the choices I made were the right ones for me. I am still happily married to the same man, now retired from the Coast Guard and teaching mathematics, and our four children are adults. Two are following me in higher education, in economics and philosophy respectively, a third is a university program director, and the fourth is a Coast Guard officer. All are living full and interesting lives; they and Ted continue to support my work, encourage me, and act as sounding boards for my ideas on history. Raising them, moving in and out of history as I have, and taking advantage of the options open to me have taught me that there are many kinds of historians one can become. With a few more productive years before me, issues, events, and life circumstances will most likely present me with new opportunities and challenges that will allow me to continue learning more about history and to continue making a difference in the communities I serve.

JOHN R. GILLIS

Detours

Some are born historians, but I am not one of them. I can find nothing in my upbringing or in my early education that would have led me to be a historian, and certainly not the kind of historian I have been over the past thirty years or more. Past and place did not weigh heavily on my parents, who had been constantly on the move since their college days. My father's career as a talented electrical engineer required mobility and my mother was expert in turning a sequence of residences into comfortable homes. Descendents of people who had broken their westward journey to settle the Iowa and Minnesota frontiers, and survivors of the Great Depression, my mother and father had no regrets about putting the past behind them. My father's passion for new technology found expression in the new Packard automobiles, which appeared in our driveway every other year and in the series of houses which he designed and had custom-built on the crabgrass frontiers of western New York. My mother was equally enthusiastic about everything new. Trained in the science of home economics, she was quite prepared to try out novel theories of nutrition and hygiene on her only child. Their faith in technology was tested only by the crabgrass, which threatened each summer to defeat their quest for the perfect lawn.

My parents traveled light, disposing of rather than moving furniture as they went. When they retired to California in the 1960s, they carried their possessions in a station wagon, taking care to leave room to see out the back. In effect, they were resuming the westward trek begun by their grandparents a century earlier. But having finally reached the land of the future, my parents moved several more times before Father died soon after customizing yet another house, this time in the desert hills above San Diego, where the crabgrass was no longer a problem. My mother stayed on for only a couple of years before moving back east to be near to us in New Jersey. Her journey came to a symbolic end only recently when I buried her ashes next to those of my father in the Gillis family plot in Osage, Iowa.

With their gaze so firmly fixed on imagined futures, my parents had little use for rearview mirrors. They were a people innocent of historical consciousness. Having long since forgotten their European origins, they were unhyphenated Americans. Protestants, but without denomination, they no longer attended church but insisted that I go to Sunday school in something called a Community Church, whose creed was pure American civil religion and whose chief attraction to boys like me was the bowling alley in the basement. In the world of the Buffalo suburbs, the only other group I was aware of were the Catholics, who were identified with Italians, Poles, and other immigrant groups. Jews lived beyond the pale in Buffalo itself, as did people of color. I came into contact with African Americans only through my years as a camper and then as a counselor in the Buffalo YMCA summer Camp Weona, which proudly proclaimed itself to be a place "where only good prevails." My experiences there reinforced my faith in a set of universal values, which, if only everyone would simply subscribe to them, would erase the historical legacies of racism and religious prejudice. Blessedly free of any sense of ethnic or religious roots, I too had little use for rearview mirrors.

Ours was a true nuclear family, incorporating but two generations and as detached from kin as from ancestry. I remember the rare visits of relatives more as unwelcome intrusions than enjoyable reunions. My parents were plain livers, allergic to ceremony and ritual. Our home contained no family mementos, no ancestral portraits and few photographs of the midwestern past. As far as my parents were concerned, time began with my birth. It was at this point that my mother, true to her training in scientific childrearing, began to record my progress, including my weight and regularity of bowel movements. And I was the star of my father's carefully crafted home movies, which documented little John from crib to college. In Father's productions, home was more a stage set than a place in its own right, and grandparents, aunts, and uncles appeared only in supporting roles. I continued to star up through my wedding day, but this was to be the last scene that my father cared to record. Soon thereafter, he gave me his old Kodak. When the camera had passed from his hands to mine, it was clear that one nuclear family had ended and another had begun.

It was not until I met my wife, Christina, who grew up deeply embedded in an immigrant Scots-English community in Rhode Island, that I discovered that families could extend beyond two generations. She had lived for a time with her grandparents; and both sides of her family had storied pasts that continued to shape day-to-day relationships. As a stranger to such a world, I felt uncomfortable, even threatened, when confronted with such powerful collective memories. Tina was the first in her family to go away to college, but our decision to marry upon graduation and further our studies in California did not entirely sever her ties with her eastern roots. Even today, she remains far more attached to family past and family place, the keeper of memories and traditions that would have long since been extinguished by my forgetfulness.

During my childhood, history was something that happened to other people, somewhere else. I was not born at a propitious moment—1939— but the war did not intrude directly on our lives. My father was too old to be drafted. He served his country through war production and as the neighborhood air raid warden, sporting a helmet and silver whistle. An occasional drill interrupted my sleep, but the war itself remained at a safe distance. The only invasion threat to New Jersey was an infestation of Japanese beetles that struck our small victory garden. And I can remember only two occasions of real fear, once I had to leave a Lassie movie when the courageous canine was captured by Nazis, and another time when watching a military parade from curbside, I found myself staring up at the seemingly real bodies of Hitler, Mussolini, and Tojo, hung in effigy on a passing float. Otherwise, war was a game I played with my large collection of toy soldiers.

Real events always seemed far away, brought to us by radio. Family dinner was timed to allow for listening to the evening news. This meant that there was little mealtime conversation. Indeed, I do not remember my parents ever discussing events, much less debating issues. They were born Republicans of a moderate, midwestern kind, hostile to the New Deal, to trade unions, and to what my father referred to as the "feds." But, as far as I know, my parents were uninvolved politically. Voting was for them a kind of civic ritual, done as much out of duty as conviction. This was wholly consistent with the ideal of citizenship that prevailed during my childhood and adolescence. At school, we were trained in the rituals of democracy. In 1952 our class was divided into little Democrats and little Republicans.

I played the role of Adlai Stevenson and won when my next door neighbor, Carl Henson, betrayed his assigned party, suggesting friendship was more important than politics.

Apart from the glory days of the Erie Canal, history seemed to bypass Buffalo and its suburbs. Mrs. Polster, our seventh grade teacher, encouraged us to do local history and this resulted in several inspired projects on the social history of the canal, but in high school the subject was taught mainly by coaches and administrators, who relied on the media of filmstrips, examined only on facts and shielded us from interpretations that might have provoked controversy. I managed to get near perfect scores on the New York State regents exams by memorizing amazing amounts of material, but I felt no engagement with or real connection to history itself. Like so many boys of my generation, only one subject really gripped me, namely Hitler and the Second World War. It was the nightmare from which we had awoken, but now it too seemed to belong to a distant past, not really connected to the present or to the future we were about to enter.

I had always taken it for granted that I would go away to college. In the 1950s separation from home and family was considered an essential step in becoming a young adult. The farther away the school, the greater its prestige. I applied to only two colleges, Dartmouth and Amherst. In high school, I had always felt most comfortable in the company of other boys, and a homosocial environment appealed to me. Both places had reputations for academic excellence, but I remember deciding on Amherst because all students were guaranteed access to its fraternity system.

As it turned out Amherst was like one great fraternity. The administration still condoned the hazing of freshmen, who were easily recognized by the purple beanies we were required to wear. During freshman orientation we were informed that we were the best and the brightest ever admitted to the college, and that we were destined for brilliant careers if we applied ourselves with sufficient diligence. I was surrounded by young men who came from famous private schools and whose futures were already guaranteed by family fortunes and connections; and I sensed that my social acceptance depended on distancing myself from my own past and taking on the coloration of those around me. Over the next four years, I devoted myself to becoming an Amherst man, active in sports and my fraternity, and dating a young woman at nearby Mount Holyoke College, whom I was later to marry.

Amherst was very good at preparing us for the public dimension of life, which was then an exclusively male domain. We were vaguely aware that family life also awaited us, but Amherst did nothing to ready us for what was still regarded as a woman's world. It was assumed that we would become good husbands and fathers, but the only concession to our domestic futures was a one-credit course on marriage and family offered only to seniors. It was taught by a biologist, who provided sound advice on birth control but had nothing much to say about the emotional or social dimensions of sexuality. I do not remember his mentioning homosexuality, much whispered about but never openly discussed. The idea that private life might have a history worth studying was unthinkable.

College was its own little world where time was momentarily suspended. It came as close to being a total institution as anything I would ever encounter, geared to produce among the young men cloistered there what Erik Erikson correctly called a moratorium, a wholly absorbing moment that effectively erased our diverse pasts to shape us into a more or less coherent elite focused on what we were told would be a future of endless possibilities. The liberal arts curriculum was perfectly suited to this end. For the first two years we all took a common core of courses in the humanities and sciences, economics being the only social science we were exposed to. The Amherst curriculum was a rarefied one, preprofessional but devoid of practical applications and absent those internships that are routinely offered to today's students. The Western civilization course I took along with all the other freshmen in the fall of 1956 was based on extensive readings in primary sources, not quite the great books approach, but a form of rarified intellectual history. It was deeply influenced by Amherst's famous English I-II, a course invented under the sign of the New Criticism by Reuben Brower and his colleagues in Amherst's prestigious literature department, which emphasized close reading of texts completely abstracted from historical context. It provided rigorous training in critical thinking and exacting writing, but it left us with the impression that history consisted of a parade of disembodied ideas, wholly without connection to our own life experience.

At Amherst we lived as if in two parallel universes, a mind-body split that is difficult even to imagine today when the boundaries between academic and social life are so much more porous. This compartmentalization was sustained by the college's geographical isolation but also by its sex, race, and class segregation. The youth cultures of which we were a part, our adolescent sexuality, and the social dilemmas that confronted us on a daily basis were wholly unacknowledged by the curriculum and made to appear less real, and certainly less significant, than the distant, abstract subjects that were presented to us as worth studying. The noble ideal of objectivity reigned during these years at Amherst. All our courses were designed to create the greatest possible distance between subject and object, the reader and the text, scientist and nature, the historian and history. The result was to erect a firewall between our own subjectivity and the various fields we were preparing to enter.

Even though it still required chapel attendance two days a week, Amherst was also relentlessly secular, even to the extent of denying religion much of a role in history itself. I had encountered myth and ritual in a course taught by the religion department, but it was *logos*, not *mythos*, which dominated every other dimension of the curriculum. Even psychology was dominated by a behaviorist perspective, foreclosing any further exploration of the nonrational aspects of life that we were encountering in every other dimension of our adolescence existence. At Amherst, Freud was an idea, not a practice.

One of the teachers I most admired, Richard Douglas, talked a great deal about cultivating perspective, convincing me that the more one was removed from one's own subjectivity the better. We were warned away from contemporary history; and, as Amherst had no sociology or anthropology department, the study of everyday life was wholly off limits. There were no non-Western courses offered, and the closest thing to world history was Europe, still an exotic place as far as most of us were concerned. Young women at Smith and Mount Holyoke were encouraged to take advantage of junior-year-abroad programs, but Amherst students were not. The faculty themselves rarely did research abroad and students were guided to subjects for which there were adequate resources in American libraries, which meant that a vast range of subjects was closed to them.

There were among my classmates young men, including the grandson of a president, who had a personal connection with the kind of political and intellectual history that Amherst and other elite institutions offered, but for those like myself it was a mental exercise, productive of critical acumen and writing skill, opening rather than closing the distance I felt between present and past. Apart from the "Guns and Boats" course taught by Dwight "Bucky" Salmon, there was very little about the experience of ordinary men (and none about ordinary women) in any of Amherst's offerings. In other advanced courses, we were encouraged to enter into conversation with Plato, Aquinas, Machiavelli, Marx, and Mill. Amherst's well-known American studies program was somewhat more grounded in social context, but it too focused mainly on ideas.

The cold war encouraged the development of area studies at major universities, but the small elite colleges prided themselves on producing those who would make policy on the basis of the expertise provided by the graduates of these other places. The possibilities of African or Asian studies may have existed at the nearby University of Massachusetts, but we were not encouraged to look beyond Amherst's offerings. Needless to say there were no women or people of color on the faculty. Distinguished female scholars abounded at nearby Smith and Mount Holyoke, but I do not remember any of my classmates going there except to search for suitable dates. The number of outstanding historians of my generation who attended women's colleges suggests that they may well have gotten an education superior to that offered at all-male institutions, but our sense of superiority precluded exploring that possibility. Even though I did my senior thesis on the role of churches in the Third Reich, it never occurred to me or my Amherst mentors that I should consult with Peter Viereck, who taught at Mount Holyoke and whose study of the irrational dimensions of Nazism intrigued me but found no reflection in my work.

The college was a place and time apart. Few of us had any contact with the surrounding community; none of us worked, apart from the summers. A few souls read the *New York Times*, but most of us did not listen to the news or watch television. History was something worthy of study but not participation. Too young to vote and exempt from the draft, we were largely ignorant of politics and the civil rights movement that was coming to life at the time. The idea of activism was unknown to us. Our extended adolescent moratorium was so complete as to be invisible to those passing through it. Most of us were content with our liminal existence. A few of my classmates deemed to be serious "underachievers" were asked take a year off, but most of us graduated right on schedule, in lockstep with the designated male life course that would have us start careers, marry, and begin families in roughly that sequence.

Amherst was very good at guiding students to medical and law schools, but it offered little mentoring when it came to graduate study. While our teachers all had advanced degrees from prestigious universities, they were for the most part not publishing scholars or professionally active. By the time I was a senior, I had been seized by the ambition to be a teacher of history. Amherst provided some excellent models to emulate, and my experience as a camp counselor suggested that I might be good at teaching. But, when I talked with my mentors about further education, they were not all that encouraging. Perhaps it was the fact that I was not among the very best of my graduating cohort; perhaps it was their own ambivalence about the profession itself, but I was given only the vaguest notion of what graduate school was all about. I never met a graduate student until I actually became one. At Amherst there was none of the professional training that today's undergraduates are exposed to. The college thought it appropriate to send me off with a tiny fellowship, endowed sometime in the nineteenth century for future high school teachers, and this was more than sufficient given my ambitions at the time.

I applied only to Cornell and Stanford, choosing the latter because Christina and I were getting married and California seemed the more exciting place to begin our new life. As we honeymooned across the country in August 1960, I still had no clear notion of what a Ph.D. involved. I viewed graduate school as an extension of college; and Stanford, which was just beginning to organize its graduate offerings in a coherent manner, did little to disabuse me of that illusion. In many respects, the first years at Stanford were an extension of my liberal arts education. I remained a generalist, pursuing that which piqued my curiosity, thinking of myself more as teacher than scholar.

I was still not sure why I was pursuing an advanced degree, but I did well enough in my first couple of years to think that I should try for the Ph.D. In any case, with the draft breathing down my neck and a child (Christopher) on the way, there were no obvious alternatives. Most of the courses I took in my first year were large undergraduate lectures, taught by master-teachers like T. A. Baily, David Harris, and Gordon Wright. My future mentor, Gordon Craig, joined the faculty the next year, and in addition to becoming a star in a galaxy which by then included Lewis Spitz and Richard Lyman, began to shape the graduate program on the model of Princeton, Harvard, and Berkeley. The Stanford curriculum was less rarified than that at Amherst, yet there was no social or cultural history on offer, and little encouragement to bring personal experience to bear on historical subjects.

I ultimately chose for my dissertation the politics of the Prussian bureaucracy in the Revolutions of 1848–49; with the help of Gordon Craig I won financial support for a year of research in Germany. Our little family spent a miserable year in Cologne, 1963–64, causing me to doubt whether I really wanted to continue to do research, especially in Germany. We returned to Stanford where I taught a year in its famed Western Civilization program while finishing the dissertation. The pleasure of teaching a course where I could apply so much of what I had learned at Amherst saw me through the toil and uncertainty of writing. I continued to think of myself as a generalist, for whom the graduate degree was a license to teach rather than an initiation into a profession. The still strong job market of the mid-1960s sustained a sense of options. The proto-professionals in our ranks were still looked upon with a certain suspicion and even scorn by those of my friends who came from the same liberal arts tradition as I had. Many spent far too long on their dissertations, finding themselves at a disadvantage when the job market tightened in the 1970s.

I finished my dissertation in 1965 and applied for positions at a number of small colleges, receiving an offer from Colorado College that I would have readily accepted had I not a gotten a phone call, quite out of the blue, from the chairman of the Princeton department, Jerome Blum, offering me a position. In those days of male privilege, a word from that old Princetonian, Gordon Craig, was sufficient recommendation. It is still hard to believe that this happened with no interview, no campus visit, and no job talk. At Colorado College, with its innovative interdisciplinary curriculum, I would have joined an excellent teaching faculty, resolving once and for all my ambivalence about specialized scholarship. But Princeton also promised to allow me to put off a choice about professional identity for a little longer. I was to be hired as an instructor and employed as a preceptor (Princeton's name for a section teacher) in the lecture courses of its senior faculty, an ideal position for a generalist like myself. Despite some anxiety about joining such a high-powered department, it was an offer that I could not refuse.

Princeton was known to be a revolving door, and, as I had my doubts whether my dissertation would ever become a book, I had few illusions about gaining tenure there. I was still thinking of myself primarily as a teacher and in this respect Princeton was a marvelous apprenticeship. The preceptorial exposed me to another set of superior lecturers—Arno Mayer, Carl Schorske, and James Billington—who deepened my understanding of European history. Teaching in a variety of courses encouraged the generalist in me, but it was intensive contact with small groups of students that I found most satisfying. Precepts met once a week to discuss the lectures and assigned readings. My task was to bring out and explore key ideas, known to the students as "cepts." Here my Amherst training in close reading and critical analysis proved invaluable, and I soon gained a reputation as a discussion leader and thesis advisor, which led to being asked to teach my own lecture course and ultimately take on the large responsibility of History 1, the department's introduction to modern Europe. In time, I was also asked to teach a graduate colloquium, something of an honor among the junior faculty. The expansion of my teaching duties occupied most of my waking time during these years, but I found it a very gratifying process, wholly consistent with my sense of self. Work on my scholarship was confined largely to the summer months. The research trips to Germany and the weeks writing in the sticky heat of Princeton do not conjure anything like the pleasant memories I have of the teaching year at Princeton.

Princeton in the late 1960s and early 1970s was, without a doubt, the most exciting place that any young historian could hope to be. The department that had been built by Joseph Strayer in the 1950s and 1960s, which included the likes of Cyril Black, Jerome Blum, Marius Jansen, Thomas Kuhn, Charles Gillispie, Eric Goldman, Stanley Stein, and Frank Wesley Craven, was being expanded and reenergized by Mayer, Schorske, and Lawrence Stone. Stone had left Oxford, frustrated by its internal rivalries and scholarly ossification. Princeton provided a perfect venue for his immense energies and formidable organizational talents. He was a missionary for the new social history, bringing to Princeton its brightest lights from both Britain and France, including Peter Laslett, François Furet, and Emmanuel Leroi Ladurie, and creating an atmosphere of intellectual excitement that was ultimately to result in the founding of the Davis Center for Historical Studies. Stone and Mayer were remarkably open to interdisciplinary approaches, making us aware of the importance of demography and sociology to our work as historians. But in one respect, Princeton drew the line. It was open to the exploration of the social dimensions of historical experience, but not the psychological. Martin Duberman, then a young associate professor whose work in this area was to bring him great distinction, encountered resistance and soon departed.

While we were not necessarily aware of it, we were at the center of a seismic shift in historical research; and many of the junior faculty were already experimenting with dimensions of the new social and cultural histories. Bob Darnton and Jim McPherson were already well known; while others, including Jack Talbott, Ted Rabb, Bob Tignor, Fred Starr, Richard Andrews, James Henretta, Don Mathews, Nancy Weiss, Sheldon Hackney, Theodore Brown, Gary Nash, Jim Banner, David Flaherty, and Peter Winn were establishing reputations for innovative research. A remarkably egalitarian spirit prevailed at the time. The bond was particularly strong among those of us who lived in Princeton's faculty housing and lunched daily in the little faculty dining room atop Firestone Library. Princeton had no faculty club in those days, and there was little of the genteel snobbery, sometimes reinforced by residual anti-Semitism, that still shaped the life of the all-male undergraduate body at the time.

But in one respect our collegiality was very Princetonian. Apart from Nancy, we were all men, mostly of similar social and educational background. And, with the exception of a few bachelors, we were all married, a condition that was an unstated condition of success in a place where social and intellectual life were so tightly joined. Junior and senior faculty found themselves in one another's houses almost every Saturday evening, a situation made possible by the fact that at this time faculty wives were expected to be helpmates to their husbands, whatever their own educational attainments. There were almost no women tenured at Princeton, and none in the history department. Jeanne Stone, a formidable intellect in her own right, set the tone through her introduction of the English tradition of "at homes," where she and Lawrence adroitly mixed all ranks over drinks and dessert. A few faculty wives like Lois Banner and Jane De-Hart Matthews taught down the road at a place called Douglass College, while my own spouse took part-time jobs at the local community college while deciding whether she wanted to enter graduate school. No one questioned, however, the priority of the man's career.

Despite its intellectual ferment, Princeton was a very conservative place. The faculty, many of whom had connections with the CIA and the military, initially favored the Vietnam War. A senior member of the department, Eric Goldman, was intellectual-in-residence at the Johnson White House. We thought of him as our connection to the real world and listened respectfully to what he was willing to reveal to us as the ultimate inside dopester. As the opposition to the war mounted, Eric made fewer and fewer appearances at the lunch table. We were too polite to confront him directly, but we made our opposition to the war known in other ways. To be sure, those of us who traveled to Washington to demonstrate were in the minority. We staged a small protest when Governor George Wallace spoke on campus, but it was not until the assassination of Martin Luther King, Jr., that Princeton was awakened to the nature of the national crisis. Even then, the campus group Students for a Democratic Society was so small as to be easily accommodated in a junior seminar I taught on the history of university politics. I was drawn to these young dissenters. I marched but was never arrested. Drugs were more a rumor than reality in Princeton, where the counterculture was practically nonexistent. I convinced myself that I was contributing to progressive causes through my teaching and writing, a not unreasonable position, but one that I remain uneasy about to this very day.

In 1969–70 a Princeton faculty fellowship allowed us to spend a year at Oxford, where I was a visiting fellow at St. Anthony's College. Now we had two boys, Chris and Ben, both enrolled at the Squirrel School on the Woodstock Road. Tina took advantage of university lectures to prepare herself for an eventual return to graduate study in English. I had convinced myself, somewhat reluctantly, to do another German project, this time on generational relations in the early nineteenth century, a project that built on my earlier work but marked a decided turn away from political to social history. We rented the Stones' house on the Woodstock Road and had the advantage of introductions to their friends as well as the connections available at the college.

We had barely settled in, however, when I found myself with a topic for which there were no sources. I had expected the Bodleian collections to be the equal if not superior to the Firestone's and was confounded to learn that two world wars had severely constrained the Bodleian's acquisition of German materials. It was too late to change location; the only option was to change subjects. After the initial shock came the realization that I now had a chance to explore new directions, to extricate myself from the field of German history to which I no longer felt any real connection. Fortunately for me, I found myself in a place at a time when a revolution in historical practice was about to happen.

My first exposure to what was to become the new British social history movement took place on a winter's evening in the buttery of St. Anthony's. Tim Mason invited me to attend a talk by Raphael Samuel, someone I had never heard of. We had several rounds of drinks while we waited for the speaker to arrive; and it was already late when Raph finally came, carrying a huge sheaf of papers, which he then proceeded to organize while still more beer was consumed. Finally, he proceeded to narrate the events that had occurred late in the previous century in the nearby quarrymen's village of Headington, a story of popular protest so minutely researched and vividly told that I can remember its details as if the talk had been given yesterday.

This was my first encounter with that most original group of historians, which included Anna Davin, Gareth Stedman-Jones, and Catherine Hall, who were in the process of forming the History Workshop collective. A few months later my friend Richard Andrews took me to a seminar given by Richard Cobb in his rooms at Balliol, where I heard his famous paper on one of the notorious criminal bands during the French Revolution. Later that spring I journeyed with Richard Andrews to Warwick University to a small conference on the social history of criminality, organized by Edward Thompson and his students Cal Winslow and Peter Linebaugh. On display were further brilliant examples of the kind of deeply researched, gripping narratives that were to become the standard of the neo-Marxist labor and social history movements inspired by Thompson, Eric Hobsbawm, and George Rudé. The new social history reflected an intense engagement with the experience and consciousness of ordinary people. Its practitioners felt free to explore areas of subjectivity that had been previously off limits to historians. Here was the inspiration and the permission I had been looking for.

As part of a generation that had been too young to be involved in the Second World War or the Korean War, and a little too old to be a part of the youth movements themselves, I was intensely curious about these phenomena. Condemned at the time as expressions of self-indulgent irrationality, they cried out for explanation in historical terms. That year at Oxford, 1969–70, provided the opportunity I was looking for. I plunged into research in the sources most readily available to me, namely those of the university and the city of Oxford, searching for evidence of the lives of young people. By the end of the year, I had a treasure trove of materials culled from school and court records, from the archives of boys clubs, Scouts, and Boys Brigades. My plan was to do similar digging in German sources with respect to the Wandervogel and youth cultures there, but I already felt far more at home in British history. For the first time, I felt engaged to a particular past in a particular place, but also connected to my own experiences as a young person, which had previously been off limits, but now provided valuable insights. What at Amherst and Stanford were made to seem irrelevant, now gained significance, not just to me but to a whole generation of young scholars who were opening up a range of subjects previously beyond the purview of historical research.

The new social history represented something more than just a change in method. It was not so much a new academic field as a new social movement, originating in Britain outside the academic establishment in places like Ruskin College and Warwick University, often associated with trade unions and community organizations. Its leading figures were political activists, who had come to history not by way of graduate study but through a realization of the importance of history to their engagement with the great issues of the day. Edward Thompson later described how he was "seized" by history only when he began teaching the subject to adult working people in the north of England; Ruskin College's connections with the trade unionists moved Raph Samuel in a similar way. Stephen and Eileen Yeo created a community publishing project in Brighton. The first History Workshop, held at Ruskin in 1969, felt more like a religious revival than an academic meeting. The fact that its plenary session was held in a vacant church only added to a sense of being present at new beginnings. For me, it had a powerful emotional as well as intellectual impact. For the first time, I felt myself connected to history, moved to draw on my own experience to illuminate the generational relations that had become increasingly problematic in the 1960s.

What previously had seemed to be purely personal, idiosyncratic youthful experiences became for me historical subjects worthy of exploration. Wherever I looked I found analogues to the rites of passage, generational conflicts, and countercultural impulses that had been an unexamined part of my own youth. What previously seemed to exist outside time was now revealed to be a product of history itself; and I found myself at the forefront of an emerging field of research when I published *Youth and History* in 1974. I too felt seized by history. The personal, previously perceived at odds with the professional, now gave access to an array of previously unexplored subjects. In addition to labor history and ethnic history, there was women's history, Afro-American history, psychohistory, and the history of family, producing an excitement not seen before in the groves of academe. This explosion of new subjects coincided with a period of remarkable expansion in higher education, providing access to minorities and largely ending same-sex education.

In the United States, universities were in a habit of absorbing new fields. At Princeton, the Davis Center under the leadership of Lawrence Stone was a major agent of assimilation, while at nearby Rutgers, Peter Stearns was building a department around a core of younger scholars immersed in labor, women's, and social history. When Princeton decided to dispense with my services in 1971, I was more than delighted to accept a tenured position at a place where the *Annales* tradition, represented by Traian Stoianovich, and psychohistory, as practiced by Philip Greven, were already well established. A host of younger scholars, including Daniel and Judith Walkowitz, Jim Reed, Rudy Bell, Calvin Martin, Michael Adas, and Al Howard joined us in forming what we called the Social History Group, which met regularly to read one another's papers. Rutgers was the site of the first Anglo-American Labor History conference, which was the beginnings of an ongoing exchange that eventually brought Dorothy and Edward Thompson, Christopher Hill, Tim Mason, and Leonore Davidoff for extended stays. It was also the location of the first Berkshire Conference, organized by Lois Banner and Mary Hartman, which laid the groundwork for Rutgers becoming the nation's premier graduate program in women's history by the end of the 1970s.

Rutgers expanded rapidly in the 1970s, and I was fortunate to be a part of the building process, which included the foundation of Livingston College, a new undergraduate unit devoted to bringing diversity to higher education and placing the university, which had not long before been a private institution, at the service of the people of New Jersey. Livingston's group of ten historians exemplified both goals. We represented an unusual mix of men and women of varied racial backgrounds engaged in the new histories not just of the United States and Europe, but of China, Latin America, and Africa. We often had to do battle with our more traditional colleagues on the Rutgers and Douglass College campuses, but bringing a college to life was an energizing struggle and, for me, a formative experience.

Teaching at a large state university initially presented something of a challenge, but I found social history offered a means of engaging students from working class and immigrant backgrounds. My goal as a teacher has always been to make history as alive and relevant as possible, to ground even the big events in lived experience of ordinary people, and thus to reveal the hidden connections between past and present. Courses on youth, marriage, and family culture offered a wonderful opportunity for students to see themselves as participating in history rather than passively learning about lives far removed from their own. But some of my greatest pleasures have come from teaching survey courses. In collaboration with my colleagues in African and Latin American studies, I began eventually to teach global history focused on the formation of the Atlantic world, tracing transnational connections to give students a sense of their place in an increasingly global economy and society.

At Livingston we not only taught and wrote history, but lived it on a day-to-day basis. The creation of the college was the direct result of the Newark riots of 1969 and represented an effort to close the racial divide in higher education. To the intense generational issues that absorbed American society at the time were added an explosive mix of racial and ethnic struggles. Livingston was a microcosm of the larger society, and attracted more than its share of adverse publicity. Issues of race and ethnicity were built into its fabric; and by the 1970s women's issues were no less pressing. I found myself department chair and speaker of the faculty assembly at a time when controversies buffeted the college. History was no longer something that happened elsewhere, to someone else. And while my involvement with college affairs seemed at times to be distraction, it is easier to see in retrospect how they affected my writing, particularly about the history of age and gender relations.

During the 1980s the ferment that had given birth to Livingston and other experimental colleges like it had ebbed considerably. By that time social and women's history were well established at Rutgers, making its graduate program one of the most dynamic and progressive in the country. Our connections with Britain were reinforced through the extended visits by Edward and Dorothy Thompson, Leonore Davidoff, and Christopher Hill; and through a series of conferences that resulted in my editing collections on a wide range of topics, including fertility decline, militarization, and the role of memory in national identity. The creation of the Rutgers Center for Historical Analysis in 1988 reinforced the university's growing reputation. As its first director, I had the pleasure of hosting a number of international scholars, including Rhys Isaac, Roger Bartra, Robert Thornton, and Tamas Hofer, whose work on identity formation and collective memory had a profound effect on my own work. I began to focus on the social history of family, resulting in a study of British marriages, a work that owed much to the encouragement of Peter Laslett and his colleagues at the Cambridge Group for the Study of Population and Social Structure.

By the 1990s the social history movement was firmly established and the history of family was becoming, as such things tend to do, yet another specialty, with its own journals, conferences, and pecking orders. It had developed in close alignment with historical demography and sociology, benefiting from their quantitative methods and behavioral approaches. It was still under the thrall of modernization theory, which had displaced old-fashioned Whiggish narratives in the 1960s. According to prevailing structural-functionalist assumptions, modern family life was moving inexorably toward ever-greater nuclearization and secularization. This was an attractive proposition, which I had indeed advocated in my earlier work, but there was now good reason to think that it was inadequate to account for the fact that the nuclear family had become increasingly unstable and dysfunctional.

Furthermore, it was becoming clear that behaviorism had wholly ignored the cultural dimension of family life, namely the ways in which
family is a mental construct, a kind of imagined community. I had documented in my studies of British courtship and marriage practices the increasing importance of ritual, beginning in the Victorian period, and was
intrigued by the power of symbols, images, and myths in modern family
life. Anthropologists had written extensively about such things in non-
Western cultures, and medieval and early modern historians made much
of them in their respective periods, but most scholars assumed *mythos* was
incompatible with modernity. Evidence of myth and ritual in the contemporary Europe and America was regarded as survivals of that which have
no place in the modern world. Yet, there was evidence of the proliferation
rather than extinction.

Although I had accumulated a great deal of evidence of ritual and myth
in contemporary family life, it had not occurred to me to write a book
about what still seemed to me to be a marginal phenomenon. Like most
men of my generation, the symbolic activities that sustained my own family life had been something that I had taken for granted. But in late 1991 an
event occurred that made me painfully aware of the power of ritual in my
own life. Our son Ben, who was a pilot in East Africa, was killed in an accident at Christmas. In an instant, all meaning was drained from our world.
The future ceased to matter and the past became a void. Time ceased to
flow and family life suddenly seemed empty, though we continued to go
through the motions. We brought back his ashes from Nairobi and arranged
a memorial service in Princeton. Later that year, we planned for a burial
at Gotts Island, Maine, our summer home. Having no formal religious
affiliation, we did all these things ourselves, finding in ceremony a sense of
both consolation and community. But the true power of symbolic acts became painfully clear as the anniversary of Ben's death approached. Preparations for that Christmas brought such painful memories to the surface
that we were considering avoiding the holiday altogether until Ben's brother proposed that he cook dinner, substituting a vegetarian chili for the
traditional roast. Bringing something new had a transformative effect. We
were able to celebrate not only Christmas but positive memories of Ben,
something that seemed impossible only a few days earlier.

This experience impelled me to consider more deeply what I came to
think of as the families we live *by* in contrast to the families we live *with*.
In the next few years, I found my work taking a cultural turn, exploring

the role of imagination in everyday life. I began to write about the history of notions of family time and family place that earlier I had been barely aware of but now I began to see all around me. This resulted in a book on Anglo-American family cultures, *A World of Their Own Making: Myth, Ritual, and the Quest for Family Values*. Dimensions of experience—myth, ritual, and imagination—which I had been previously encouraged to think of as purely subjective and beyond the bounds of history proper were now moving to the very center of my interests. I found myself in the company of other historians who had come to appreciate these nonrational aspects, who were also turning to anthropology and cultural studies to make sense of the accumulating evidence not just of the persistence of *mythos* in the modern world, but its increasing grip on contemporary politics and social existence. I was also impelled to engage more fully with the politics of family life and to become one of the founding members of the Council on Contemporary Families, which has taken a leading role in confronting media distortions of family realities.

It was perhaps inevitable that my explorations of family time would bring me to an awareness of the centrality of place in modern family life. I had grown up in an America fascinated with space exploration, moving as quickly as possible to subordinate the entire earth to its commercial and political will. Frequent changes of location had eroded what little sense of place I had developed as a child. I had experienced a wide range of environments, each of which had its own intense appeal. I transferred my affections from the Connecticut Valley to California, then to Oxford, and later to rural New Jersey, where we lived for a time in an eighteenth-century farmhouse on a dirt road. As a peripatetic academic family, we had become adept at picking up and moving about, careful not to become too attached to any one place.

But in 1965 we acquired, through my wife's family, a house on a small island off the coast of Maine. We had spent the previous summer there, when I began writing my dissertation, frequently distracted by vistas of the open Atlantic that surged only a few yards below the tiny cabin we rented, called the Box on the Rocks. My parents would never have thought of owning a summer place. Our vacations had always been road trips and I initially resisted being committed to a place so insular and remote. The possibility of owning property on Great Gott Island was too good to pass up, but we were still living in California and we had no idea how central this decision would be to our lives in future years. Princeton and Rutgers brought us to the east coast, but Downeast Maine was still very distant, a day's drive and a complicated journey by boat away. Accessible only during summer months, the island was equally remote in time.

Little did we know that Great Gott Island would become the central place in our lives, not only physically, but emotionally. More than forty years of roundtrip journeys have established it as a kind of mecca, complete with its own rituals of arrival and departure. Over time, Gotts has become central to imagining ourselves as family, for the more we moved about the larger it loomed. It is the central place in our mental maps, but equally for us a marker of time. The year still turns on the annual island sojourn. Some summers stand out more than others—the summer we buried Ben's ashes, the summer of Chris and Kathy's island wedding, the first visits of grandchildren—but the island also condenses time, brings the past, present, and future into a sense of flow that is absent in everyday mainland existence. Here time and space are fused into an intense sense of place unavailable elsewhere.

It took me some time to adjust to an islanded existence. Even now I often feel restless after even a few days, intensely aware of the tension between our romance with island life and the challenges that this isolated place actually presents. Yet, these very tensions led me to reflect on the nature of place itself and were the motivation for the explorations in cultural geography that ultimately resulted in the publication of *Islands of the Mind* in 2004. In that book I tell the story of western islomania and the singular capacity of islands to stir imagination and confer identity. It is a study in mythical geography, which Mircea Eliade once called "the only geography man can never do without," and was inspired by the writings of Yi-Fu Tuan, Adam Nicolson, and my dear friend David Lowenthal. But it owes much to Gotts Island itself, where the power of place first became apparent, an unexpected gift which I have tried to repay in my writings about islands and, more recently, about coasts.

Yet, I remain keenly aware of the fact that I am, in the eyes of Mainers, someone "from away." I am not an islander, and can, by their standards, never be one. Even our house on Gotts, now in our possession for over forty years, will always be known as the Moore place. So, I find myself in a relationship to islands much the same as I was to all my other historical subjects. As in the case with youth cultures and, to some extent, with family cultures, I occupy the position of the outsider, intrigued by something that I can never fully know. But, then, is this not the source of all curiosity? True islanders do not often write about islands. They feel no need to do so.

My liberal arts education at Amherst placed me in the position of the outsider, the anti-specialist, ever curious about a range of subjects that have drawn me into their orbit ever since. When I look back on my life as a historian I can see that it is a continuous remediation project. If it is true that the mark of an educated person is an awareness of what he or she does not know, then Amherst provided an excellent starting point. In graduate school, I began to recognize what I did not know about sociology and demography; later it was anthropology and cultural studies that piqued my curiosity and propelled me into what I like to think of as a third graduate education. Most recently, I have been learning to be a geographer, something sadly lacking in the training of historians in the United States. Once again, I found myself seized by a subject I had been previously oblivious to, making detours that take me off the conventional highways of the historical profession.

Today's students arrive at graduate school already decided on a field of study, often already highly trained in a particular specialization. I admire their protoprofessionalism, but I worry that the trajectories they have set for themselves will not afford the kinds of detours that have so enhanced my own explorations of the past. As part of a generation that experienced a virtual revolution in historical practice, I am concerned that however well they may be prepared in particular fields, they will not be open to the changes, such as the challenge of global or world history, that are already looming on the horizon.

Becoming a historian has not been for me a linear process. In most respects, I have remained a generalist in both my teaching and writing, true to the liberal arts ideal I first encountered at Amherst. But my interests have shifted unpredictably, even illogically, from period to period, from place to place. However, through hindsight, it is possible to see how certain dimensions of my experience, often inaccessible to me at the time, ultimately found me and directed my attention to certain subjects, first to adolescence and youth, then to courtship and marriage, later to family cultures, and now to mythical geographies.

Like my parents, I have traveled light, freer than those rooted in a particular past or place, to roam through time and space, sometimes far from the domain of history itself. There were even moments when I thought of changing fields, of becoming a sociologist or an anthropologist, though I have always found my way back to history. It remains my compass, something much more than a profession, a basic condition of my day-to-day existence, my being in the world. There have been times when I have felt quite disconnected from the past, lost in the vastness of time and space, but it is precisely at those moments that something out of my own experience has focused my attention on some underexplored dimension of history, demonstrating Thoreau's observation that it is "not till we are lost in the world, do we begin to find ourselves, and realize where we are and the infinite extent of our relations."

Becoming would seem to imply a telos, a destination, a terminus. It is true that a career in full-time teaching does have an end point. This is something we all confront sooner or later. Retirement often means separation from worlds grown familiar and comfortable over time. Some find they miss the teaching; I certainly do. My decision to retire was eased by knowing several older historians, Bill Bouswma, David Lowenthal, and Gene Brucker, who provided me with splendid models of what life can be in retirement. I am particularly grateful to one friend, the late Cambridge philosopher-historian-demographer Peter Laslett, who wrote *The Fresh Map of Life*, in which he explored the emerging reality of what he called the Third Age, an active phase between retirement and true old age, for him the Fourth Age. Peter was already a founder of one remarkable institution in Britain, the Open University. Never contented to just articulate an idea, he put his latest vision into practice, inventing what is now known as the University of the Third Age, a grassroots self-education cooperative that has now spread around the world.

The idea of the third age encouraged me to retire a few years early so as to make way for younger scholars in my field. That turned out to be not the end of becoming, but yet another beginning, another detour, this time into the unexplored territories of global history. I learned early on that taking detours has its costs in terms of the status and recognition normally reserved for those who follow the prescribed road maps, but, in retrospect, I do not regret any of the unanticipated turns my work has taken. It is also an excellent preparation for my third age. A British friend of mine told me recently that he had retired from retirement and was now looking forward to new teaching assignments in Australia and Sweden. I have done something of the same, teaching global history at Berkeley, organizing an NEH summer institute on the same subject for college teachers at the Library of Congress, and going abroad as a Fulbright Senior Specialist in island studies.

It strikes me that historians may well be more comfortable with becoming than are people in other fields. After all, telling the stories about change is the core of the assignment that culture has assigned to us. We are quite good at narrating how peoples become nations; and in recent decades we have taken on the same task at the subnational and transnational levels. We are more familiar with contingency, and therefore perhaps better equipped to deal with the unpredictable than are those who approach the world as a steady state of being. I feel very fortunate to have spent my life thinking and writing about becoming, something that is openended and therefore ultimately unknowable and infinitely intriguing. History has been for me a meaningful life's work rather than a mere career. Because my own becoming is still unfinished, it is impossible to give here an account that will satisfy those who want to know how things will turn out. That I must leave to others.

FRANKLIN W. KNIGHT

A Caribbean Quest for the Muse of History

Until I entered the university I did not even know that being a historian could be a useful occupation. I had never seriously thought about what historians did, although all through my high school, students took a specialized course in history. All reading was the same to me—a sort of diversion that exercised the imagination and occasionally provided grist for reflection on world affairs. Both history and literature at their best, however, required a superb use of language. I liked creative writing and I liked foreign languages. The nearest I came during my teenage years in high school to defining a vocation was a fleeting fancy to become a creative writer or a translator of poetry. Two of my teachers were published novelists and in the upper school many of my friends and I fancied that we would be great writers or poets. Our notion of great, however, was probably restricted to occasional publication in the leading daily newspaper. I wrote a lot of imaginary material for the high school newspaper, and I translated from Spanish the entire volume of *Rimas* of Gustavo Adolfo Becquer. I really liked the idealistic romanticism of Becquer as well as the sonorous solemnity of his Spanish. Nevertheless, the idea of being a full time professional writer never appealed to me strongly, and in any case, I never discussed the prospect with anyone.

Indeed, as far as I can recall, no one ever discussed my career prospects with me, and neither did I think much about them. That may probably be the case with the majority of children, not only those who turn out to be historians. I cannot recall my parents asking me what I wanted to do as an adult. But then my parents never spoke about what happened when their children were no longer dependent offspring. Vocational aptitude simply did not form part of the repertoire of childhood discussions for me. None of the teachers I had in elementary or secondary school talked about what I wanted to be later in life, although their range of conversation was wider than that of my parents. That was hardly surprising. There were lots of things that never entered the conversations between the important adults in my life and me. Nobody talked about sex or any of the interesting subjects that occupy young minds. It was simply assumed that we would grow up eventually and, if we could, do something useful. The assumption, I suppose, was that a good education would eventually resolve all the problems of adolescence and adulthood, so my parents strove to provide all their children with the best education available.

But had vocational interests been specifically discussed, I doubt that my parents would have considered becoming a historian an attractive or wise proposition. History, to them, was what some people did in their leisure time. In my family desirable professions were narrowly restricted to medicine, law, teaching, or as in the case of my father, the government bureaucracy. Of all those options, only teaching faintly appealed to me in my youth.

Looking back now after all these years I realize that I simply muddled through life aided by a series of fortuitous circumstances that led me to a career in history. My formal and informal education was profoundly influenced by time, place, and circumstances as it is for all. In my case I am the product of a late British Caribbean colonial society and the commingling of a British and United States higher education. The confident but undisciplined impetuosity of my youth slowly matured in college and university into a reflective individual with a broader and more complex worldview. Nevertheless, I became a historian through repeated coincidences rather than by directed vocational attraction.

Growing up in Jamaica at the middle of the twentieth century was part of my good fortune. The period between the late 1940s and the early 1970s were halcyon years for the island. The British government poured a lot of resources into education both at home as well as overseas in the empire and I was a beneficiary of that largesse. The curriculum was obviously British-biased in a number of ways, but academic selection was made on merit and there were no special categories. Everyone, regardless of color, class, or condition, had to sit the eleven-plus examination, the prerequisite for entrance to any of the island's secondary schools. The competent, and this was especially crucial in the colonies, could make it on their own. Considerations of race and class were not manifest in decision-making. Neither during my high school nor university years did I experience the negative consequences of race and colonialism that strongly permeate the writings of Frantz Fanon, Albert Memmi, or Octave Manoni.

British colonialism did not scar all of my generation for a number of reasons. By the time we came to maturity after the Second World War, Great Britain had lost viability as an imperial power along with its self-confidence. British political and economic influence throughout the Caribbean was waning and everywhere locals were taking over. Certainly in Jamaica, where blacks comprised the overwhelming majority of the population, there was not any obvious inferiority complex. On the contrary, color was subordinate to class in many social situations and most schools tried very hard to negate those differences. My high school peers and I confidently felt that we could accomplish anything we wanted to in our society. No one had to tell me that. Like the character Jackson Philip in Derek Walcott's *Pantomime*, I felt that the roles in life were not circumscribed by race, color, or colonial condition. Racism, however, was not a major issue for most young people at that time and Caribbean political discourse was not yet infected by the North American race-conscious rhetoric of the civil rights movement. But at no time in my early youth did I recall being politically active. I was entirely a product of my time, politically indifferent until I entered the university.

For anyone born during or immediately after the Second World War the times were especially propitious. This was true everywhere but even more in the British Caribbean. The second half of the twentieth century was quite unusual. I could never understand, and still refuse to accept, the contrary idea expressed in 1997 by American Historical Association president Joyce Appleby that "it is the conceit of all contemporaries to think theirs is a time of particularly momentous changes." The record is clear for anyone to see. During the 1950s momentous changes were definitely taking place across the Caribbean. The Puerto Ricans were crafting a dynamic form of colonialism that fundamentally transformed both their island and its political relations with the United States. The Cubans embarked on a revolution that would eventually rank among the most profound in the history of the world. Winds of change were moving across the British, French, and Dutch Antilles, too, affecting all levels of Caribbean life although obviously not to the same degree everywhere or to everyone equally. It was also a time of incredible technological changes and I lived through those tumultuous times. The saturating presence of radio and the emerging medium of television meant that increasingly the world was truly becoming a global village.

The decades-long rivalry between the United States and the Soviet Union indelibly colored all sorts of relations in societies that had nothing to do with the conflict. Jamaica was inescapably caught up in the wake of the Cuban revolution led by Fidel Castro ninety miles away during the late 1950s. The Cuban revolution was an integral component of my intellectual maturation, as it was for generations of young people around the world. My initial interest in Cuba was derived, however, less from the ongoing revolution that none of us teenagers really understood than from the sensational and sometimes salacious pictures carried in *Bohemia* magazine that we shared surreptitiously in my all-male boarding school, compliments of the few Cuban exile students who also attended.

It was very easy to capture the sense of viewing history unfold in the Caribbean of the 1950s. Enormous local changes were taking place independent of the internationally recognized Cuban revolution. Even before that event, Luis Muñoz Marín was dramatically transforming the island of Puerto Rico through his progressive department of development in a process that came to be called "Operation Bootstrap." The Puerto Rican events were headline news in Jamaica and discussed even in my household. My father and his friends talked a lot about Muñoz, but I was never a party to their conversations. The French and Dutch Antilles were adjusting to their new political statuses, but that got far less press in the British West Indies. In 1946 Martinique, Guadeloupe, and French Guiana (along with Réunion in the Indian Ocean) became French Overseas Departments, losing their administrative designation as tropical colonies. In 1954 the Netherlands Antilles gained associate status with their metropolis, Holland. The British West Indies began to implement universal adult suffrage in competitive local elections across the British Caribbean colonies beginning with a general election in Jamaica in 1944. This calculated move toward internal self-government presaged the eventual disintegration of the British Empire in the Caribbean. Anxious to relieve itself of the Caribbean territories, which were then past their glory days, the British government encouraged the formation of a federal structure. Ten units joined together in an ill-fated federation in 1958, but by May 1962 it dissolved in dismal and acrimonious failure. The federal elections constituted my first foray into politics and forced me to learn a lot about the rest of the English-speaking Caribbean; I would tour the region during my first year in college.

The development of the United Nations in the late 1940s also had an appreciable impact on Jamaica and the rest of the Caribbean. Although the domination of the United States deeply marred the development and performance of the newly established United Nations, its organization was big news in Jamaica. If the United Nations was quite familiar to us, the important international monetary and financial institutions created to facilitate the reconstruction of the West after the Second World War escaped our attention, or were deeply overshadowed by the cold war conflict between East and West. I was born during the Second World War and so have no recollection of that great global undertaking. My earliest consciousness of events of the wider world beyond my island home probably began with the Korean War, remembered patchily as large maps on the front page of the principal daily newspaper of the island. I cannot recall reading the reports, but do recall vividly that the war stimulated excited discussions among the adult acquaintances of my father. The cancellation of the new constitution of British Guiana (now Guyana) in 1953 also made the news and agitated the adult gatherings at my home since everyone was convinced that the Guyanese were turning communist. That alone, to them, justified the British action.

Yet I was too young to understand the importance of wars or communist threats, or revocations of colonial constitutions. That was of interest to the adults. I was more interested in the repeated showing in local cinemas of the coronation of Queen Elizabeth II, new shorts about the independence of Ghana, and the cricket tests between Australia and the West Indies. The coronation was advertised as "brought to you in living color," a phrase that still remains a puzzle to me. The independence of Ghana and the cricket matches played outside the Caribbean formed part of newsreels shorts shown repeatedly before feature events. International cricket matches transmitted by radio from Australia to the West Indies in the middle of the night local time in the Caribbean reinforced the reality of the relativity of time and the enormity of distance. England was only six hours difference from Jamaica. Australia was almost a full day ahead. These realizations were never lost on me and would eventually become important dimensions of my later historical consciousness. In my world, relativity did not automatically connote hierarchy. Other factors were surreptitiously influencing me throughout my youth. Urbanization was rapidly transforming the city of Kingston. Between 1955 and 1960, while I was at a boarding school in the suburban foothills, the city limits moved out and engulfed many formerly isolated localities. Housing developments became a regular feature of the urban expansion in every direction and the city was gradually modernized before our eyes. Buses replaced electric streetcars and increased interurban mobility. A favorite pastime on Sunday afternoons when we were allowed out of school was to ride various buses along their entire routes. This reinforced the changes that were taking place at the time. Colorful new shopping centers overwhelmed small individual entrepreneurs and undermined the itinerant peddlers.

Clearly not everyone at the time would have been conscious of history in the making. But even in my small Caribbean island there was a tremendous awareness of something ominously imminent not just locally but internationally and I recall the events as fleeting, unconnected episodes of an interesting time. There was a pervasive sentiment of an uncontrollable onrush of overwhelming events like the perennial Caribbean hurricanes that nullified individual national readiness with an exhilarating destruction. Caribbean hurricane seasons, for those who live in the region, provide important general lessons in geography, civics, and politics. They temporarily reduce insularity and accentuate the urgent need for cooperative action despite ingrained political and linguistic differences. Any neighbor in distress instantly became a friend in need and it was unimportant that the neighbor spoke a different language or had a different political system, or was oriented to a different European (or North American) country. At least that was the prevailing local Caribbean view during my childhood. We were never insular. Moreover, our daily lives were anything but parochial. From a very young age I can recall listening frequently to adults who had returned from distant lands with fascinating stories. Jamaicans of my generation, as my teenaged peers throughout the region, minded in such a cosmopolitan world.

For most prominent Jamaicans, high school was a formative experience because of the quality of education available and the duration of the time spent. High school friendships often lasted a lifetime. This was certainly so in my case. At age twelve I was sent as a boarding student to Calabar High School, where I spent six years that truly prepared me for an adult life, although not necessarily for a career in history. Run by the British Baptists, the curriculum followed the conventional English model so it was not strange that important local events were never discussed by any of my teachers, although we had a regular class in current affairs. But the quality of instruction was excellent and great emphasis was placed on thinking and expressing oneself. All examinations involved essay writing and the simplistic answer was frowned upon. We were taught to see the world as a complex collection of peoples whose trajectory was anything but linear.

We were not especially inquisitive nor intellectually curious. We took everything for granted then, as young adults are sometimes wont to do. Later I realized that the school was not only academically exceptional but also remarkably cosmopolitan. It had teachers from England, Scotland, Canada, Jamaica, Barbados, Panama, Belize, and Cuba. Teachers had degrees from some of the most prestigious universities in the British Isles, Canada, or the United States. Others were graduates of the new University College of the West Indies. We treated their qualifications all the same, although our British teachers tended to exalt their own degrees. A few teachers, such as the Canadian-born prize-winning novelist John Hearne, already had an international reputation in their field. The students came from Australia, the Bahamas, Belize, Bermuda, Cuba, and Venezuela. This rich diversity inculcated an essential plurality to the world that would become normal in my intellectual formation. At Calabar I learned that, in the phrase of Rudyard Kipling, one could talk with crowds and not lose one's virtue; and walk with kings and not lose the common touch. Almost astonishing, there was never any overt racial incident. Neither did the school experience discussions, heated or otherwise, about race, color and class divisions or of world affairs outside the British Empire. Team sports were a big part of student life but one belonged to several teams involving an ever-widening circle of teammates. Enduring friendships were easily made across lines of native language, race, class, and nationality. For its part the school operated as though such distinctions were irrelevant. Of course they were not; but postponing the confrontations provided an opportunity for increased maturity.

My Calabar experience prepared me for the demands of studying history at the university. Calabar was a school that enjoyed a reputation for stressing the basics of a good general education, at a time and in a society where education was given inordinately high social value. I was a quiet but good student. I played several sports, as did all students, and excelled at track. I was promising at soccer, cricket, and field hockey, and indifferent at most of the others. I was given responsibility at an early age becoming a school prefect and deputy head boy. The boys under my charge were not troublesome and in those times the most serious delinquencies had to do with tardiness and leaving the school grounds without prior permission. Being a school prefect meant that one had frequent contact with the teaching staff and had to explain school policy to fellow students as well as new teachers. The sixth forms, with students aged seventeen and above, offered the equivalent of an American junior college curriculum.

There was not, however, any coordinated preparation for higher education—simply a prevailing assumption that all sixth formers would continue to university (preferably in the British Isles) and continue to do well there. The school had no counselors of any kind. No one overtly mentioned occupational role models, or discussed professional careers, or emphasized the importance of public service. The school had a well-substantiated confidence in the adequacy of its preparation although no one knew precisely how that was measured. It was simply assumed that good general education test results reflected good preparation. In the British colonial system at that time high school students represented the sort of potential intellectual elite as Eric Williams and C. L. R. James have described so memorably. The Calabar High School motto, written on every notebook, declared, "When you play, play hard. When you work, don't play at all." A number of students, including me, took the motto seriously. Fifteen of the seventeen boys in my upper school cohort continued afterward to university. At Calabar I learned that one's ambitions, like one's imagination, were restrained only by one's volition. I left Calabar High School at the age of nineteen with a solid conviction of who I was and what I could do with my intellectual talents. No doubt I was mentally as well as physically tough and both aspects would be tested later. Nevertheless, I did not have the slightest clue about what I would do with my life, or even how university life differed from that in high school. I left Calabar and entered the University College of the West Indies, then an external college of the University of London established in 1948. It was a logical progression, aided by a generous stipend from the university; still overcome by naïveté, I had no idea what lay ahead for me.

I selected history honors at the University of the West Indies, but the process of selection during that first bewildering week on campus was based on elimination of other attractive options—in this case Spanish and English Literature—and, like so many undergraduate decisions, the misperception that the history curriculum was both conveniently arranged and easy to fulfill. The courses were easy enough—a series of lectures that everyone considered to be optional and a required weekly meeting in a small group with a designated tutor. The weekly history tutorials required discussion of an essay written either individually or collectively. There were no examinations before the end of the final year.

I gradually discovered that history could be not only intellectually challenging but also immensely pleasurable; by the end of my first year I never thought of doing anything else. Yet in making that fateful decision to become a historian I was, perhaps, unconsciously responding to the persuasive technique of some excellent college instructors of the craft as well as to something permeating the Caribbean air of the turbulent early 1960s. I was fully a product of my time. Nationalism was rampant across the Caribbean and I caught the fever.

A number of the university professors were British expatriates. The student body, however, reflected the full variety of Caribbean nationalities and phenotypes. The untimely demise of the West Indies Federation spawned a rapid proliferation of independent Caribbean ministates in the 1960s and 1970s, so nationalism was a part of our daily conversation and deeply influenced, albeit unconsciously, my later historical studies. My acquaintances and friends at the university were as likely to be from Barbados, Trinidad, Grenada, Guyana, the Bahamas or Belize as from Jamaica. I arrived on campus just as the university vice chancellor, the Nobel Prize winner in economics Sir Arthur Lewis from St. Lucia, was leaving for Princeton University. One highlight of my freshman year was having dinner with the vice chancellor and listening to his recollections of his own university days in Great Britain. I was struck by his modesty and command of regional politics and society.

A number of students were then on the campus who would distinguish themselves later in various fields. I lived in Chancellor Hall along with Walter Rodney, Gordon Rohlehr, and Geoffrey Woo Ming of Guyana, as well as young men from the entire range of British Caribbean territories. In other halls at the time were Orlando Patterson, Richard Fletcher, Norman Girvan, and Maureen Warner-Lewis. In my history tutorials were Colin Palmer of Jamaica, John Cumberbatch and Betty Gollop of Barbados, as well as Pauline Sahoy from Guyana. Equally important, my undergraduate peers ranged in age from the late teens to the late thirties. Some of my fellow classmates had served in their countries' civil service or had been gainfully employed before entering the university. They brought a maturity, wisdom, and experience to our discussion that I certainly lacked. At the University at Mona, and later at the University of Wisconsin–Madison, I began to appreciate the fortuitous, intangible value of belonging to a good academic cohort. Undoubtedly, I learned as much from my peers as from my professors. At the University of the West Indies I learned the value of listening carefully to my peers and thinking carefully before speaking. Some of them could be savagely unkind to careless assertions. Nevertheless, I could hold my own among the upper class students. In my first year I was elected to edit the major undergraduate magazine and I was also chosen to be an interhall debater along with Walter Rodney. I reveled in both the formal and informal aspects of university life. Unfortunately, my penchant for long hours at the student's union proved incompatible with my previous sports career, leaving me an enthusiastic sideline supporter of intramural and international competitions.

The history department at Mona was a stimulating place in the early 1960s. It followed the guidelines of the University of London, with a strong emphasis on British and European history, although history majors could do a special yearlong field in Caribbean history. Historians were also required to do a field in political philosophy. John Parry left shortly before I arrived, but his various publications appeared on our required reading lists and would have a very strong influence on my studies, not only at Mona but also later at the University of Wisconsin–Madison.

The two individuals who influenced me most at Mona were Professor Sir Roy Augier and Professor Elsa Vesta Goveia, both then young dynamic members of the department of history. With their markedly different styles they taught an indelible type of historical methodology that seamlessly integrated primary and secondary sources while eroding the boundaries of theory and practice, of narrative and analysis. Both were passionately interested in establishing Caribbean history as a major field of research and writing. Moreover they demonstrated that in order to understand Caribbean history well one had to be quite familiar with the histories of Europe, Africa, Asia, and the United States. Roy Augier, from St. Lucia, was of a different temperament but demonstrated the same sterling qualities of intellectual acuity as Elsa Vesta Goveia. His empathy, generosity, and encyclopedic bibliographical knowledge invariably intimidated but also endeared him to generations of students. If Goveia emphasized that every book or document deserved to be closely and carefully read, Augier stressed the importance of careful listening to everything that was said. Both practiced what they preached and inspired in their students an appreciation for the importance of history to knowledge but also to community and nation building. They had a remarkable way of connecting their ideas to something relevant to the Caribbean. Both Augier and Goveia were

extremely exacting while also approachable and supportive. Their demanding tutorials were excellent models for training good historians as well as
occasions for personal humility. Having a hastily prepared paper ripped
apart constructively communicated a lesson not lost later when I entered
graduate school. I spent much more time thinking about what and how I
would present the arguments of my written and oral presentations.

Goveia, Guyanese by birth, was already a legend on the Mona campus.
The first woman to win the highly competitive and enormously prestigious
British Guiana Scholarship in 1944, she read history at the University of
London, where she became the first West Indian to win the prestigious
Pollard Prize in English History along with a First Class Honours in 1948.
Her doctoral dissertation, completed in 1952, was published in 1965 with
the title "Slave Society in the British Leeward Islands at the end of the
Eighteenth Century." When I entered the college in 1961 Elsa Goveia
had just been designated professor of West Indian History—the first female professor in the history of British higher education. She was also the
first West Indian, and the first female, to be awarded a chair, but neither
she nor her students made much of her accomplishments either then or
later. Rather, students were attracted to the unassuming Goveia because
she was a brilliant lecturer with a beautifully modulated voice generously
infused with equal proportions of contagious charm, engaging wit, and
matchless erudition. She was an extraordinarily rigorous scholar, as well
as a highly original thinker. Her intellectual range and depth were simply
astonishing. A voracious reader, her command of several literatures was
exemplary. Yet she was spontaneously encouraging of most students and
retained a life-long interest in the careers of some. I qualified for Professor Goveia's tutorials—she tested aspirants before accepting any to her
group—and worked very hard to hold my own. I never got more than a
B+ in any written paper, and never knew anyone who had got an excellent grade, but she was copious in her suggestions and occasionally wrote
that some idea was very good and worth pursuing more fully. I would frequently go back to her throughout my graduate school days for support
and inspiration.

Goveia patiently and methodically postulated the importance of good
questions, carefully explained the varieties of approaches to historical
writing, the importance of data, and the connections between geographical regions, periods of time, and the production of history. Her forte was
the close reading of documents and books, but she recognized that historical sources were not restricted to just documents and books. She had

recently published *A Study on the Historiography of the British West Indies to the End of the Nineteenth Century,* which illustrates very well her approach to history in general and the British West Indies in particular. It deeply influenced my own work then and it remains one of my most frequently consulted volumes. Goveia's selected sources included works in Spanish, French, Latin, and Dutch and she showed that even among writers of the relatively distant past in the Caribbean, the local was invariably linked to the global. Good history, she repeatedly emphasized, required a good working command of several languages and monumental patience. Equally important, Goveia looked not just at what was written but she also tried to fathom the mind of the author. She brought a clearly defined philosophy of history to her work and she revolutionized the way in which the British West Indies, and by extension the wider Caribbean, was seen and written about. In her quiet and effective way she postulated that the Caribbean experience constituted an integral part of human experience. Learning about the Caribbean could, therefore, inform about the broader human condition worldwide. That is the theme that I too try to convey in all my courses and writings on the Caribbean and Latin America. The local may be connected to the global in important ways. This approach is much more readily acceptable today than it was in the 1960s.

The centrality of the Caribbean to modern world history appears clearly in Goveia's better-known magisterial publication, *Slave Society in the British Leeward Islands.* In this work she coined the term "slave society" although it appeared often in her lectures and discussions on the Caribbean. Along with many of her students, I would adopt the phrase and use it frequently. The notion that the Caribbean colonies represented a complex type of society was relatively novel at the time and impressed me powerfully. Goveia explained the term (placed within quotation marks) in the preface to her book on the British Leeward Islands. "The term 'slave society' in the title of this book refers to the whole community based on slavery, including masters and freedmen as well as slaves. My object has been to study the political, economic, and social organizations of this society and the interrelationships of its component groups and to investigate how it was affected by its dependence on the institution of slavery." Today the term "slave society" is casually thrown about, but in the early 1960s it represented an entirely new way of understanding the complex nature of plantation societies and slave systems. By the time that I got to graduate school in the mid 1960s I had acquired an appreciation of the complexities of slave systems and the inherent difficulties in comparing them. At Wisconsin I became convinced that my understanding of slave systems in general was way ahead of my non-Caribbean peers. They continued to talk of disaggregated groups of dichotomously divided masters and slaves. I saw a social complex that changed through time and reacted reciprocally to time, place, and circumstances. But slavery was only one dimension of the importance of the Caribbean to modern history.

By the time I got to Mona, Anglocentric assertions about the Caribbean were unfashionable. Clearly much had been discovered and written about the Caribbean between the generation of Eric Williams (or Lowell Ragatz), writing in the first part of the twentieth century, and mine. My generation knew better partly because we read more widely from a rapidly growing field of literature, but also because more local archives were offering a variety of new information as well as new ways to examine it. We had much greater detail about the early development of the Caribbean and the Americas after 1492. Local histories were becoming plentiful indicating that the period before slavery overtook the Caribbean was important. Barbados and St. Kitts began as settler societies of English immigrants. Guadeloupe and Martinique along with some of the smaller nearby islands were established with permanent French settlements in mind. And many early Spanish considered the Caribbean islands to be their permanent homes. How did these essentially European settlements come to reflect the wide demographic variety of the middle of the twentieth century? How did the Caribbean move from the mainstream of empire to the periphery? These questions endlessly fascinated us. That we knew more about the Caribbean did not lead us to rashly discard what was accurate and acceptable in the earlier works of John Parry or Lowell Ragatz. In our tutorials at Mona we learned that we ourselves could err in some ways and yet get some things right. Learning was a constant effort in shifting, winnowing, and refining.

From Elsa Goveia we learned that there were positive dimensions to Caribbean history and that it was the inescapable responsibility of Caribbean historians to discover and promulgate these. History should serve as a tool in the construction of the nation, however the nation was defined and wherever it was found. To Goveia, the history of the Caribbean was far more than European activities in the region, and it certainly predated the arrival of Christopher Columbus. As one of her students, therefore, I looked for the continuities and discontinuities in the construction of the societies of the Caribbean and eventually believed that the past was important for the present as well as the future. The history of slavery constituted an important aspect of the complex development of Caribbean societies, but it was not the alpha and omega of the Caribbean experience. As she explained, "It is essential for West Indians to grasp in all its complexity the nature of the influence which slavery has exercised over their history. But they will not be able to do so until they can see the white colonists, the free people of colour, and the Negro slaves as joint participants in a human situation which shaped all their lives.... Good intentions are not enough, and the road to hell is paved with authoritative half-truths. No one is ever liberated from the past by being taught how easy it is to substitute new shibboleths for old."

Those were words that she wrote, and spoke meaningfully and persuasively to generations of students. I took them to heart and have tried to ensure that my considered opinions reflected serious considerations of the complexities of the subject. I probably would never be an advisor to any government, but maybe someone reading what I wrote could be persuaded about the relevance of the past to the present, of the intrinsic value of history to the construction of civil society. When I started to develop my interest in the history of slavery and American slave systems, I was convinced that this theme offered an important window not only into the construction of a tropical colonial Creole society but also that it had intrinsic value to the wider world.

At the end of my second year I began a yearlong research project that ended up in a long and undistinguished paper on the role of slavery in Caribbean history. I gathered a lot of data on Caribbean slave societies but could not make many useful generalizations about the system as a whole because my data was unevenly drawn from the British West Indies. How did the slave systems change through time? What essential differences, if any, existed across imperial boundaries? How pervasive was slavery in social values? I could not answer those simple questions. If my overall results were unimpressive then I nevertheless learned a lot about locating and analyzing primary sources, and the patent shortcomings of many publications by internationally distinguished historians. My Mona experience sharpened my academic tools, but also infused in me a healthy skepticism about the printed word.

On graduation from the University of the West Indies I set off for the University of Wisconsin on a scholarship offered by its Program in Comparative Tropical History under the direction of Philip Curtin. I consulted Goveia and other colleagues about the program. Most were dismissive, if not downright condescending. Goveia was highly encouraging. She

pointed out that the University of Wisconsin had one of the best departments of history anywhere and that Curtin had written an excellent book
on Jamaica. She also stressed that its interdisciplinary approach would be
invaluable. I reread Curtin's book on Jamaica but made no other intellectual preparation for what would be, for me, a profoundly transformational
change.

I left Jamaica in the summer of 1964 to attend the University of
Wisconsin–Madison. I was about to enter serious postgraduate training in
history, yet I had never asked myself what I would do with a graduate degree in history, nor did I question the value of history as a suitable career
choice. I never examined the inherent bias toward political and economic
history that I had unconsciously acquired along the way. I still thought
wars, dates, and dynasties were interesting, informative, and the basic requirements for history. I went off to graduate school more casually than
I went on vacation. I never looked up the strengths of the department at
Wisconsin, nor did I read any research by the faculty there. Frankly, I
knew nothing about the university beyond its limited promotional literature. I went to Wisconsin thinking that I would study for a higher degree
and return to Jamaica either to teach at the university level or to find appropriate employment in government. That was the profile of graduates
of the University of the West Indies during my time there. I preferred to
concentrate on the present and let the future take care of itself. If I had to
get a job, any adequately paid employment would do. Things did not turn
out quite like that. Wisconsin provided an entirely new experience for me
and tested me in many ways, academic and otherwise, before I graduated
with a doctorate in history and the irrevocable decision to become an academic and a professional historian.

Getting accustomed to life outside the classroom in Madison was extremely challenging at first. It was a culture shock. People in the Caribbean were not, generally speaking, nasty and antisocial. Rather, they tended
to be extremely courteous to strangers. Nowhere in the Caribbean was
there the inescapable preoccupation with race, color, and geographical
origin that permeated North American society in the early 1960s. Madison,
as a university town, was the most liberal area in the state of Wisconsin,
but it still strongly reflected all the traditions of institutionalized discrimination and racist segregation that characterized the broader American
society. Many townsfolk strongly disliked the out-of-state students at the
university and were openly hostile to foreign students. Some folks were
crudely racist. Finding a barber or an off-campus apartment was no easy

matter for a non-European, nonwhite resident of the city. Indeed it was much easier to live, when I went to do research in Madrid, Spain, under Generalissimo Francisco Franco than in self-styled democratic Madison. My idealistic preconceptions of American democracy were shattered during my sojourn there. Since at that time I never intended to reside permanently in the United States, the racism never bothered me too much. I could hold my own verbally with bigots and fortunately I was never physically attacked. Neither colonialism nor bigotry scarred me psychologically but in any case I bulked up a bit should the need arise to defend myself or my family physically. Jamaicans generally were usually not aggressive people until provoked. Then all Christian charity immediately evaporated. I was not in Madison, however, to prove my machismo on the streets but to get a degree at the university. Most of my time, therefore, was spent on campus.

The department of history at the University of Wisconsin in Madison was larger and better than I could have expected. It had about sixty members covering just about every field. It was exceptional in two areas. It had a very large African studies department, a rarity in any university; and it had a newly instituted program in comparative tropical history to which I had been admitted along with a number of students from Ghana, Nigeria, Kenya, Germany, Canada, and the United States. Although it was difficult to adjust to the extreme Wisconsin weather, especially the long, harsh winters, or, for me, the idiosyncratic local culture, the university community in those days before the United States became fully engaged in the Vietnam War effervesced with interesting people and stimulating ideas. Some students, partly out of ignorance and partly out of envy, referred to the program in comparative history as "swamp history"—a mischievous, comically misguided reference to its apparent concentration on the tropical regions with large rivers and aquatic civilizations. But it was a creative development in the training of historians. I immediately loved it. Comparative tropical history was not narrowly tropical at all. It was genuine world history from a non-European perspective. It required majoring in one geographical area of the world with a minor in another. The program later evolved into a distinguished operation in comparative world history but at the time I participated, it was centered on African studies with complementary areas in the Americas, India, and Asia. I focused on Latin America under the direction of John Leddy Phelan, an extroverted, likeable, and articulate ex-Jesuit with a penchant for clear writing who, like Elsa Goveia, died unexpectedly at an early age. Phelan, like many Latin

Americanists, trained students across the full range of colonial and modern Latin America. I also took courses and seminars in African history with Curtin and Jan Vansina and on India with John Smail. All the better professors at Wisconsin were extremely accessible and open-minded.

At Wisconsin my decision to specialize in Latin American history and minor in African history exposed me to two academic fields in which I was previously dismally unprepared. Although I was reasonably familiar with its geography, I did not know much about Latin American history at all. Mexico was the only Latin American country that I had briefly visited as an undergraduate. As an undergraduate I had studied modern history with its excessive reliance on British and European history. That focus, however, would serve me well later. At Mona the single course in Latin American history was offered by a non-Spanish-speaking Caribbean economic historian whose cavalier attitude to the field reflected many of the major shortcomings of a British-style graduate education. At best it described the activities of the English in Latin America especially during the nineteenth century and at worst it was history by analogy. Latin American area studies and Latin American literature were booming and Wisconsin was at the forefront of this. I was curious about the peoples and cultures surrounding my Caribbean and the countries that had, in many cases, played host to large numbers of Caribbean migrants. I read avidly in that field and was especially excited by the poetry of Pablo Neruda and Nicolás Guillén. Moreover, since I was still clinging to the idea that I would go back to the Caribbean to teach history, Spanish and Portuguese America appeared to be obviously relevant, although manifestly neglected in University of the West Indies course offerings.

The academic system at Wisconsin was very different from that of the University of the West Indies, especially in the graduate program. At the University of the West Indies, like most English universities, graduate students spent three isolated years researching and writing their thesis. Graduate school at Wisconsin was a more focused and serious coordinated training operation. As an undergraduate I had sacrificed sports for activities like drama and student government but had managed to keep up my eclectic general reading. Wisconsin, alas, required more personal sacrifices. My dismal ignorance of my two major fields, Latin America and Africa, meant that I had to abandon any notions of nonacademic interests. My first meeting with John Leddy Phelan, my faculty advisor, immediately put me somewhat at ease. He abruptly switched our conversation to Spanish and appreciated the fact that I was not in any way disconcerted by his strange exercise. I would have to study French and Portuguese during the summers, he told me, and gave me a long reading list along with a sermon on his notoriously high expectations of graduate students. We were, in his opinion, expected to know everything about every book that was already published or about to be published. And in every field we were expected to know more than he did. Fortunately, since I did not know what he knew at the time the implausibility of the remark completely escaped my attention. Otherwise, I would probably have caught the first plane back to Jamaica. Despite his off-hand remark about the high "mortality" rates of graduate students in Latin American history, I was not dismayed and suspected that he spoke in jest, or at least, exaggerated. Graduate school was all about history and its affiliated requirements, about spurning delights to live laborious days. There was much to do and relatively little time in which to do it. There was much writing and many courses and seminars in different fields. Before long, getting accustomed to a cranky duplicating machine in the poorly lit basement of Bascom Hall was a common tale of woe among all graduate students. That eccentric machine was a perpetual exercise in humility for four long years.

African history was the toughest field for me. I had never had a course in the field, had never done any reading beyond a few novels by Peter Abrahams, Nadine Gordimer, and Chinua Achebe. Unlike many of my returning ex-Peace Corps colleagues I had never been to Africa. Competing in African history required supreme effort. Although I seemed so ill-prepared for a demanding graduate program, I never despaired. The unfriendly weather of those unbelievably long winters made it easy to manage my time and keep indoors, especially in the reading rooms of the two great libraries on campus. I had never been exposed to so many books and such ample resources for study. Going through the card catalogs—in both the old Dewey decimal system and the newer Library of Congress classification scheme—was like a foretaste of literary paradise. I quickly formulated a personal modus operandi for those pre-Internet days: book reviews and publishers catalogs would become almost daily reading material. Like my peers I became adept at note-taking on multicolored 3×5 and 5×8 note cards. The smaller cards were for bibliographical references and the larger ones for notes. Quickly I learned, as did so many others, that book reviews could be as misleading as the publishers' promotional material and that a well-constructed index was like a gift from the gods.

By the end of my first year I had done well enough academically to surprise myself, fulfilling all the requirements for the master's of arts in history and writing a thesis on the Cuban Ten Year's War of 1868–78. By the end of my first year in Madison I had acquired some good time management skills and begun to understand how historians thought and the basics of historical methodology.

I made the transition, but not easily, from undergraduate school in a warm, pleasant tropical island to graduate school in a challengingly cold northern locale without too much difficulty. The distance between Kingston, Jamaica, and Madison, Wisconsin, is far less than the distance across the United States. But the two cities were worlds apart. The scale of the operation at Wisconsin was overwhelming at first. The university had more students than most British Caribbean towns, and might even have approximated the population of some of the smaller islands at the time. The Wisconsin graduate school alone had more students than the entire student body at Mona. In Madison the array of outstanding historians and varieties of historical methods were bewildering but the accessibility of the faculty made communication outside one's field of specialization relatively easy. The doctoral program in Latin American history required a number of courses in anthropology and political science. Phelan strongly encouraged consultations with other faculty, especially suggesting that his Latin American history students discuss relevant questions with professors in American history such as William Appleman Williams, or William Taylor, who several years later would join me on the faculty at the State University of New York. Every student I knew dropped in on the exciting lectures by George Mosse and Harvey Goldberg, who were competing vigorously with each other to see who could attract the larger audience on campus. I was comfortable with my command of British and European history, but in every other field I was starting from scratch. I was very fortunate to have someone as patient, extroverted, and broadly based as John Phelan as my academic advisor.

Phelan was gregarious, inquisitive, informed, and insatiably curious, a fact illustrated in his outstanding professional productions. An Irish Catholic from Boston, he easily blended a genteel political activism with rigorous scholarship and expected his students to do the same. As a foreigner on a student visa, political activism for me would have been imprudent, but I managed to acquire some scholarly rigor. I started by reading all the publications of my professors, something that nowadays every prospective graduate student routinely does. Phelan wrote much better than his oral presentations. His work illustrated two highly appealing qualities to me. The first was a sound appreciation of the other social sciences as well as literatures that informed his lectures and his writing. While I had read widely as an undergraduate, I paid less attention to disciplinary differences; I could not really identify the precise ways in which academic disciplines differed methodologically until I went to Wisconsin. The second impressive Phelan attribute was a remarkable competence that spanned the entire region of Latin America as well as the Caribbean. He knew every country intimately and had visited most of them. John Phelan convinced most of his students that span was important and allowed one to appreciate the consummate importance of geography to community construction. I slowly realized during my graduate studies with Phelan that Latin America was not any single country on a larger scale. Moreover, every country was a disconcerting combination of perplexing variety. Just as I was acutely aware of inter-Caribbean differences I would also have to become intimately acquainted with the enormous variety of that immense region called Latin America. That was a challenge that I accepted with gusto.

Phelan knew a range of Latin American scholars and had worked in several archives in Spain as well as across Latin America. He was an excellent academic advisor and role model. He frequently took his graduate students to lunches or dinners in outrageously expensive restaurants where the discussions could range freely from academic interests to the architecture of Frank Lloyd Wright, the pleasures of Ibiza, or the comparative qualities of specific wines. He was also an excellent cook, frequently treating his seminar participants to private dinners where, by desert, the enthusiastic consumption loosened and emboldened both tongues and minds. Phelan was not paternalistic, patronizing, or arrogant, and encouraged his graduate students to give him spontaneous evaluations of his classes and seminars. He was surprisingly receptive to criticism and treated his favorite graduate students just like junior colleagues. I cannot, however, recall any outrageous indiscretion on such occasions. Phelan gave and received respect from his students. He became a professional role model for me although our personal worlds were so different. I got to like him and I think the feelings were mutual. Later he would always remember the names of my wife and children, and until his unexpected death we corresponded frequently.

My Caribbean academic preparation served me well in graduate school. I thought that I was, in general, more widely read than my North American counterparts and less discriminating in disciplinary divisions. I classified books and authors informally by fields rather than by disciplines.

In the Caribbean it really did not matter to what field an author belonged as long as his work was relevant to an understanding of the theme pursued. I had never heard anyone described as a public intellectual. Nor did the race or color of the author become a prerequisite for evaluating the quality of the work. In the Caribbean invidious distinctions of color were not routinely applied to authors and so students were able to read books by scholars such as W. E. B. DuBois without caring much about his race or his personal politics or letting those considerations influence the importance of his ideas. DuBois's idea of the talented tenth and the importance of Africa and Africans resonated throughout the Caribbean with its long tradition of back-to-Africa movements. At Wisconsin most of my brightest white student colleagues had never heard of DuBois, or Marcus Garvey, or even read Gunnar Myrdal's outstanding compilation on race relations in the United States. As a result much of what DuBois was railing about in his books was lost. It was very difficult for an outsider to understand society and politics in the United States. I was incredulous that schools and public accommodations could be still legally segregated in the middle of the twentieth century. But then, the 1960s were the decade of American civil rights indicating that many Americans were not only incredulous but impatient for change.

History seminars at Wisconsin in the early 1960s were delightful but challenging. They tended to be small, with about six participants who quickly developed a strong camaraderie. It seemed that everyone generously shared their ideas and were spontaneously helpful. In my first semester a fellow student who majored in African history and shared many courses with me agreed that we would split the cost of purchasing all the assigned and recommended books for all our common courses. Soon we had a comprehensive library of relevant books in African and Latin American history, and read far more than the minimal course requirements. Not surprisingly, we were always among the most prepared for each class. My student colleagues were an invigorating and intellectually generous group, many of whom later became distinguished historians including Joe Alagoa, Joe Miller, Phil Shea, Patrick Manning, Colin Palmer, Myron Echenberg, Matilde Zimmerman, Mary Karasch, David Cohen, Allen Isaacman, Jane Loy Rausch, Patricia Progre, David Sweet, and Ann Zulawski. There were exceptions, though. Several graduate students were returning Peace Corps volunteers who had seen some exotic part of the world and shared that arrogant conviction that how they saw the world was how it really

was. Seminars were sometimes exceptionally lively, but the really insightful discussions took place in informal sessions late at nights in smoke-filled
student meeting places like Glenn and Ann's, or Paisan's, or at the enormous Student Union.

I had always loved reading and I also loved books. I liked to read not
only to expand my informational base, but equally important I read with
an eye for the basic quality of the research, or the originality of the insights, or the stylistic precision and elegance of the language. I loved language before I loved history and as I advanced through graduate school I
gradually realized the importance of the essential compatibility between
language and history. Good history required clear, precise writing. Historians were supposed to be not just good storytellers but persuasive interpreters of the human past and the human condition. Historians had a
responsibility to retrieve relevant lessons from the past in order to inform
the present and provide guidelines for the future. I could see the relevance of the solid foundation laid with my earlier studies at Mona. In four
years at Wisconsin it all came together.

Apart from Phelan's writings, two works that especially impressed me
were Philip Curtin's *Two Jamaicas*, which Elsa Goveia had recommended
to me when I was an undergraduate, and William H. McNeill's *The Rise
of the West*. In their different ways these are truly outstanding, highly original models of historical scholarship. Both are based on meticulous
research and exemplify superb writing skills. Like Goveia, Curtin considered Jamaica around the middle of the nineteenth century to be an
autonomous society rather than a marginal appendage of British society. Using the conventional manuscript and printed sources available in
Britain and Jamaica, Curtin offered a strikingly original interpretation
and revealed a complexity and nuance that escaped previous historians.
He also coined the marvelously useful phrase "South Atlantic System"
to describe the complex overlapping pattern of trades and demographic
exchanges that has often misleadingly been described as an Atlantic Tri-
angular Trade. Curtin linked the developing political consciousness of a
small Caribbean colony with the events and ideas of the wider Atlantic
world and demonstrated how carefully chosen case studies could inform
broad generalizations in history. He did more to bring awareness and
academic respectability to African history than any of his contemporaries. His lectures were illustrated with slides of his travels across Africa
and Latin America and his command of esoteric information was simply

astonishing. I strongly admired Curtin's technique in recentering history away from the north Atlantic axis. That was how I too wanted to see the world and its peoples. I wanted to see them on their own terms.

McNeill's *Rise of the West* was required reading in Curtin's courses and seminars. This large, strange book ranges boldly across geography and time like some energetic muralist working on an oversized wall. The bibliographical command is, not surprisingly, extremely outstanding. But two aspects of the *Rise of the West* especially impressed me. The first was that it was a model global history (when the term had not yet gained currency) that did not privilege Europe and the Europeans the way that most college textbooks in Western civilization did at that time. The second is that it cleverly used artwork and illustrations not as appendages to the text but as integral parts of the textual explanations. McNeill's approach paralleled Fernand Braudel and the *Annales* school by giving inordinate importance to economics, art, literature, geography, and culture. History was more than politics, war, and diplomacy. History was also about how people responded to their changing environment. Both Curtin and McNeil forced me to include many other factors than social, political, and economic into my historical equations, and inadvertently helped me to realize the severe limitations of Marxist or Positivist schools of history. But they also helped me conceptualize Latin American and Caribbean history without the conventional chronological divisions created by dynasties, wars, and international treaties. What I had acquired at Wisconsin was a keen appreciation of the new social history with its generous borrowing from other disciplines and its unqualified sensitivity to all orders of society. Later this was referred to as "history from below" but I have never found myself fond of that term.

For my doctoral thesis I thought initially of doing something on the economy and society of early colonial Mexico. As a specialist on colonial history in general and on Mexico in particular Phelan was encouraging although he never insisted that his disciples become his clones. My original idea, probably the result of dabbling with anthropology, was to explore the economic and social roles of *pulque*, a rather unpleasant beverage fermented from the milk of the maguey plant, in the domestic market economy during the sixteenth and seventeenth centuries. The theme was too ambitious at the time and I floundered much before abandoning the task. I collected considerable data on production but could not follow sales and distribution of the product. The paper from my initial research was never published and I never revisited the subject, although later I would contemplate writing on rum and society in the Caribbean. I faced two major obstacles for my original Mexican research study. My command of Spanish paleography was exceedingly weak and despite investing an entire summer in the Llanos de Apan, that long, semiarid plateau straddling the provinces of Hidalgo and Tlaxcala not far from Mexico City, I found that my data could not answer the simple questions I was asking. In the end it was obvious how *pulque* was produced and who consumed it, but its role in the wider society beyond the work force on the producing haciendas escaped me at the time.

Abandoning the research on *pulque* was not a disastrous setback with any prolonged consequences. My graduate fellowship did not depend on the success of that particular project. Phelan was quite sympathetic to my plight and we discussed my obvious shortcomings. He advised that I find something else that I could do more comfortably. I told myself that I would concentrate on an age where the documents were printed and information more accessible. I decided that I would try to do a comparative study of the slave societies of Cuba and Brazil during the nineteenth centuries. This would allow me to use my Spanish and Portuguese language skills as well as visit two countries that fascinated me, although it was no easier to travel to Cuba in 1967 than in 2008. Given the restricted funding sources for foreign students, I could not get support to go to Brazil. Instead, I went to Spain and worked for a year in the Archivo General de la Nación and in the Biblioteca Nacional in Madrid, as well as the Archivo General de Indias in Seville. The military archives in Segovia were not then open to the public. In those days when General Franco was active, the archives were not as accessible as they are today, but Spanish society and politics were fascinating and complex.

The idea of doing a dissertation on slavery did not come out of the blue. I had dabbled with the theme under Elsa Goveia. The transatlantic slave trade was a staple of Philip Curtin's Comparative Tropical History Program and I had tentatively explored the idea in an earlier seminar paper with John Phelan. As preparation for that seminar we all had to read carefully Frank Tannenbaum's *Slave and Citizen,* a remarkable book by a most remarkable author. Tannenbaum himself visited the university and we had a session with him. He was a thoughtful, prolific, and talented writer as well as one of the founders of Latin American studies in the United States. His book was truly seminal and was widely read and exceedingly influential in the 1960s. Nevertheless, it grew out of a modest seminar at Columbia University in the late 1930s and while avant-garde for that time, was woefully unsatisfactory from many points of view by the mid 1960s. Not the least of its deficiencies was its lack of primary sources.

Tannenbaum's principal assumption, stated boldly in his book, dealt with the moral relationship implicit in slavery. Linking together questions of freedom, liberty, justice, law, and morality, Tannenbaum believed that Latin America provided a more conducive social atmosphere for slaves and ex-slaves as they transited from subordination to independence. But his argument was weak and largely unsubstantiated. The principal value of Tannenbaum's study rested on its firm conviction that comparative study afforded illumination of specific cases, and examining slavery elsewhere in the Americas could enhance an understanding of slavery in the United States. There were a lot of provocative questions raised by Tannenbaum's insightful work. Tannenbaum treated slavery as a static institution unchanging across geographical space as well as over centuries. He assumed, like many others, that imperial divisions provided reliable boundaries for discrete colonial cultures and he remained convinced that material and moral conditions of slavery provided a reliable basis for predicting future race relations in postemancipation societies and that all societies developed in a linear fashion. He vastly overestimated the number of Africans brought to the New World as slaves, estimating the number at probably twenty millions.

By the late 1960s, it was possible to do a lot more with the study of slavery and the prolific bibliography on the subject reflected this. For one thing, Philip Curtin brought some order to the vast range of figures used to estimate the number of Africans brought to the Americas as slaves. Examining a large variety of sources, Curtin arrived at a total of approximately ten million Africans—with a margin of error of about twenty percent—sold in the Americas and that figure has stood the test of time very well. Before his study appeared in 1969 he generously allowed me access to this work and that influenced both my dissertation and my first book. Also, by the end of the 1960s, the subject of slavery had become a veritable growth industry, attracting attention from scholars on both sides of the Atlantic, although many of the publications followed the old Tannenbaum school of thought. I did not begin my study, however, using Tannenbaum as a straw man. I began with some open-ended questions on the nature of slavery in Cuba and how it could reasonably be compared with the other Caribbean and Latin American cases.

Connections are important to a fledgling historian. In my research on Cuban slave society my contacts certainly were. The initial generosity of

Philip Curtin and John Phelan to a young, foreign graduate student was paralleled by equally surprising encouragement and support from many other distinguished scholars who were complete strangers at the time. On the suggestion of John Phelan, I wrote to many senior scholars in the field asking for advice and comments on my proposed research. I got some very helpful replies. Roland Ely wrote me a long encouraging letter from Venezuela with extensive suggestions on possible primary sources. Magnus Mörner from Sweden sent me a copy of the latest *Guía del Archivo Nacional* of Cuba that permitted me to get an excellent idea of the extraordinarily rich archival sources available for the study of Cuban history. The major problem was how to get to Cuba. Sidney Mintz replied to me from Iran and suggested that I look carefully at the recent publication of Manuel Moreno Fraginals, *El ingenio: El complejo económico social cubano del azúcar.* That was the first I had heard of that publication. While I was doing research in Madrid, Horacio Fuentes Martínez of the Cuban Embassy magnanimously offered to get a copy of Moreno's book from Cuba so that I could consult it while I was in Madrid. Later Moreno Fraginals and I would become great friends and he would render enormous assistance in Cuba, showing me around the research facilities and introducing me to many of the leading Cuba scholars to whom I remain greatly indebted for all they taught me about the history, society, and culture of their island. These scholars and others like Peter Smith, Eugene Genovese, Hugh Cleland, David Trask, and Bernard Semmel made invaluable contributions to my developing the ideas that are found in my first major publication, *Slave Society in Cuba during the Nineteenth Century.* Their questions forced me to clarify fuzzy passages and substantiate loose assertions. Together they made the work considerably better than the original dissertation on which it was based.

Luck followed me throughout my academic career. When I finished my doctoral dissertation in 1968 there were more jobs for Latin Americanists than qualified applicants that year. My original desire to return to the University of the West Indies suffered an irreversible setback when the head of the history department wrote that they had no opening for me. I went on the teaching market in the United States and got several attractive offers. Over Phelan's reservations, I accepted a teaching position at the newly established State University of New York at Stony Brook, which seemed to be the least cold location available in the United States. I made a promise to myself in Madison that I would never live anyplace as cold as that. I had absolutely no university teaching experience before accepting my job at Stony Brook so my initial two years acquiring the requisite skills were difficult ones. My first assignments were to teach a year-long course on comparative world history and to teach another on the history of Mexico. It never occurred to me that the teaching load was light. At the time it seemed as though, having studied slavery, I was experiencing it. I would stay up late at night preparing my classes, invariably overpreparing and fretting excessively about whether I could ever cover all the points I felt absolutely necessary for my students to hear. Sometimes I would work through the night and still feel invigorated for my eight o'clock morning class.

I eventually became a good historian through the generous help of others, but developing the skills of a good teacher was a solitary assignment. I worked at it as hard as I had during my formal courses to become a historian. Stony Brook was an excellent first job with wonderful colleagues and challenging students at both the graduate and undergraduate levels. From among both students and faculty I would make life-long friends.

In my first major published work I tried to do several things, not all of them successfully. The case study of Cuba in the nineteenth century demonstrated emphatically that American slave societies were uniquely dynamic constructs that varied in their genesis as well as in their disintegration. In doing the research I learned a lot of things that I never knew before, or grossly underestimated the importance of the information. Not all Africans in the Americas arrived as slaves or in servile conditions, therefore not all African Americans were descendants of slaves. How did this affect contemporary societies? African slavery in the Americas was fundamentally different from slavery in any other part of the world, and indeed from other forms of servitude. This certainly affected the way we should compare slave systems. Comparisons of slavery either across the Americas or around the world were best done systadially—that is selecting comparative stages of socio-economic development—rather than synchronically—that is, simply during a specific period of time. Any good comparison of Caribbean slave societies should focus on predominantly sugar producing territories at the peak of their productive stages. This would range over time from Barbados in the seventeenth century, Jamaica and Saint-Domingue in the eighteenth century and Cuba, Puerto Rico, Trinidad, and the Guianas in the nineteenth century. I also suggested that Africans enslaved in the Americas did not lose their culture mysteriously in transit across the Atlantic Ocean or experience any of the symptoms of what later the sociologist Orlando Patterson would misleadingly call "social death." Africans were vitally instrumental in every phase of the construction of the Americas after 1492, negating any reasonable assumption of intellectual or social inferiority despite their subordinate social and economic roles. Anyone who has studied the Haitian revolution could have no doubts about the innate creative abilities of Africans and their descendants in the New World. Strangely, no one paid much attention to the importance of the Haitian revolution in the 1960s and 1970s. By looking at slavery within the broader context of Cuban society, as Elsa Goveia conceived it, I could determine that African slaves were effectively disfranchised immigrants who were ruthlessly exploited and brutally abused. This coercion and subordination did not diminish their humanity in any way. Nor should that obscure the reciprocal way in which Africans and their descendants contributed to the all-round development of their host societies. One could more easily examine these African and African American contributions by exploring the complex interrelated changes brought about by the sugar revolutions that converted overseas European settler societies into efficient and unprecedented exploitation societies. These overseas sugar revolutions fundamentally changed both the American tropics and Europe.

My later publications derived mainly from my attempts to think through problems I found in what I had read or questions I could not answer satisfactorily from my teaching. I do owe one publication, *The Caribbean: The Genesis of a Fragmented Nationalism,* to Sheldon Meyer, the venerable and sadly missed editor of Oxford University Press. He was a rare type of scholarly editor, as deeply interested in ideas as in the potential revenue of a publication. When Meyer approached me at one of those famous Oxford University Press receptions at the AHA meeting and asked if I would be interested in writing a general history of the Caribbean, I had never taught a course on Caribbean history. I was busily teaching various courses on several national units in Latin America covering the entire region from before Columbus to Fidel Castro. I had never contemplated doing a general study of the region, although I had frequently fulminated against the shortcomings of a range of books that pretended to be regional histories of the Caribbean. I myself had frequently treated the Caribbean as an integral dimension of the wider Latin American and comparative world history. Nevertheless, I accepted the challenge. When I presented the outline, Meyer admitted that it was unconventional and different from what he had in mind. But he liked the concept very much. I conceived of a series of themes in Caribbean history that had a coherent framework but did not adhere strictly to chronology or follow the conventional periods dictated by previous subregional histories. I tried for something that would resonate across Caribbean linguistic boundaries adhering consistently to a regional approach. Since Meyer liked it, I wrote the book. It reflected how I saw Caribbean history and how I have tried to teach it. As I wrote in the introduction to the first edition: "It is a history, therefore without designated heroes and significant dates.... The heroes are what the Cuban poet, Nicolás Guillén would call *Juan Nadies*, or common folk, too numerous to mention; the dates are not specific years, but varying periods slipping almost imperceptibly by. Such has been the history of the Caribbean and the nature of change in that part of the world. The history of the Caribbean is the examination of fragments that, like looking at a broken vase, still provide clues to the form, beauty, and value of the past."

In retrospect, becoming a historian for me was not all that difficult. Only in graduate school did I realize what was truly required and by then I was mature enough to set my goals and pursue them. I had time, place, and circumstances on my side. I never experienced the crippling handicaps of segregation and legally enforced discrimination. I could think freely from a very early age. I came from an area of the world where stereotypes such as "black" and "white" were neither permanently damaging nor insuperably obstructionist and debilitating. In my early Jamaican and Caribbean world, an author could write a serious book entitled "my mother who fathered me" based on sound scientific research. Gender roles existed but never constituted formidable boundaries. Women handled sexism courageously. We did not get hung up with inventing labels, we just got about doing things. Mentoring had no name but came intrinsically linked to any responsible position. All my teachers along the way were mentors and my entire career I have worked in a nurturing community of serious, intellectually curious scholars. That gave me the psychological freedom to define myself and my expectations independent of the expectations of the wider community. I was very lucky always to be my own man. That resulted in a sort of objectivity that served me well in foreign countries, especially in the United States. I could be detached without being indifferent—and that is a valuable tool to have in historical research. Of course, I must confess that I never became the narrow, single-minded nationalist historian I envisioned at the beginning of my undergraduate career. The confident impetuosity of my youth matured into a complex vision of history and of the world.

My fortuitous experience with a number of powerfully inspirational teachers permitted me to navigate my way into a professional career with a minimum of pain. The obstacles in my way were few and always insignificant. My timing, through no effort on my part, was perfect. I grew up in a genuinely democratic society and entered high school when the government of Jamaica subsidized a secondary education open to everyone based solely on intellectual merit. I attended the local university at a time when the overwhelming majority of students were, unlike succeeding generations, paid handsomely to be there and provided the flexibility to do whatever they wanted, even to fail. The competitive scholarship I received to pursue graduate study at the University of Wisconsin in the 1960s placed me within an intellectually supportive atmosphere of highly productive faculty and unusually stimulating students. At Wisconsin I learned to think constructively and work diligently to become a historian. Most important of all, I learned good historical methodology. I have been incredibly fortunate with my departmental colleagues along the way. Both at the State University of New York at Stony Brook where I began my career, and later at the Johns Hopkins University, my colleagues have graciously and patiently read my work and helped me as I sifted and winnowed my rough ideas and clarified my thinking. They respected me and respected my scholarship. I was able to work with minimal distraction, free from excessive institutional committee obligations. Both institutions provided a desirably conducive atmosphere in which a scholar could keep growing intellectually. Without that unbroken sequence of good fortune I probably would not have become a historian.

TEMMA KAPLAN

My Way

As a historian who frequently carries out interviews, I'm conscious that what people recall often tells more about intervening events than about the periods they purportedly describe. Memories often depend on the context in which one expresses herself and the purposes to which the testimony will be put. I, for one, generally write about ordinary people sometimes caught up in extraordinary events, people who have chosen sides in some conflict they might have preferred to avoid. Since my work as a historian and activist is generally concerned with overcoming injustice, I'm undoubtedly drawn to discovering why this issue became so overpowering. But writing a memoir is a bit like doing an oral history of oneself, and looking backward, it seems that everything in my early childhood was shaped by growing up in a working-class Jewish extended family in Brooklyn during the Second World War.

Although I was far from the battlefields, and was safely ensconced in Williamsburg, my preoccupation with the war led to a fascination with extreme situations—repression, revolution, resistance, and struggles for justice, as well as the sometimes ingenious ways in which people can respond. All my work has entailed studying social movements in art and politics, and many of the activists I've considered believed, as I do, in the possibility of creating a better life and more equitable social relations. Their commitments to social justice and their decisions to participate in public affairs have fashioned most aspects of my conscious life and structured the way I do history.

Children's memories are more emotional than cognitive and usually appear as stories, as mine definitely do. My father was drafted in late 1942 shortly after I was born and was not released until I was three. Even in November 1942, one of the worst periods of the war, as a thirty-two-year-old with a ten-week-old child, he could have avoided the service, yet he chose to fight. Once my father was discharged, he never again stood up for what he believed—or believed anything else was worth the sacrifice. But his decision to confront the Nazis has drawn me to people who take political stands, has inspired almost everything I have chosen to study, and has influenced almost every political commitment I have ever made.

Despite my father's heroic decision, there is another side to the story. My twenty-seven-year-old mother had to give up her household and return with me, her infant daughter, to live with her parents, sisters, and brother-in-law. She was withdrawn and relatively quiet, while the rest of the extended family talked constantly and had strong opinions about everything. From the time I could remember—and for some reason I have very early memories—I thought that all interactions with my relatives were tests to see if I got the joke or could uncover the moral embedded in their stories. Of course, I couldn't have thought this when I was a small child, but I can't remember any time when I imagined otherwise. I also recall a feeling critic Marianne Hirsch calls "post-memory," the sensation that some are responsible for what happened to their families before they were born or when they were small children; I felt responsible for protecting my mother and other defenseless people. My teenaged Aunt Jean, on the other hand, seemed fearless. She told stories like the "Billy-goats Gruff," "The Three Pigs," and "Peter and the Wolf," which involved triumphing over the trolls and the big, bad wolves of the world. Some of my faith in resistance developed from growing up with these stories, though other children might have drawn other conclusions from them.

Even as a toddler, I began hearing stories about my father's army experiences, which helped me feel as if I participated in his life, though he was largely absent from mine. One of my earliest memories is of how I inadvertently helped my father. While home on his last furlough, when I was about two years old, my father was amused that I liked to nibble vegetables before they were cooked. As the story went, when the American troops were starving on the British transport ship that took them to England in November 1944, my father said that if his little daughter could eat raw vegetables, so could he. He gathered cabbage cores and potato peels to fight off hunger, and the other men followed suit, causing such a tumult that the British finally started rationing the peelings.

Although I've never suffered real poverty, I was conscious of scarcity, about which I have written extensively. Because of rationing during the Second World War, chocolate was hard to come by. My mother kept one box of cocoa, cautiously taking it down to prepare hot chocolate on especially bad days. Conflicts over food supplies were even more immediate. One of the stories my family told was how I confronted the local butcher when he drove my mother to tears by short-changing her on her ration tickets.

My interest in injustice was also related to my early knowledge about Nazi brutality. I was still a toddler when my father was demobilized in November 1945. The previous April he had been among the troops that liberated Halberstadt-Langenstein-Zweiberge, a part of the Buchenwald concentration camp where the Nazis were developing a buzz bomb. The camp directors kept Polish slave laborers in line with a whip called a "cat of twenty-four tails," two examples of which my father had brought home. He also insisted on showing visitors photographs he had taken of the scarred backs of liberated prisoners. I could never look at the pictures; I hated having them in the house. Knowing more than I wanted to know about the evil in the world, I took solace in the fact that my father had fought against it.

My longtime fascination with small communities and my sense that they could be unfair to rebels and outsiders was shaped by my rebellion against my father's extended family and by living in Williamsburg. Once my father returned from the war, we spent every other Sunday visiting his family in the Bronx. Like my mother's family, with whom I lived until I was twelve, members of my father's family were clannish. They distrusted all outsiders–including my mother and her family–but felt passionately loyal to one another, at least after my paternal grandfather, a garment worker, died leaving ten children. At sixteen, my father became the family's main breadwinner. Four of the unmarried siblings in their twenties and thirties shared an apartment near the Grand Concourse when I was growing up, and most of my paternal family gathered there on Sundays. I remember them as highly conspiratorial, determined to win me, a small child, to side with them, but I'm not sure over what. They constantly talked to me about the need to support the family and to stay away from others. And, although I was not supposed to fight with grown-ups, I taunted them by challenging a lot of what they said. My father's family had originally lived in East Harlem when it was largely a Sicilian and Jewish neighborhood. Their congressional representative had been the leftist populist Vito Marcantonio who had supplied food when the family was in great need. Yet my four paternal uncles seemed obsessed with whether he was, in fact "a communist," who was trying to win their support by helping them. As a child, I liked the stories about Vito Marcantonio and associated him with Robin Hood.

Apart from family outings to my father's family, I spent most of my life in Williamsburg, Brooklyn, which provided me with additional insights about how conservative small communities could be. The neighborhood was home to two groups of Jews who had moved over the Williamsburg Bridge from the tenements of the Lower East Side to subdivided brownstones abandoned by somewhat more prosperous Italians. Unlike my family, whose Judaism consisted primarily of eating roast chicken and drinking chicken soup on Friday nights, many of our neighbors were ultra Orthodox, including some Hasidic people. Descendents of an exuberant Jewish sect formed in eighteenth-century Ukraine and Belarus to counteract the increasing formalism of other Jews, the Hasidic men wore beards and long black silk coats and black hats rimmed in fur. The boys had long, curled sideburns and wore skull caps. The women and even young girls wore long-sleeved dresses with heavy stockings, summer and winter. Married women shaved their heads and wore wigs or head scarves. As I was growing up I was fascinated by my neighbors and could observe men vigorously praying and dancing in a converted brownstone-synagogue across the street on Friday nights. They had little or no interest in me or my family since they considered secular Jews outsiders, maybe even pagans. The insularity of my neighbors became evident in the way they vigorously upheld the sanctity of the Sabbath, once throwing stones at my young aunt who returned home dressed in her nurse's uniform late one Friday night.

While horrified and frightened about the potential violence of crowds, I also had enormous sympathy for people who managed to survive the worst people could do to them. As a curious child, I gradually became conscious of more and more Hasidim moving into the neighborhood and noticed that they, like the Roma (whom we called gypsies then) who lived above my aunt and uncle's small grocery store on the Lower East Side of Manhattan, had navy-blue numbers tattooed on their arms. In the years before I went to kindergarten, my mother, a crypto socialist who secretly voted for Norman Thomas, told me that my father had fought against an evil dictator called Adolf Hitler who had taken Jews and gypsies to camps where they were tattooed and forced to work as slaves until they died or were killed. My grandmother told other stories that horrified me. On my sixth birthday she told me about what happened to her and her younger sister Jennie, who both worked in a textile factory in Jaşi, Romania, before the First World War. One day when my grandmother was six and her sister, Jennie, was five, they woke up to find their mother lying dead in the bed they all shared. The girls went to neighbors, who pooled their money to send a telegram to Montreal, where some of the older siblings were factory workers. They sent money and the two children were passed from shtetl to shtetl until they reached Bremen, Germany, where someone had money for their passage in steerage to Canada. One moral I drew from this story is that private life is never secure and that I wanted to be a part of the kind of community that got those two little girls to Canada.

By present standards of childrearing, my grandmother was traumatizing me. Knowing that there was a moral to her story, I said, "Grandma, Grandma, how did you manage?" She said, "You survive!" I'm not sure that this scene ever really took place though I remember it vividly. As someone who has interviewed many people about dramatic events in their lives, I've learned to consider such stories as explanations people give for how they view the world as they do, and I certainly derived many insights from my grandmother. She was the dominant force in the household and was clearly the model for many of the working-class women I have studied. I have no doubt that I've been sensitized to different forms of women's leadership by my early experiences trying to understand the main heroine of my early life.

Despite the ways my grandmother tried to toughen me, I remained fearful about the world around me and far too conscious about current events that I really couldn't understand. The way I dealt with my fears as a school child was to close out as much news as I could. Many historians and novelists have written about growing up in the conformist suburbs in the fifties, but I would have been happy for a greater sense of security. For me that period, until I reached the third grade, was terrifying, and I was afraid that my life would be filled with the horrendous events my grandmother suffered. I went to P.S. 16 in Williamsburg, where we were forced to carry out air raid drills. Williamsburg is only seven miles from the Empire State Building, thought to be ground zero for a possible Soviet nuclear attack on the United States. My schoolmates and I learned two kinds of drills.

Supposedly, if we got sufficient warning, we were to follow procedures developed for fire drills. But, instead of leaving the building, we were to go downstairs to the school basement. If, however, there was a sneak attack, we were to put our arms behind our heads, go under our desks, and face away from the windows. I also remember being issued dog tags with our fathers', but not our mothers', names on them. I began to dream of annihilation. For about six months I ran from the room whenever I heard the news, especially the right-wing commentator Walter Winchell, to whom my father listened every Sunday night on the radio.

Once I learned more about the involvement of ordinary people in history, I overcame many of my fears and began to believe that I could make a difference in the world. For me the process began in the fourth grade when we studied the history of New York state, including the history of the Seneca, Iroquois, and Algonquin Indians and their displacement by the Dutch, British, and French. Perhaps because our teacher, Mildred Katz, was especially gifted, we learned about Native American families, about the Indian governmental systems, and about the positions Indian women held in political institutions. I don't know whether Mrs. Katz had read Lewis Morgan or Friedrich Engels or was a feminist, but we simulated councils in which the Indian women played a leading role. When I later became involved in women's history, I had a context into which to fit these observations.

As parochial as the course on New York state history might have been, it actually convinced me that I could and should understand worlds very different from my own. As a working-class girl whose family never traveled, I was a provincial New Yorker. I knew a lot about Brooklyn, the Bronx, and Manhattan, but had very little firsthand knowledge about the rest of the world. My family sometimes went to nearby public beaches, so I was familiar with the ocean but knew almost nothing about rivers. I was fascinated by the study of the industrial growth of the state and the various products that had shaped the urban development of cities and mill towns. Since the only rivers I had ever seen were the Hudson River and the East River, I couldn't imagine how you would dam them to construct water wheels for power to drive the factories. I lined up blocks to form a pool in the bathtub and then built a water wheel out of popsicle-sticks, nearly flooding the bathroom but figuring out how manufacturing established itself in upper New York state.

I remember the story of the water wheel because it taught me that I could understand things that went beyond my own limited experience.

And most of my early education reinforced that lesson. Although the course on New York State history had been mandated by the Department of Education, the rest of my studies until I was twelve developed according to the best principles of progressive education, which emphasized learning by doing. I'm quite ambivalent about the process of "tracking" children, singling them out at seven or eight according to standardized tests, but a small class for gifted children gave me the intellectual skills and openness to cross-cultural and interdisciplinary practices I don't think I would have developed otherwise.

The other children and I were generally curious about the world, and when someone in the class raised a question about the Middle Ages, our teacher arranged to take us to the Cloisters Museum in Fort Tyron Park in upper Manhattan. Opened in 1938, the Cloisters focuses on medieval art from the twelfth to the fifteenth century. The museum includes the work of craftsmen who created stained glass, metal boxes, enamels, works with ivory, and textiles like the unicorn tapestries, and it makes little or no distinction between fine arts and crafts. All this revealed to us that history was filled with possibilities. We studied Carolingian ivories on trips to the Metropolitan Museum of Art and shaped soapstone sculptures. I liked the objects but craved the stories of ordinary people. Since my grandparents were the owner-operators of a little workshop where they sewed button holes, I was familiar with skilled workers, including women, and wanted to learn more about similar people in the past.

My community in Williamsburg consisted mainly of garment workers and small shopkeepers who lived alongside Hasidic jewelers, and I have drawn upon my own experiences when studying local history of similar neighborhoods. There was a lot of surveillance and a lot of bickering among neighbors. But until my parents, two younger sisters, and I moved north of New York to a working-class neighborhood in suburban Yonkers when I was twelve, I had never lived in a nuclear family, and I begged to be allowed to stay with my grandparents and schoolmates in Brooklyn. Lonely and angry about the exile to Yonkers, I turned to novels and later to history to find the stories I craved. Alienated from junior high school where we were forced to memorize patriotic chants like Henry Holcomb Bennett's "Along the street there comes the blare of bugles, the ruffle of drums, a flash of color beneath the sky, hats off, the flag is passing by," I took refuge in the Yonkers Public Library and read every novel longer than nine-hundred pages, from A to Z.

Several novels I read there focused on Anne Boleyn, and they led me
to read actual histories of the Tudor period in which women played significant roles. I found Garrett Mattingly, whose *Catherine of Aragon* included the kind of significant details that novelists often use and attracted
me to the history of Spain. His book, *The Spanish Armada*, published during my last year in high school, opens with the execution of Mary, Queen
of Scots. He portrays her as wearing a red dress, the color of martyrdom,
explaining in a long footnote that he "opted for the crimson, not so much
because it is in more early MSS than any other, but because if Mary had
crimson undergarments (and we know she had) I think that she would
have worn them." Whether he was right or wrong, Mattingly taught me
that women had altered history. He also convinced me that arguments
could be made visually as well as verbally, confirming my sense that stories could be found in a variety of places, even in inventories.

Reading became a form of escape, but paradoxically drew me toward
engagement with other people's lives. A high-school English teacher soon
made me realize that I might like to write stories of my own. I had never
thought about how people narrated stories, but my teacher's focus on
style made me realize that there was a certain art to storytelling that went
beyond gathering facts. She told us to go to the old cemetery in downtown Yonkers and find a person, family, or incident about whom we could
write a fifteen-page paper in the style of Thomas Babington Macaulay or
Thomas Carlyle. I soon discovered that I liked piecing together historical
puzzles. It was my first experience using primary sources, let alone objects, and provided me with a sense that history entailed interpreting material. Some of the students and parents were outraged at our being sent
into the cemetery, but I was delighted to reconstruct family histories from
tombstones.

My senior year in high school was pivotal to my development as a historian and an activist and enhanced my sense of being an engaged intellectual. The events of that year, 1959–60, alerted me to stories of repression
overcome and the heroism of ordinary people. A friend became involved
in the national campaign to picket Woolworth's and other drug stores to
force them to integrate lunch counters in the South. Yonkers was a pretty
racist place, and although there was a Woolworth's not far from where I
lived, there was no picketing going on there. But Columbia University students gathered on Saturdays at the Woolworth's branch on Broadway near
the university, and I joined them. Standing around on Saturday afternoons,

I learned a lot about Rosa Parks, the Montgomery bus boycott, Martin Luther King, and the Greensboro sit-ins. My growing involvement in the civil rights movement led to curiosity about how people come together and stay together to fight for social justice. Studying the history of racial strife in various countries helped launch my interest in comparative history, especially the history of Spain and Latin America.

Current events spurred this interest. On New Year's Eve 1959 Fidel Castro and Ché Guevara had entered Havana, and in the following fall of my senior year, Herbert L. Matthews, a reporter from the *New York Times,* came to my high school. As a young man, Matthews had gone to Ethiopia to chart Mussolini's invasion, and then he went to Spain to cover the Republican side during the Spanish Civil War. He was the first journalist Fidel Castro and Ché Guevara welcomed to their camp in the Sierra Maestra mountains, and Matthews was convinced that the Mafia-ridden, bloody dictatorship of Fulgencio Batista, which was supported by the United States, had run its course in Cuba but required a revolution to overthrow it. Matthews, though critical of many of Castro's policies, believed that the revolution was capable of democratic reforms. My Spanish teacher, who had been educated in convent schools in Havana, strongly disagreed. I was impressed that adults I respected had different opinions and wanted to understand the conflict for myself. I went to work studying Cuban history, especially the role of Antonio Maceo and other Afro-Cubans in the struggle for liberation from Spain, and subsequently I became curious about the history of other countries in Latin America.

In my last year of high school, I developed friendships with five or six college-bound seniors, who tutored me about college applications. While it was always presumed that I would go to college, my family and I knew almost nothing about what that entailed. All I knew was that I wanted to leave home to study, and I made my choice of colleges almost completely arbitrarily. A woman I met went to Radcliffe, so I applied there; the cousin of a friend went to Brandeis, where I also applied. After huge fights with my father, who wanted me to stay home and commute to a local college, I received a big scholarship from Brandeis.

Going to Brandeis in 1960 was the major turning point in my life: it was like traveling to a foreign land. The fierce and vibrant intellectual and political atmosphere there took me farther from home than I had ever imagined. My school work and political commitments had already supplanted my family as the center of my life, and Brandeis completed the process. In fact, for a long time, my membership in intellectual and political groups was my personal life, the only life that I wanted.

My time at Brandeis also heightened my belief that current events provided a context for historical studies. My freshman year began fifteen years after the end of the Second World War, and all first-year students were required to take a course called "Western Civilization," which, despite its name, focused largely on Europe. The outstanding professors who lectured in this course constantly made reference to the war. Frank E. Manuel, who had recently published *The Eighteenth Century Confronts the Gods* about the anthropological ideas of Enlightenment thinkers, taught us about the French Revolution and worried that mass movements might lead to irrational behavior. Herbert Marcuse (at that time just an especially beloved professor but later a guru of the New Left) gave a stirring lecture on the Albigensian Crusade, which he called the greatest turning point in history before the advent of the Nazis and the Second World War. He romantically portrayed the aristocracy of the entire Languedoc region and Catalonia as part of an open society, free of political, religious, or sexual repression. Much of what I remember from that lecture turned out not to be true, but it taught me about a world of which I had previously known very little and aroused my interest in more stories about turning points in history, especially in southern France and northeastern Spain.

A huge proportion of the faculty at Brandeis was made up of European émigré intellectuals or others with strong political commitments, and contemporary events permeated almost every class. A history course on the Civil War and Reconstruction in the spring of 1961 spent an inordinate amount of time digressing to the Eichmann trial that was going on in Israel at the time. Debates ensued over what constituted justice then and in the period following the American Civil War. Although I believe that the cultural and political maelstrom we think of as "the sixties" generally began in 1963 or 1964, at Brandeis political movements flourished along with sex, drugs, and rock and roll even earlier. One program brought activists from the Student Non-Violent Coordinating Committee from their struggles for integration in the South for six-month stays at Brandeis, and they vigorously participated in classes and at public lectures. Listening to them speak, I began to see the impact people could have in shaping history.

Among my closest friends at Brandeis were students from Africa and Latin America. We had numerous birthday parties as various African nations became independent states. My friends from Latin America, especially

Clara Lida and Juan Corradi tutored me in their views of history. In addition to taking anthropology, political science, and history courses about Latin America, I jumped at the chance in the summer of 1962 to go for three months on a travel seminar that arranged home visits as well as seminars with student leaders and members of unions in Colombia, Peru, Bolivia, Chile, Argentina, and Brazil. It was the first time I had lived outside the United States; I saw the Andes before seeing the Rockies. When I returned, I took history and anthropology courses dealing with Latin American peasant movements going back to the resistance of the Araucanian Indians in Chile to the Spanish conquerors; I became fascinated with Peru and Chile. I wanted to understand how certain communities developed and sustained revolutionary traditions and wound up writing an undergraduate thesis on José Carlos Mariátegui, an early-twentieth-century Peruvian Marxist who viewed indigenous people as the only group capable of the social transformation of Peru.

I took many courses on political philosophy with Marcuse, who one day asked me which graduate school I planned to attend. I had enjoyed writing papers for him, for Ray Ginger, a muckraking U.S. labor historian, and for Leo Bronstein, with whom I took courses in Islamic art. One of my professors of Latin American history wanted me to apply to graduate schools at Princeton and the University of Texas, but since I was already familiar with Widener Library at Harvard, I arbitrarily decided to apply there. I won a fellowship and thought I was set for the foreseeable future.

Brandeis had been equally divided between men and women, and I felt intellectually challenged and completely cherished there. It was only when I got to Harvard that I realized how difficult it was to be a woman intellectual and activist. The graduate program of the History Department at Harvard admitted about twenty-five students a year, about four or five of whom were women. In fact there were so few women students in any graduate department that we knew all the women in the arts and sciences departments by name, which didn't help much since about half of all women admitted generally left by the end of their first year. By chance or design, one professor of U.S. history drove at least one woman or gay man to tears every year. I myself would not have survived had it not been for Ellen Edwards and Gabrielle Spiegel, who, having studied at feminist Bryn Mawr College, periodically whisked me away from the intensely competitive history reading room at Widener Library to the Radcliffe College library (later the Schlesinger Library). We studied, took breaks to discuss the ideas permeating the histories we were reading, dug out works by women intellectuals, like the economist Joan Robinson, and continued our probing discussions over the dinners we prepared together. Tom Cohen, Lewis Bateman, and Lutz Berkner in history and Edward Baker in Spanish were like supportive brothers, but I mainly felt like a sexual and class pariah in the very tweedy male world, where women were not even allowed into the Harvard College Library.

When I arrived at Harvard, there were two assistant professors of Latin American history, but neither could offer the all-important graduate seminar. So I went to talk to David Landes, who had just come from Berkeley and was teaching a seminar on something called "social history." My previous readings of Eric Hobsbawm's *Primitive Rebels* and E. P. Thompson's *The Making of the English Working Class* provided models for what I wanted to write in Latin American history. Reading their work, as well as that of George Rudé and Richard Cobb, made me believe that I could write about ordinary people who changed the world. Although I had read Marx as a nineteenth-century intellectual and had written about Mariátegui, I hadn't used Marxist theory in the historical work I did in college. But these British Marxists (and Richard Cobb) were studying people more like the community organizers, indigenous people, and women activists in whom I was really interested, and I wanted to apply their kind of social history to Latin America.

Landes told me that he didn't know anything about Latin America, but since I read Spanish and Portuguese (though not Catalan at that time), I might consider working on Spain. Although I was interested in Catherine of Aragon and the Catalans in the Albigensian Crusade, and was fascinated by the Spanish Civil War, I had never studied Spanish history. So I joined the seminar and began research on the making of the Barcelona working class, which I actually completed almost thirty years later as *Red City, Blue Period: Social Movements in Picasso's Barcelona*. Drawing on Thompson, I started to explore the ways that Catalan nationalism and anarchist internationalism figured in the mutual creation of the Barcelona bourgeoisie and working class. My experiences as a foot soldier in various civil rights organizations and my growing opposition to U.S. engagement in Southeast Asia provided me with insights about decentralized associations committed to internationalism. In these groups and in SDS (Students for a Democratic Society), a New Left organization that I joined in graduate school, I became committed to creating popular associations that would allow people to govern their own lives. As usual, I turned to history books to understand current events, but I also joined various study

groups that were reading Marx's early political writings that dealt with
people attempting to carry out revolutionary change.

Hoping to blend my increasing desire to teach with my political commitments to the social movements emerging around me, I passed my comprehensive examinations and went to Mississippi. For three months in the
summer of 1966, I taught Rousseau and Voltaire to politically progressive
Christian, fundamentalist students at Tougaloo College, worked in voter
registration drives, and participated in the marches and rallies following
the attempt on the life of James Meredith, the first African American
to enroll in the University of Mississippi. My students defied stereotypes
about liberalism and radicalism. They believed in civil rights but hated
Voltaire and even the Beatles because the previous spring John Lennon
had claimed that the Beatles were greater than Jesus Christ. When I returned to Cambridge in the fall, I thought I'd finish out the year and apply
to law school so that I could work full time in the civil rights movement.
But as the war in Southeast Asia escalated, I increasingly came to believe
that studying and teaching history was crucial to developing the kind of
social movements that could win civil rights and stop further incursions
into political conflicts abroad. That left me the task of finding a topic for
my dissertation.

I had very little guidance, and, in fact, had four different thesis directors before H. Stuart Hughes agreed to be the nominal director of my
thesis. I had hoped to write about the Spanish anarchists, but in the mid-
to late-1960s, when the Spanish government was increasingly repressive
during the last days of the Franco dictatorship, everyone said it would be
impossible to study a subject as controversial as anarchism. So I wrote
a dissertation about Luis Simarro, who became famous for his defense
of anarchists and freethinkers. In the dissertation, I explored the connection between his political commitments to the rule of law and his work
as a professor of neurology and head of the Spanish Free Masons. I was
fascinated by his passionate defense of Fernando Ferrer, a progressive
educator whom the government tried and executed as the alleged organizer of the 1909 uprising in Barcelona known as Tragic Week. I scoured
archives in Madrid, Valencia, and Barcelona, where I was lucky enough to
be guided by José María López Piñero, Josep Termes, and Josep Fontana.
At the time, Termes and Fontana were excluded from university jobs but
were reinventing Spanish history through the informal seminars they organized. I also worked in the Spanish archives alongside young historians

such as Susana Tavera and Mary Nash, who are now among the foremost historians of women in Spain.

My concern with current events reached a crescendo in 1967–68. I left for Spain to begin research on my dissertation just after the race riots in Newark and was abroad during the assassination of Martin Luther King, the May protests in Paris, the liberalization in Czechoslovakia, and the assassination of Robert Kennedy. In July 1968, I joined the demonstrations outside the Democratic National Convention in Chicago and wept over the Soviet invasion of Czechoslovakia in August. In the fall, I became a member of "Bread and Roses," a broad-based women's movement that was attracting over 150 women a week to general meetings in Boston. I started writing my dissertation and worked on an underground newspaper called the *Old Mole*. Putting out a newspaper with Dick Cluster, Linda Gordon, Amy Merrill, Danny Schechter, Meredith Tax, and Jon Wiener gave me a language for both my political ideas and my dissertation. As the war in Southeast Asia escalated, I joined with fellow students in the Students for a Democratic Society in occupying the administration building at Harvard shortly after turning in my thesis.

While I was working on my dissertation and just before the job market dried up, UCLA hired me to teach Spanish history. It's hard to imagine now, but I got my job with a minimum of effort. Hayden White interviewed me at the American Historical Association meeting in late 1968 and then invited me for a campus visit in early January 1969. The interview consisted of dinner with a few people from the European field and some polite conversation about my thesis. Three days later the department chair offered me the job. Much later, a colleague opposed to affirmative action explained that he and his colleagues had hired me before they "had to hire women and blacks." They hired me because I was "good." I knew he was trying to explain himself and include me in a community of scholars in which he earnestly believed. But I reminded him that although I might have been asked to give a public lecture and respond to searching questions, I had done nothing of the kind. The only thing our colleagues knew about me when I was hired was that I was getting a degree from Harvard. Undoubtedly my professors had praised me and might even have spoken on the phone to acquaintances at UCLA, but people at other graduate schools also supported their students. I strongly believe that no matter how much support a woman from a less prestigious school received, UCLA would never have hired her.

As ambivalent as I still feel about the selection process, I have no doubt that being on the faculty at UCLA at the time was one of the best things that ever happened to me. When I began to teach in 1969, there were over seventy faculty members in history, working on subjects ranging from Medieval Islam to revolutionary movements in Tanzania. I attended public lectures all over the university and even audited courses so that I could continue exploring my interests in art, politics, and social movements, and develop new areas of study. Suddenly, I stopped feeling like an outsider and could pursue comparative historical studies with some of the most learned people in the country. My partner, Jon Wiener, a fellow graduate student and political activist at Harvard, had come to Los Angeles with me, and, with great faith in each other and the future, we decided to get married at the end of 1969.

Around the same time, my students convinced me to apply my skills as a historian to the study of women. Two history graduate students had started teaching an experimental course on women's history, and they focused on the supposedly feminine qualities of "nurturance" and "submissiveness." Some leftist feminist graduate students and I were furious at what other feminists later called "essentialism." And to counter what we viewed as an outrageous set of premises, the students and I organized our own seminar dealing with comparative historical studies of women. In a separate but related development, my new colleague, Terry Ranger, had just come to UCLA following the publication of his book *The African Voice in Southern Rhodesia, 1898–1930* that dealt with the political role of religious seers in early revolutionary struggles in Zimbabwe. One reviewer had criticized him for overlooking the fact that a large number of those revolutionary prophets were women. One of the most principled and creative intellectuals I have ever met, and subsequently the coauthor with Eric Hobsbawm of the formative collection, *The Invention of Tradition*, Terry Ranger asked me to co-chair a year-long lecture series called "Women in Africa," and we invited some of the scholars who basically invented the fields of African women and gender history. From Terry and other African historians, such as Edward A. Alpers, Iris Berger, Chris Ehret, and Marcia Wright, I learned the importance of studying local religion, rituals, and crafts and of reading oral testimony to avoid an overreliance on government documents. I've applied these methods to all my subsequent studies, no matter the country or period.

Once again a social movement of which I became a part reoriented my historical studies. I became a historian of women in the first seminars

and study groups I taught in women's history; these courses drew Rachel
Biale, Alice Clement, Nancy Hollander, Jean Quataert, Nancy Northrup,
Margaret Strobel, and others writing dissertations on women in African,
European, Latin American, and U.S. history. Since there were few books
that dealt with women's history at any time or in any place, we began
to create comparative women's history by reading a vast array of ethnographic studies of women's movements in West Africa. Judith Van Allan, then a graduate student in political science at Berkeley, gave a lecture about what the British called the "Aba Riots" and locals called the
"Women's War." She argued that in 1929 women's groups in southeast-
ern Nigeria applied collective rituals commonly used to shame abusive
husbands to alert British authorities about how they were violating local customs. From this early study, I learned to look at ritual elements in
almost every area of life.

Early-twentieth-century British historians Alice Clark, Margaret Hewitt, and Ivy Pinchbeck shaped many of the questions we asked about
work, sexuality, childbirth practices, and women's rituals all over the
world. From the beginning, we considered how sexuality influenced work.
We also discussed maternity and cloistered women—from medieval nuns
to women in the village harems of Iraq. Undergraduate courses I taught
on women and revolution raised questions about why women constituted
about one-third of the participants in radical groups such as the Norodnik
in Russia and the Jewish Labor Bund in Poland and what part women
had played in the Chinese Revolution. I encouraged students to interview
female relatives and women workers on campus; to read ethnographies,
government reports, and religious accounts; and to study crafts such as
quilting in which women engaged.

Like many other feminists in the mid-1970s, I was attracted to psychoanalysis. Before the Second World War, my teacher Herbert Marcuse
and his colleagues at the Institute for Social Research in Frankfurt had
attempted to link Marx and Freud in the study of culture. My own concern with the history of women and gender led me to combine the ideas of
Marxist theorist Antonio Gramsci and British psychoanalyst D. W. Win-
nicott with Freud's case studies of female sexuality as he developed them in
Dora, Anna O., and related papers. In various seminars and unpublished
lectures, I examined class, culture, and sexual identity in historical contexts. Because the History Department at UCLA was so large when I was
there, I taught what I liked. But I couldn't have taught such varied courses
in women's history in the 1970s and early 1980s without the pioneering

works of my friends and colleagues Joyce Appleby, Ruth Bloch, Nikki Keddie, Deborah Silverman, Katherine Kish Sklar, and Mary Yeager in history and Dolores Hayden in architecture and urban planning.

Political events and membership in activist groups again determined what I would study. As the war in Southeast Asia escalated in the early 1970s, I had become increasingly intrigued by peasant revolutions, sustained resistance to outside aggressors, and women's involvement in these movements. I published a few articles from my dissertation and revised most of the chapters, but I made the fateful decision not to turn my thesis into a book. Some of my friends thought this might be committing academic suicide, but returning to the study of the anarchists offered me opportunities to pursue so many of the social and cultural issues that continued to shape my intellectual and political life that I decided to follow my own path; I've never doubted that I made the right choice.

At first, I thought about the history of anarchism and women's history as two discrete categories, but some discoveries in the archives showed me that they were connected. While reading late-nineteenth-century Spanish anarchist newspapers at the Institute for Social Research in Amsterdam, I discovered repeated coverage of anarchist women presenting newborns with anarchist pamphlets while singing anarchist songs. It seemed like an infant initiation into the anarchists, a form of secular baptism, and it made me realize that people do not give up something for nothing. Even though the anarchists were anticlerical, they still wanted to celebrate significant events, and the birth of a child was a powerful incentive for a party. On another research trip, this time to the Hoover Institution of War, Revolution, and Peace at Stanford University, I found a few issues of *Mujeres Libres* (Free women), a largely forgotten 1930s Spanish newspaper and an anarchist women's organization by the same name. I analyzed six or seven issues and published a brief note as "Spanish Anarchism and Women's Liberation." Although I certainly would write it differently today, it was a political as well as an intellectual statement. The article confronted the contradictions between anarchists' theoretical commitments to sexual equality and their failure to include the women anarchists of Mujeres Libres as full members of their movement. The article was as much about the growing consciousness among women that they were second-class citizens in movements for social emancipation they had helped create as it was about the Spanish anarchist women of Mujeres Libres.

For better and worse, I began writing about past struggles that were similar to those in which I participated. Although I admire people who assume leadership, I have always preferred belonging to ensembles, doing my part, but not taking authority—or responsibility—for directing any organization. I became concerned with how collective leadership developed in earlier movements and read the great studies of European anarchism by James Joll and George Woodcock. Yet no one could explain to my satisfaction how the ideas of Russian political philosophers Michael Bakunin and Peter Kropotkin had filtered down to some of the supposedly most backward peasants in Europe. Once again, the British Marxist historians E. P. Thompson and Eric J. Hobsbawm, who influenced me and so many other social historians of my generation, had laid a path by writing about people with skills and vocations: the printers, shoemakers, tailors, and prophets who had led political mobilizations. I thought the explanation for anarchist persistence in certain areas over long periods of time lay with rural and urban craftsmen and viewed them as extremely rational in trying to achieve a high degree of local control over the politics (they called it "administration") that governed their lives.

My involvement as a historian of women's movements made me sensitive to anarchist cultural projects. I realized that the anarchists were committed to what later became known as "social construction," the belief that society, not "human nature" or biology, shapes people's personalities and their sexuality. With great intellectual awareness of nuances of power, anarchists were concerned with relations between the sexes, and they were also highly internationalist, a characteristic that helped them shape public opinion in Europe and the Americas as government repression increased in the late nineteenth and early twentieth centuries.

My youthful participation in the relatively autonomous branches of SDS structured my later historical understanding of anarchist ideas about local control of politics. I focused my study of anarchism on one city, Jerez de la Frontera, the home of the sherry industry as well as a center of late nineteenth-century Spanish anarchism. I discovered that the pruners, vintners, and blenders of the city united with women workers and landless day laborers. Together these groups periodically formed communes through which anarchists attempted to seize power over the region and govern their own affairs. Although I wanted to call the book that resulted from these studies *Anarchy and Sherry Wine*, I was in the throes of successfully getting tenure at UCLA in 1975 and regretfully deferred to the publishers who regarded that title as frivolous. Instead it was called *Anarchists of Andalusia, 1868–1903*.

While continuing to study the motivations of activist women and skilled workers, I went through one of the most depressing periods of my life. In 1980 my marriage broke up, and although I loved California and my women colleagues at UCLA, I decided to leave. With a grant from the Rockefeller Foundation to write the Barcelona book I had begun as my first seminar paper in graduate school, I went to Spain and then to the East Coast, where old friends took me in. Cable television was just beginning to take hold, and I had several contacts with HBO. While I contemplated writing and producing feminist situation comedies, I never made the necessary phone calls to initiate the process. Instead, in the spring of 1983, I found a job as director of the Barnard Center for Research on Women at Barnard College, Columbia University. It enabled me to continue to write and teach while developing programs to attract a popular audience of people who had not had an opportunity to study women's history.

The Barnard Center for Research on Women—or the Women's Center, as it was originally known—was a unique institution, part sounding board for the New York feminist community, part research center, part feminist college within a women's college. In 1975, the Center launched an annual conference known as the "Scholar and the Feminist." It was the first and most important feminist interdisciplinary conference of its time. As the second director of the Center, I emphasized the multicultural and international dimensions of women's activism in our programs and research projects. Along with Robert G. Moeller, then teaching European social history at Columbia University, I began a seminar on women's history, where scholars like Claudia Koonz, Denise Riley, and Ellen Ross discussed drafts of their first books before popular as well as academic audiences. Life at the Center was all-encompassing, and increasing conflicts over racial differences, the immigrant and refugee status of women in the developing world, and women's relationship to religious fundamentalism gave a continued urgency to historical studies.

Being a historian at that time and place allowed me to introduce a historical dimension to every issue that our programs explored. By asking people to examine historical differences between the ways certain issues of gender were posed now and in the past, we were able to overcome a notion that certain forms of discrimination were timeless. For example, feminists like Adrienne Ashe, who was active in the disability rights movement, asked why the Victorian period that viewed dependency and frailty as desirable qualities in women did not view disabled women as the cultural ideal. The Center also engaged in political activity, exploring the relationship between gender and warfare with students who were organizing opposition to the U.S. shipment of cruise and Pershing missiles to bases in England and Italy during the last stages of the cold war. By relating contemporary political developments with historical patterns, the Center was able to serve as a cultural organization that enhanced political activity. Although the Center occupied me day and night, I managed in 1985 to join a ready-made family with a partner, Bennett Sims, and a stepdaughter, Abby Sims, who supported my engagement in grassroots movements and joined me in political demonstrations.

At Barnard one Saturday a month for two years a few other engaged feminist intellectuals and I met to study what we jokingly referred to as "motherist movements." In my last year at UCLA, I had written an article on "female consciousness," the ideas some women hold about their rights to confront authorities to protect their families and communities when survival is at stake. The Barnard seminar was a diverse group of historians and other scholars from four continents: Marjorie Agosín, Dana Frank, Ynestra King, Anne McClintock, Marysa Navarro, Ann Snitow, Amy Swerdlow, Meredeth Tax, Marilyn Young, and Teresa Valdez. We gathered each month to study testimonial literature and histories of militant women who had fought against repressive governments. As leftist feminists, we generally identified ourselves as sisters and citizens rather than as mothers, even though we were mothers, and one a grandmother. Separately and together, we had been involved in feminist movements that established the rights of women to be serious and have fun; to speak openly about sexuality and to practice any form of it we liked; to hold any job, gain equal salaries, and have as many or as few children as we wished. Yet, in the Barnard seminar, we studied movements of other kinds of women, those who denied their own needs and legitimated themselves by reference to dire circumstances entailing the loss of life and the survival of their communities.

After nearly a decade as director of the Center, it was time for new leadership, and I moved on to join the faculty at the State University of New York at Stony Brook, where I again became deeply involved in teaching and writing Latin American history along with Brooke Larson and Barbara Weinstein. In 1992–93, the year between leaving Barnard and going to Stony Brook, I won a fellowship to the National Humanities Center in North Carolina, an experience that set my life and work on yet another trajectory. Even before going to North Carolina, my own voice had gradually been creeping into what I wrote. Part of this was due to my domestic partner Bennett Sims who was not an academic and encouraged me to discard even the smallest pretence of distance from my subject. Chapters in *Red City, Blue Period*, which appeared before I went to the National Humanities Center, occasionally began with my own observations, but then I quickly disappeared from the story.

At a seminar on subjectivity and personal scholarship at the National Humanities Center, two new friends, Leo Spitzer and Marianne Hirsch, urged me to write more subjectively, and yet I fiercely resisted their suggestions. I wasn't so much constrained by a belief in objectivity as I was shy and in awe of the people about whom I wrote. I chose the documents that made people come alive on the page, but the subjects were the actors, and I was interested in their agency rather than my own. What turned me around was my reintroduction to interviewing participants and using their testimonies as another historical source. I was at the Humanities Center to write a book about the history of six related events, and one of the segments pertained to a group of women activists in northeastern North Carolina. After examining local historical documents, I made contact with Dollie Burwell, who had launched the environmental justice movement in the United States. Burwell is a storyteller like many of the people I grew up with, and taping her life history and her accounts of how she and her neighbors fought against the pollution of the land around them led me to carry out other interviews. Although I had taught Latin American testimonial literature in my courses, I had never used interviews as a major historical source. Though far more rigorous than merely gathering information through stories, integrating people's memories calls on skills I have been developing since childhood. Just as the stories I related at the beginning of this essay have become part of my repertoire, part of my explanation of who I am as a historian, so too, many of the people I began talking to or whose interviews I've read in preparation for my own investigations have also honed their storytelling over many years. As a historian, I am increasingly conscious that stories change and that people integrate new observations and insights into their memories of the past. This is a theme that is apparent in both *Crazy for Democracy*, which features histories of women activists in South Africa and the United States, and *Taking Back the Streets*, which uses oral and written sources to deal with social movements and rituals of resistance in Spain, Chile, and Argentina during their transitions to democracy.

As has probably become clear, my life as a historian continually focuses on politics and people's assessments of what politics means to them. But the attack on the World Trade Center and the Pentagon on September 11, 2001, involved both and marked a turning point in my life and work. I returned to New York from a conference late on Monday night, September 10, 2001. When I heard the news and ran out into the smoke-filled streets the next morning, I felt that New York might be under attack and that the rest of the country would not care. But instead of having my old dreams of annihilation, I felt a sense of collective purpose and spent the day trying to donate blood, getting supplies for rescue workers, and talking to friends and strangers in the street.

Other historians and journalists would not be surprised that I also wanted to document what was happening, to make sure that the perceptions and insights of my neighbors would not be lost. I joined a project organized by Mary Marshall Clark, director of the Oral History Office at Columbia University, to record responses to the attacks. Even though I was now comfortable weaving people's recollections with written sources, I had never before been involved in collecting testimonies designed to remember a single historical event, least of all one that affected me so directly. On September 21, 2001, ten days after the attack, I joined another woman to interview people at Union Square. At that time, most of lower Manhattan was closed to anyone but local residents and rescue workers, and Union Square was the furthest south the public could go. The square had become a place of collective mourning and was filled with impromptu shrines of teddy bears, candles, drawings, and keepsakes of people who disappeared in the World Trade Center.

For the *September 11, 2001 Telling Lives Oral History Project,* we interviewed people right after the attack, so we couldn't employ the life history method, one of the most important techniques in oral history. In doing life histories, participants have an opportunity to discuss their personal backgrounds by presenting their own setting for their stories. By providing historical depth, the life history interview places individuals in a larger historical context. Most of the people we talked to on September 21, 2001, were so traumatized by the loss of a friend or the recollection of some previous horrendous experience that all they could do was talk about what they felt at the moment. Their emotions were too raw to reflect, analyze, and interpret what had happened to them. On the other hand, hearing their stories helped me to cope with my own sadness.

Several of the participants on the project had interviewed people who had survived the Holocaust and many had read literature by survivors of other atrocities. Initially, members of the group chose the people whom they would interview, and after my experiences in Union Square, I decided to focus on owners and employees of some of the small shops surrounding the World Trade Center and on immigrant women, particularly Latinas. My usual concern with the perceptions and voices of ordinary people continued as I tried to come to grips with the disaster. One thing that surprised me was the tenderness strangers expressed for one another, a quality I have often found in accounts of collective crises. Before the attack, the shopkeepers and their employees talked to hundreds of people a day on their way to all kinds of jobs around the World Trade Center. When people bought their lunch, purchased medicine or health food, or got cigarettes or candy, they discussed their lives. The shopkeepers and their customers knew about each other's children and the schools and camps they attended. With the collapse of the buildings, many of the customers simply disappeared, and for a long time the shopkeepers did not know who was alive and who was dead. The majority of the workers I spoke to were Chinese and Eastern European immigrants. A young Chinese man ran a health spa that had become a shelter for rescue workers. A young Bulgarian man who enjoyed ballroom dancing and had won many prizes had protected dozens of people in his postage-stamp-sized dry cleaning shop on Fulton Street. A retired policeman had opened his health food store just two weeks before the attack. When I returned to reinterview these people in February 2002, most of their shops had closed down, and their contact numbers and addresses were no longer functional.

The Latina women I talked to were concerned in the first days with finding undocumented workers who worked in the World Trade Center or were messengers in the surrounding blocks. Some of these people roomed in boarding houses to which they never returned. One man who lived across from a police station in the Bronx disappeared for days after the attack, afraid to come close to any person in authority since he didn't have identity papers. One woman I interviewed came to my house and asked me to raise her nephew if she and her sister were deported. I wrote it all down, conscious more than ever that historians like me would want this kind of personal information in the future.

During this difficult period after the attack, and after Bennett died, six months later, collective intellectual and political activity sustained me. I had just moved to Rutgers, the State University of New Jersey, in the winter of 2002, to join what is widely considered to be the country's foremost program in women's history. I sometimes regard the History Department at Rutgers as a bus where feminist scholars get on at the front and off at the back. I consider every one who has ever taught there to be a faculty colleague: Carolyn Brown, Belinda Davis, Victoria de Grazia, John Gillis, Alice Kessler Harris, Nancy Hewitt, Martha Howell, Samantha Kelly, Seth Koven, Suzanne Lebsock, Phyllis Mack, Bonnie Smith, Judith Walkowitz, and Deborah Grey White. These scholars are equally members of the historical community at Rutgers, and I engage with their work in almost everything I do in my continuing practice of trying to be a good historian.

Several of my friends have taken early retirement, and they generally say that it's like having a Guggenheim every year. I've enjoyed my years of leave, but I always feel thrilled to go back to teaching and participating in seminars. I'm hungry for the company of historians and feminist scholars from a variety of disciplines and love the world that colleagues and students keep opening up to me. I like hearing their arguments and welcome a growing ability of historians to combine cultural and social history. All my work has considered how people come to believe what they do and how they change their minds or contend with ideologies that others believe. My work on Picasso as a largely apolitical bystander forced to choose sides in the social conflicts in Barcelona expressed my conviction that almost everyone must sometime stand up for what he or she believes. Wars, especially the Cuban war for independence from Spain and the Spanish-American War, have captured my interest along with the editorial cartoons and ads that were so important during those conflicts. Increasingly, gender analysis, especially investigations into how racism and sexism has contributed to a sense of masculinity among liberal imperialists, has reshaped the way I analyze material in the history of art and politics.

Becoming and being a historian means many things, but my sense of vocation has always been tied to the search for social justice that I have carried on along with a community of largely feminist activists. For me history is similar to the kind of truth Antjie Krog, a poet and journalist, hoped the Truth and Reconciliation Commission might offer in South Africa. She wanted to hear "the widest possible compilation of people's perceptions, stories, myths and experiences to restore memory and foster a new humanity." For Krog, this connected to "justice in its deepest sense." Of course historians do more than compile memories and myths, but many work precisely in this way. I think that by seeking truths, historians can help sustain decency against lies told to preserve the status quo and to prevent a sense that ordinary people can change history. Paradoxically, at a time when politicians make more and more allusions to the meaning of history, there is less knowledge about how variable the lessons of history really are.

In a confusing period of history, I feel increasingly engaged as a historian who writes about storytelling, oral history, women's movements, rituals, and resistance. Since the time I built the waterwheel in my bathtub, I have been the kind of historian who tries to understand what others find obvious. But it is precisely because history and the pursuit of social justice are so connected that historical writing is even more important to me now than it ever was.

PAUL ROBINSON

Becoming a Gay Historian

I feel slightly fraudulent writing an essay about how I became a historian. Truth to tell, I am not sure that I am a historian, even though I have spent forty years as a member of the Stanford History Department. My sense of identification with the historical profession is less than complete, and I often think that history has simply provided a convenient intellectual home for my diverse and unconventional interests. I suspect that intellectual historians are especially apt to consider themselves outliers within the profession. Often they feel greater affinity with members of the literature and philosophy departments than with their fellow historians. Of course one might argue that history's great virtue is precisely its tolerance for diversity, its willingness to let individual scholars pursue their demons.

My early years, spent in and around San Diego, gave little indication that I would one day become an intellectual, never mind a historian. I was always an overachiever and a grade-grubber, but I had no real intellectual interests. Most striking for someone who would spend his life writing books, I was not a reader. The only exception was L. Frank Baum's *The Wizard of Oz*, which I practically committed to memory, without any awareness, apparently, that it might mark me as queer. I was exquisitely attuned to the pleasures and conventions of Southern California life in the 1950s. My neighborhood of three-bedroom homes was completely white, without even a Jew, all the mothers housewives, and everyone, except my parents, Republican. I was devoted to being with-it, which meant wearing the right clothes (my t-shirt sleeves turned up exactly two times) and driving a cool car (a 1951 Mercury, lowered, leaded, with pipes).

Ironically, my obsession with cars provided me with the first occasion to exercise my mind. I collected automobile advertisements from magazines. I also made trips to the local dealerships to gather brochures. The intellectual exercise consisted in my organizing these ads and brochures into a strict hierarchy from Cadillacs, Lincolns, and Chryslers at the top to Chevrolets, Fords, and Plymouths at the bottom. My collection perfectly reflected the vulgar commodity culture of the 1950s, but at the same time it let me apply my powers of analysis and judgment to bringing order to a mass of random particulars. Today I own a Cadillac, proving Freud's contention that our deepest wishes originate in childhood.

My high school singularly failed to introduce me to the charms of history. There were no courses on European or world history, only a state-required U.S. survey, which was badly taught and consisted mainly of dates and personalities. My one brush with genuine intellectual passion came from two dedicated teachers of English and American literature. In the American class I became transfixed by Thomas Wolfe's *Look Homeward, Angel*, which was the subject of my first extended piece of writing. I have avoided looking at the novel since, for fear that it would confirm my baleful adolescent tastes. My paper advanced the ludicrously provincial thesis that *Look Homeward, Angel* was "the great American novel." Still, it marked an important step in my emerging identity as an intellectual and a writer.

Although I lacked intellectual interests, I became deeply interested in politics. I date the onset of my political awareness to the 1948 election, when my family voted for Truman while the rest of the neighborhood voted for Dewey. My father must have been impressed by my precocious convictions, because he asked me if I understood the difference between Democrats and Republicans. "Yes," I answered, "Democrats are from the South, while Republicans are from the North." He immediately corrected me: "No, Democrats are for the poor, Republicans for the rich." In that moment my ideological formation was complete.

Even more central to my young life than politics, however, was music. Early on music became the source of my most intense emotional experiences, and it also contributed more substantially to my intellectual growth than did either books or teachers. As a small child I listened repeatedly to my paternal grandmother's 78 rpm recordings of two pieces by Beethoven: the Emperor Concerto (performed by Artur Schnabel) and the Appassionata Sonata (performed by Artur Rubenstein). Although neither of my parents was musical, they gave me piano lessons, and, most important, they let me buy my own record player. In the 1950s I became a member of the Columbia Long-Playing Record Club, through which I gradually acquired a collection of orchestral classics from the long nineteenth century. To this day musical Romanticism remains my aesthetic center of gravity, and when I later came to appreciate literary Romanticism (above all, Wordsworth), it was as an extension of my earlier love for the music of the era. In my career as a historian, I eventually figured out how to incorporate music into my scholarly work, notably in *Opera and Ideas*, which I consider my best book. It is the most striking instance of continuity in my intellectual and emotional life.

Listening to my records and later playing some of the pieces in the local youth orchestra introduced me to a distinctly historical way of thinking. Essential to my experience of this music was the idea of development. First at the level of individual careers, above all Beethoven's, I attended to the evolution of the composer's art—from the Haydnesque classicism of the First Symphony to the grandiose romanticism of the Ninth. More important, the entire history of orchestral music in the nineteenth century impressed me as a single story of development, in which the harmonic, rhythmic, and orchestral techniques of Beethoven were elaborated and enriched by his successors, from Schubert to Strauss. When I became an intellectual historian, I imported this conception from the history of music to the history of ideas. But I must immediately add that the idea of development was not the same as the idea of progress, for it did not follow that the later (more developed) works were of greater merit. I believe the same is true of the history of thought: it is a story of development but not necessarily of progress. Music, then, provided me with a powerful yet supple idea for thinking about the past.

I should not overstate the intellectual nature of my response to music. In *Opera and Ideas* I argue that intellectual history can illuminate the history of music, but from the beginning my response to music has always been more visceral than conceptual. Whenever I felt gloomy (about which more in a moment), I would closet myself in my bedroom and put on a Toscanini or Szell recording of one of the Beethoven symphonies, and my spirits would lift. You could say there was a tension in my reaction to music: it had an important mental dimension—it was good for thought—but it also drew me away from the mental into a realm of unutterable emotion. Today I still spend a great deal of time listening to music—admittedly,

more opera than instrumental music—yet, even though I have made a career writing on the ties between music and ideas, my primary response
remains emotional.

Unmentioned to this point is the subject about which I thought more
intensely (certainly more anxiously) than any other, and to which much of
my scholarly work would be devoted: sex. Until puberty I had led a conventional, if uneventful, heterosexual life. I pursued a series of childhood
romances with little girls in the neighborhood—usually with remarkable
persistence and reasonable success. True, I was a disappointment to my
athletic father, but otherwise I was a manly little boy. Indeed, my automobile collection put me at the stereotypical end of the 1950s masculinity
spectrum. But when I entered puberty, I discovered a sudden and myste-
rious attraction to boys. It was a profoundly distressing experience, which
I remember comparing to the earlier discovery that I suffered from a seiz-
ure disorder: "You thought that was bad," I reflected, "but it was nothing compared to this." Just as I had kept my seizures hidden (until my attentive mother confronted me about them), I knew instinctively that my
untoward sexual desires must remain secret. Outside of a few enclaves like
New York and San Francisco, homosexuality was unthinkable in the 1950s:
there was not even a public language for it. I don't recall whether I entertained the vain hope that it was just a phase and I would eventually return
to the heterosexual ways of my childhood. But, given the intensity of my
feelings, I think I knew I was in for a long, hard siege.

In freshman year of high school, homosexuality, as it were, went from
theory to practice. I was seduced by the oboe player in the band, a senior.
The experience was ecstatic, confirming in spades that my attraction was
neither passing nor trivial. It also contained important lessons for how
homosexuality was to be thought about and dealt with under conditions
of extreme repression. For one thing, the affair was conducted in utter
silence, both in bed and in our daily interactions as friends and fellow
band members. The silence was more than a matter of personal reticence:
what we were doing was unspeakable, in the literal sense that no discourse
for it had yet been invented, at least not in our middle-class suburban
universe. Even more revealing, my seducer was engaged to a flute player
in the band, whom he had got pregnant and who, in a wonderful irony,
played the Virgin Mary in our school Christmas Pageant. The lesson was
clear: regardless of what you might desire or even do, heterosexual union
was everyone's destiny. Perhaps there was a further lesson for the future

historian: things were not necessarily as they seemed. The Virgin Mary might be having sex. Joseph might be queer.

There were more "boys in the band," and over the course of the next four years I managed to have sex with at least some of them. But I was careful to maintain a heterosexual front. Calling it a "front" isn't exactly right, because, unlike the straight dating recounted in so many gay autobiographies, for me pursuing girls was neither distasteful nor entirely bogus: after all, I intended to get married eventually. I was in fact a fairly ardent wooer of one girl in particular, though I may have been relieved that her puritanical views guaranteed that we would never get beyond heavy necking. Even here there was an interesting gay twist. My chief rival for the girl's affections managed to figure out what I was doing with boys. After a party he followed me and a mutual acquaintance to an isolated location where we were carrying on in a car. He later made menacing allusions to what he knew, but, significantly, he never took advantage of his knowledge to prosecute his case with the girl we were competing over. Even for an interested party, the subject was unspeakable.

In *Gay Lives*, my study of homosexual autobiography, I complain that the story of the closet and its exit is often exaggerated. The typical American gay autobiography is constructed as a Manichean opposition between the darkness and emptiness of the closet and the authenticity and joy that come when the truth is announced. Paul Monette's *Becoming a Man* is the locus classicus of this narrative. Monette insists that his closeted existence was in fact a living death, in which nothing really happened to him and everything he accomplished was phony. From a political perspective it is a useful narrative. But I suspect that for many, perhaps most, gay men of my generation—the quintessential closet generation—it seriously misrepresents a more complex reality. Certainly it does in my case. To be sure, being in the closet was a source of constant and often intense anxiety. One could fairly say it cast a long shadow. But it did not obliterate the satisfactions of my life or render its achievements meaningless. On the contrary, I remember these years as much for their gratifications and successes as for their central misery. I enjoyed my interesting, liberal, funny parents, who were the envy of my friends and entirely devoted to my happiness. Friendship too was important and valued, especially in high school. I was also proud of my academic accomplishments. I even took pride and pleasure in my girlfriend, despite the fact that our relationship served to remind me of my shameful sexual secret. Most of all, I found an almost transcendental joy in the music making and music listening that were so central to my daily life. Historians of homosexuality properly consider the 1950s a uniquely bad time, marked by suffocating repression, McCarthyite hysteria, and a pervasive, unexamined heteronormativity. Yet when I revisit the 1950s in my mind, I think first of the warm, sensual summers at the beach, of my academic and personal successes, of the people I loved and enjoyed, and, not least, of the ecstasies (rather than the agonies) of my first sexual experience. If there was a lesson here for the future historian, it was doubtless an appreciation for ambiguity. Nothing was as bad as it seemed, even if there was always something to worry about.

Music and sex, then, were the great preoccupations of my young life, and music and sex would become the most important subjects of my work as a scholar. They might appear to inhabit opposite poles in my psychic life, music belonging to the realm of thought and aesthetic contemplation—the realm of sublimation, as Freud would say—while sex was rudely material, fleshly, and, in my particular case, illicit as well as dangerous. But in reality the two realms were not opposed to one another. The very fact that my sexual adventures took place in the band created an existential link between the two. More important, sex and music were united by the intensity of the emotions they unleashed in me. I later discovered a substantial body of aesthetic theory, from Plato to Koestenbaum, that associates the musical with the erotic. My enduring intellectual concerns are less disparate than they might at first appear, and they are deeply rooted in the experiences of my early life.

*   *   *

I went to Yale in 1958. Without question it was the most fateful event of my life. College always changes you. But in my case the intellectual distance between my mediocre, provincial high school and the sophisticated culture of Yale was categorical. I do not believe it too grandiose to say that Yale introduced me to the life of the mind. It placed me in the sustained company of powerful and charismatic thinkers who not only taught me a great deal but quickly became models for what I myself wanted to be.

Yale also confirmed my sense of my abilities. Although I got straight A's in high school, I had scored indifferently on the SATs, and no one from my school (so far as I knew) had ever gone to an Ivy League university. I feared—and Yale anticipated—that I would fall into the middle of my class. But in fact I excelled from the beginning—not, I'm sure, on raw intelligence but on determination and discipline. By the end of my sophomore year I had settled easily into the assumption that I would go to graduate school and become a scholar, indeed become an intellectual historian.

That makes too neat a story of my Yale experience. In reality my route to an academic identity was more tortured, as might be expected from the unsettled emotional state in which I departed high school. Certainly the most improbable development of my undergraduate years is that I became a serious Roman Catholic, which dramatically set me apart from the majority of my classmates, the nominally Protestant sons of New York businessmen, primarily intent on following in their fathers' footsteps and (during their sojourn in New Haven) getting laid. I am tempted to say that I was a convert to Catholicism, because it felt like a conversion, but in fact the history of my religious opinions was more complicated. My maternal grandmother had become a Catholic as a girl when her family put her in a convent. She was a lovely, modest woman, who would play an important role in my life over the next few years. Out of respect and affection for her—but ever more half-heartedly—my mother raised my brother and me as Roman Catholics, which meant Sunday mass, catechism classes, first communion, confirmation, and—the most dreaded item—confession. I can recall as a child taking a certain polemical interest in the difference between Catholicism and Protestantism, but religion was marginal to my life. The main source of my worldliness, I'm sure, was my Voltairean father, who made no secret of his anti-clericalism and whose profane and filthy mouth was a constant source of delight to me.

In the most immediate sense, my Yale conversion resulted from the powerfully seductive influence of one of my freshman roommates, a scholarship boy from New Jersey who had himself converted to Catholicism in high school. He was very smart and articulate, with a particular gift for philosophical argument, which he applied to me with relentless zeal. I recall being aware of a barely suppressed erotic undercurrent in our relationship. He was not attractive, but when we had had enough to drink (which was a large part of undergraduate life in those days, even among the pious) he became inappropriately intimate. He was the first example of what would become a pattern in my Catholic friendships: almost all of them had a distinctly homoerotic feel. And in fact many of these friends eventually came out and pursued openly gay lives. When I later sought to make sense of my Catholic phase, I concluded that sex was the key to the matter. I became alienated from my zealous and oppressive roommate even before I left the Church, and I lost track of him after college. But I heard that he had become a radio evangelist in the Midwest.

Through him I was introduced to a number of other Catholics, the most influential of whom were two graduate students from Holy Cross, one studying Renaissance history with Hajo Holborn, the other writing a dissertation on Carlyle in the English Department. What most impressed me about these two was that they combined piety with sophistication. Their devotion did not keep them from being fierce critics of the Church, with more than a suggestion of heresy. From them I also learned that becoming a Roman Catholic did not entail becoming a political reactionary. On the contrary, like most of my Yale Catholic friends, they were firmly on the left. Moreover, the fact that they were both getting Ph.D.s fed into my own emerging scholarly identity. The young historian also served another function: he was the first opera queen I met, a discovery with both sexual and aesthetic implications. He invited me to his apartment to listen to recordings. I particularly remember his trying to persuade me that Joan Sutherland's Lucia was preferable to Maria Callas's (a deeply wrong-headed judgment, as I knew even then). The faintly homoerotic atmosphere of these sessions hinted at an affinity between opera and sexual dissidence, an affinity I would explore in my essay "The Opera Queen." Later in life, without having entirely repudiated Catholicism, my historian friend got involved in the gay pornography business.

Over the course of the next three years I became deeply enmeshed in Catholic life at Yale. Before long I was going to church every day, indeed often serving mass at the crack of dawn. In the summers I went to daily mass with my maternal grandmother, whose selflessness served as a model for what I wanted to become. Inevitably I started to think that I might have a vocation. Celibacy, after all, was the permanent solution to the sexual problem. I don't know how close I came, but I could well have ended up one of those priests exposed years later for sexual misconduct with their charges. In my junior year, members of Opus Dei, the Spanish Catholic organization with Fascist connections, tried to get their fangs into me. They sent emissaries from their Boston house, where I attended more than one weekend retreat.

There was an unmistakable Oedipal element in this entire exercise. My poor father, so abjectly proud of me, was devastated by my newfound religiosity, which he viewed as a repudiation of his enlightened values. He greeted the prospect that I might become a priest with horror. I don't remember that he ever called the Church *l'infâme*, but the word exactly captures his sentiments. At the conscious level our relationship had always been good, but clearly there remained unconscious tensions, which even then I suspected had something to do with my sexual predicament. He died of a heart attack early in my senior year, just as I was beginning to liberate myself from Catholicism and embrace again the rationalist values we had long shared.

When I think about my Catholic experience in psychological terms, I am convinced that it was an effort to deal with my homosexuality. It was, in effect, a ritual of avoidance. The great practical advantage of becoming a Catholic was that it categorically prohibited me from indulging my desires. Indeed, it made even thinking about those desires illicit. In just the years when, according to Alfred Kinsey, male libido is at its peak, I invoked the aid of this ancient religious tradition to block out the very thought of sex. It was, moreover, an extremely successful strategy: I would be in my midtwenties before I again had sex with a man. At the same time, I was seduced not just by the prospect of avoiding sexual depravity. The main attraction of Christianity was the promise that it would transform you—that, in Saint Paul's words, it would replace the old man, slave to the body, with a new man, born to freedom and virtue. For three years I entertained the hope that I would undergo such a transformation, and I threw myself into the rituals that were supposed to make it happen. Precisely the failure of that effort led to my eventual disillusionment with Catholicism. Despite years of daily mass and enforced chastity, I was, I found, the same flawed creature I had been from the start. In a word, conversion didn't work. It was at this point that Freud came to my assistance: in Freud I found the great critic of conversion, the thinker who, more than any other, insists that our ability to change is drastically limited. We are condemned to remain the self we have always been.

I have spoken so far about the psychological import of my undergraduate turn to religion. But it was no less significant for my intellectual development. In an important sense, Roman Catholicism was the main vehicle through which I found my professional calling, even though it encouraged a habit of mind antithetical to that cultivated by the historical profession. Put another way, Catholicism made me a serious thinker, but not a properly disinterested one. My undergraduate education consisted of a dialectical negotiation between the believer's pursuit of theological truth and the historian's commitment to impartial understanding. Admittedly, the opposition is overdrawn, for historians are seldom morally neutral, and theologians are not immune to evidence. But there remains a fundamental difference of sensibility between the two enterprises. In my undergraduate courses and writings I was often torn between these contradictory impulses.

I did not take a history course until my sophomore year. My first inclination was to study philosophy. I enrolled in a survey of the history of philosophy, from Plato to Whitehead, taught by the senior members of the department, and then in a more specialized course in which I wrote a long essay on Anselm's ontological argument, comparing it to Karl Barth's modern appropriation of the argument. At this point in my conversion, I was persuaded that the strongest evidence for religion was supplied by philosophical proofs for the existence of God, above all Aquinas's third way, the so-called argument from contingency, which in my mind reduced itself to the question, "Why is there something rather than nothing?" I'm not sure I entirely believed the ontological argument, which I now see as an obvious verbal ruse, but my paper was as much a work of advocacy as analysis. I was eager to show that proofs for God's existence were intellectually respectable—indeed, that they posed the only really serious question.

But I was not a natural philosopher. Right from the start I sensed that philosophical debate didn't suit my talents. I would later say that I was not smart enough to be a philosopher. As a graduate student I was delighted to come across Henry Thomas Buckle's famous put-down of the historical profession: "Any author who from indolence of thought, or from natural incapacity, is unfit to deal with the highest branches of knowledge [such as philosophy] has only to pass some years in reading a certain number of books, and then he is qualified to be an historian." I no longer subscribe to Buckle's judgment. Philosophers, I've found, are perfectly capable of being stupid, while the best historians (such as Thucydides) are masterly dialecticians. But there is a real difference in the kind of intelligence required of the historian and the philosopher. In intellectual history I would discover a discipline that allowed me to address the issues that drew me to philosophy, but without the peculiarly abstract demands I found uncongenial in philosophy.

My first history course was Yale's famous European survey, History 10, the early-modern part of which was taught by a young Reformation scholar, Charles Garside. He was a colorful and partisan lecturer. I recall that after presenting the sequential careers of Charles V (good) and Philip II (bad), he ended by intoning, "I *hate* Philip the Second." In my junior year some of my Catholic friends and I took his undergraduate seminar on the Reformation. It was very much a kind of polemical confrontation, in which Garside defended Protestantism, while my friends and I argued the case for the Church. In terms of my developing professional identity, then, my work with Garside was a mixed blessing, since it encouraged my dogmatic tendencies even as it introduced me to a sophisticated understanding of a great episode in European history. There was, moreover, a troubling personal dimension to the relationship. Garside failed to get tenure at Yale and spent most of his career at Rice, where he was largely unproductive and suffered increasingly from ill health. He was already a heavy drinker at Yale, and on more than one occasion he showed up drunk at our dorm. I sensed at the time that he was another of those tortured souls suffering from "my problem," which he was trying to cope with through a combination of religious repression, alcohol, and inappropriate familiarity with his students. I think of him with a shudder of recognition, but also with gratitude for his having guided me, however inconsistently, toward my eventual career.

A more judicious model was supplied, ironically, by a scholar at the Yale Divinity School, Hans Frei, a German Jewish émigré who had become an Episcopal minister and a student of nineteenth-century Christology. His class on the history of Christianity, while not untouched by confessional passion, was very much a course in intellectual history. I readily identified not merely with his formidable powers of analysis but also with the wit and good humor he brought to the task. He seemed blessedly free of the anguish that troubled so many of my religious friends. He was exactly the sort of intellectual and pedagogue I hoped to become.

Three other undergraduate teachers influenced my decision to become a historian. The first was Stanley Mellon, the author of a book on the political uses of history in the Restoration, who had just come to Yale from Berkeley to teach French history. He was a compelling if idiosyncratic lecturer, who seemed to be speaking to a nonexistent balcony. My religious convictions were not at stake in the story of modern France, at least not the way they were in the Reformation or the history of Christianity. So I entered into the course in a more properly historical spirit. True, I learned to hate Edmund Burke when we read the *Reflections on the Revolution in France*, an antipathy that was to stay with me the rest of my life. But the role of the Catholic Church in modern France was so odious that I had no trouble siding with the Dreyfusards or against the Action Française. Mellon's lectures taught me that history, far from being the mindless string of facts lamented by Henry Thomas Buckle, was in reality a sustained argument with the past: above all it was an interpretive enterprise. He also introduced me to the use of literature as a historical source: we read Stendhal's

The Red and the Black to get a sense of the Restoration and Anatole France's *Penguin Island* to conjure up the late nineteenth century. His-torical study, I found out, was intimately connected to the sorts of ideas that had attracted me to philosophy. After the class ended, Mellon took me to lunch and listened to my plans to become an intellectual historian. He was encouraging, but he urged me to keep an open mind about just what kind of historian I wanted to be. His personal attention, as well as his intel-lectual example, made me feel that I was already a member of the guild.

A very different kind of inspiration was provided by Leonard Krieger, Hajo Holborn's prize student, whose "The Rise of the Modern State" lec-tures were a tour de force. Krieger was a surprisingly genial lecturer, ban-tering with the members of the football team in the class, but the analysis he advanced was pitched at the highest level of abstraction, more like phi-losophy than history. My friends and I struggled to follow his intricate di-alectical conception, which moved from the "structure" to the "form" and finally to the "content" of the state. It was thrilling to hear history pursued on such an elevated intellectual plane. Yet in a way it was too elevated: there was something a little bloodless about the parade of abstractions. I greatly admired Krieger's rigor, but my own brand of history, I knew, would have to be more down-to-earth. I remember buying a copy of his study *The German Idea of Freedom*, which, when I finally got around to it in graduate school, turned out to be the most difficult history book I had ever read. It was rather like reading Hegel himself.

The teacher who, more than any other, provided an example I iden-tified with was Martin Duberman, who lived in a faculty apartment in my college and from whom I took a seminar on American history. His influence was one of manner and style rather than substance. True, I ad-mired his intellectual radicalism, especially his effort to rescue the Abo-litionists from condescension. But by this point I was exclusively inter-ested in Europe and—as if in reaction to my obsession with "the great American novel" during high school—had decided that America was an intellectual wasteland. At the time I had no inkling that our lives were secretly linked or, of course, that nearly forty years later his autobiogra-phy, *Cures*, would become a subject of analysis in my book *Gay Lives*. He was already leading a double existence: during the week in New Haven he was a successful young scholar who brought attractive dates to the col-lege dining hall, while on weekends in New York he was chasing boys and subjecting himself to a punishing regimen of psychoanalytic treatment to turn himself into a straight man. I've already noted that I was sensitive to the repressed homosexual inclinations of many of my Yale friends and teachers. But in Duberman's case I remained oblivious, less because my gaydar was defective than because his heterosexual disguise was so successful. He seemed remarkably self-assured, yet also modest and candid. I especially remember a conversation after his first book—a biography of Charles Francis Adams—was published. I already identified strongly with this epochal moment in the life of a scholar, and I brought along a copy of the book for him to inscribe. Yet he surprised me by speaking about how he still felt divided between a career as a historian and one as an imaginative writer—and in fact a few years later he enjoyed a great success with his play about segregation, *In White America*. Precisely the combination of analytic intelligence, unpretentiousness, and plain speaking seemed not only admirable but something that I could reasonably hope to emulate. In *Gay Lives* I give an account of our somewhat troubled relationship over the subsequent decades, when I lagged behind him in the decision to come out professionally. I am sorry to say that he was very unhappy with my analysis of *Cures*, which, in an angry three-page letter, he denounced as "ungenerous." I thought I had created a fundamentally admiring portrait, but writing about the living, I've learned, is a treacherous business.

My last year at Yale was mainly devoted to extricating myself from the Church. I was helped along by a few of my friends, who were also undergoing deconversions, notably the Holy Cross graduate writing a dissertation on Carlyle. He introduced me to two books that, a few years later, would become the subjects of my doctoral dissertation: Herbert Marcuse's *Eros and Civilization* and Norman O. Brown's *Life against Death*. In them I found a fusion of psychoanalysis and radical politics that appealed to my disillusioned yet still hungry state of mind. They marked my first exposure to Freud, who, as already noted, served as a primary guide in my escape from religion. In particular I embraced Freud's antiphilosophical prejudice, which has stayed with me ever since, though it might more readily be associated with Wittgenstein or with the Keats of Negative Capability fame: we must forgo hankering after knowledge of things that are unknowable, indeed unthinkable, such as why there is something rather than nothing. Wisdom, in this view, rests in accepting our mental limitations. Put another way, we should think about the things we *can* think about. "Whereof one cannot speak," as the man said, "thereof one must be silent."

Two other tasks occupied my senior year. The first was applying to graduate school. I can't say that I approached the job very responsibly.

My Holy Cross friend had also directed me to H. Stuart Hughes's book *Consciousness and Society: The Reorientation of European Social Thought 1890–1930*, and after reading parts of it I got the sense that Hughes was the sort of scholar I would like to work with. But mainly I decided to apply to Harvard (and only Harvard) because of the vague impression that it was the place to go. An even weightier motive, I fear, was that Harvard did not require the Graduate Record Exam, and I knew from my earlier experience with the SAT that I was unlikely to distinguish myself. So I made no effort to find out about other scholars—such as Carl Schorske at Berkeley—who might be appropriate mentors.

The second decision I reached was to delay graduate study for a year in order to spend time in Germany. The immediate reason was to learn German, because I found my intellectual interest increasingly drawn to German-speaking figures, like Freud and Marx. I was also tired of being a student and looked forward to spending the first year of my life since kindergarten free of academic responsibilities. There was the further consideration that I was about to become a European historian and yet I had never been to Europe. At a deeper psychological level I felt I needed to leave the country to escape the web of Roman Catholic ties in which I had entangled myself as an undergraduate. Earlier I suggested that becoming a Catholic was mainly a defense mechanism against my homosexuality. But quitting the Church did not yet mean facing the truth about myself. I was far from ready for that, and, more important, neither were the times. Rather, I imagined my European sojourn in terms of a new personal project: I hoped that romance might bring me something of the happiness I had vainly sought in religion. So, like many young men before me, I went to Europe to fall in love. Moreover, it worked after a fashion: in Berlin I met a young woman whom I would marry two years later. Still, I have to say that, on the whole, I did a better job of learning German.

*   *   *

After the excitements—intellectual and emotional—of my undergraduate career, graduate school was a big disappointment. Above all it brought a drastic sense of intellectual reduction. Where for four years I had ranged over philosophy, literature, religion, and history in the company of both undergraduates and graduates from a variety of disciplines, I now found myself surrounded exclusively by would-be European historians, pursuing a course of study intended to qualify me for an academic job. Even

without the intellectual narrowing, graduate school is probably doomed
to be an unhappy experience: you are no longer in the first blush of youth,
yet you remain poor and dependent, even as your former undergraduate
friends enter the adult world of work and domesticity. Harvard, moreover, seemed to pride itself on fostering a cut-throat intellectual ethos.
One heard that students hid books on library reserve to keep their com-
petitors in the dark. The atmosphere was suffused with anxiety and alienation.

My cohort of first-year Europeanists numbered about a dozen, virtually all of whom went on to distinguished professional careers, among
them Elizabeth Fox (later Fox-Genovese) and Edward Shorter. Our main
collective enterprise was a year-long colloquium that introduced us to
some of the major issues and literature in modern European history. It
was run by Stuart Hughes and Mack Walker, who, as an assistant professor and hence destined to be exiled from Harvard, was treated like a
lackey by his senior colleagues. Other department members came when
their expertise was relevant to the topic. I was responsible for a presentation on the causes of the First World War, which was attended by the
grand old man of the department, William Langer. He was the great authority on modern European diplomatic history, so I was flattered that he
found my remarks not insensible.

Graduate school, as everyone learns, is a relatively inefficient method
of education, in which much of your work seems unrelated to your supposed area of specialization. I had come to Harvard to study modern European intellectual history with Stuart Hughes, and I eventually wrote my
dissertation under his direction. But I never took a seminar from him,
because he didn't offer one while I was in residence. Rather, like all my
classmates, I enrolled in the two European seminars being given that year,
both of which, as it happened, were on topics in early-modern social history. Thus in the first semester I found myself in Franklin Ford's course
on seventeenth-century cities. Ford—who had just become dean of arts
and sciences and taught his seminar in a university mansion on Brattle
Street—had published a book on early-modern Strasbourg. He assigned
each of us a city to write about, with a view to compiling a collective
portrait of European urban life in the era. I was assigned Basel, and I
proceeded to write a paper on the confrontation between Basel and the
encroaching French state of Louis XIV. Needless to say, it had nothing to
do with modern intellectual history, indeed with any kind of intellectual
history. Yet so fragile was my emerging professional identity that I began

to think that I should perhaps become an early-modern social historian myself. Social history, one sensed, was the coming thing, and by sticking with intellectual history I was perhaps consigning myself to a backwater of the profession. By the middle of the semester I had moved in with two of my colleagues, Bill Beik and David Hunt, who had already decided to specialize in early-modern social history. The wave of the future seemed clear.

In the spring, with the same cast of characters, I took Crane Brinton's seminar on eighteenth-century France. Once again, all the papers were on social topics, so I settled on a study of tax farmers. By this time I had begun to find the conceptual puzzles of early-modern history intriguing and to appreciate the high intellectual quality of the scholarship in the field. I also discovered that I was skilled at this kind of analysis: both of my seminar papers were well received. Everything seemed to be conspiring to direct me into the field.

I didn't need to make a decision about the matter until I chose a dissertation topic. The next stage of graduate training was the oral examination. Harvard required you to be examined in four fields, one of which had to be in ancient or medieval history. The rule of thumb was that you prepared a reading list of about fifty books in each field. I settled on medieval France under Charles Taylor, early-modern intellectual history under Crane Brinton, modern Germany under Fritz Ringer, and modern intellectual history under Stuart Hughes. Virtually the entirety of my second year was devoted to this reading. I took elaborate notes and did extensive reviews. I even conducted mock exams with some of my fellow students. Yet despite my diligent preparation my performance on the orals was unimpressive. Later I heard that my fellowship was going to be reduced in favor of my classmates who had outperformed me on the orals. I felt I was in a kind of professional no-man's land.

As I recovered from the trauma of the orals, I gradually found my way back to my original idea of becoming a modern European intellectual historian. The reading I had done to prepare for Stuart Hughes's field obviously pointed me in that direction. But more important was the teaching I did at Harvard. For two years I taught in Harvard's Social Studies program. Alongside Martin Peretz—who would later become the owner of *The New Republic*—I led discussions of the great modern social theorists, from Tocqueville and Marx through Weber, Durkheim, and Freud. These, I found, were definitely my people. I abandoned any idea of becoming an early-modern social historian and began to look in earnest for a dissertation topic that would let me pursue my real interest in modern thought. At some point I recalled my undergraduate enthusiasm for the ideas of Herbert Marcuse and Norman O. Brown, and, working almost entirely on my own, I managed to transform that enthusiasm into a feasible topic. In the end, my graduate training turned out to be largely irrelevant to the dissertation I in fact wrote and the professional career it launched.

I have overstated the case, and I should give some credit here to Stuart Hughes's example and permissive guidance. In my essay "H. Stuart Hughes and Intellectual History" (reprinted in *Opera, Sex, and Other Vital Matters*), I have already written a tribute to Hughes and recounted how our somewhat impersonal relationship at Harvard blossomed into genuine friendship after he moved to San Diego in the 1970s. He was not my teacher in the way that Charles Garside, Hans Frei, Stanley Mellon, and Martin Duberman had been at Yale. But his books were a singular illustration of the kind of history I wanted to write and, even more, of the kind of prose I hoped to emulate. Equally important, he provided just the right combination of indulgence and support when it came to my dissertation. He was in Europe on sabbatical when I began writing, but he responded to my chapters with letters that buoyed my confidence. I was especially flattered when he told me that he was reading the chapters to his wife, Judy. Albeit in absentia, he proved a true mentor.

The drama of my academic life in graduate school was nothing compared to the drama of my personal life in those same years. Moreover, the two dramas remain intermingled in my mind. I won't say that the struggle to become a European intellectual historian was inseparable from the struggle to become a gay man. But without question the sexual saga had its professional consequences.

During my first year at Harvard I proposed, by mail, to the young woman I had met and courted in Berlin the previous year. Ute Brosche was a lovely, sophisticated, and deeply good-hearted student of English literature at the Free University. Her English was in fact better than my German, though in the early years we spoke mainly the latter. When she accepted my proposal, I returned to Germany in the summer of 1964. We were married at the city hall in Bochum, where her family lived, and spent our honeymoon at her grandmother's home across the border from Salzburg. We then returned to the small third-floor apartment I had rented in North Cambridge. Our daughter, Susan, was born less than two years later.

I have much to answer for in this episode. Objectively speaking, I behaved selfishly, for I knew full well that I was not firing on all cylinders.

But I'm not going to beat up on myself. I was acting in good faith on the virtually universal sexual assumptions of the day. I felt I had enough heterosexual interest to make a go of the relationship, and I was certainly more attracted to Ute than any other woman I had met. Had I been born just a few years later—and the great cultural shifts of the 1960s had begun to kick in—I am certain I would have made a different decision. But, under the historical circumstances, I began my year of preparing for the oral exam as a new husband. To say that my heart was only half in it would be an exaggeration.

One fateful evening, perhaps already in the first year of our marriage, I went to a Boston Celtics game with some of my fellow grad students. As we walked from the subway to the sports arena, we passed the open front door of a bar. I was able to make out enough of the clientele to figure out instantly what kind of place it was, and I resolved to return. It was in fact Boston's most famous gay bar, Sporters. Why I was so alert to the significance of the establishment I don't know. I presume I must have received some early signals from the culture. The country was on the verge of a historic change, especially on the two coasts.

Over the next couple of years I returned to Sporters—and other such venues—repeatedly. Because I was married, I had to pick up men who would take me to their place, though sometimes we rented a hotel room. Later I occasionally took tricks to the office provided for me by the Social Studies program. I quickly learned two things. First, the sex was just as good as I remembered from high school—and vastly better than straight sex. Second—putting together the pieces from the stories of the men I met—I saw that these men inhabited a well-established underworld of friends and lovers, a world they considered not merely a site of fleeting and guilty pick-ups but the permanent domain of their lives. I learned, in other words, that you could live as a homosexual, even though the life might be less than ideal.

For perhaps two years, as I moved from my orals to writing my dissertation, I remained in this schizophrenic world of marriage and gay infidelity. Then at the beginning of 1967 came a series of developments that drastically changed everything. The first was that I got offered a job at Stanford. I had written Stanford that I was planning to visit my Palo Alto relatives at Christmas 1966 and suggested they might want to interview me. In those days jobs were not advertised, but I knew through the grapevine that Stanford was looking for a modern intellectual historian. In fact they had already offered the job to several candidates, who, for one reason or another, had not panned out. The "hiring process" was nothing like what it has become. I had a chat with various senior members of the department and was taken to lunch. I gave no job talk and met no graduate students. At one moment I was left alone in the chairman's office, where the letters from my Harvard professors were strewn on the table (I peeked). I suspect that Stuart Hughes's recommendation carried special weight. Several members of the Stanford department had served with him in the OSS, and he had taught there in the 1950s. A few weeks later I got the offer.

So I knew that I would be moving to California in the fall of 1967. Then the inevitable happened: in February of 1967 I met a man in Sporters with whom I rather quickly fell in love. Practically overnight, and with surprisingly little anguish, I decided I wanted to live with him. Although radical and with profound implications (for several parties), the decision seemed almost easy: what I felt for him was categorically more intense than anything I had felt for my wife (or any other woman). Indeed, not to act on the feeling, I thought, would be almost stupid. So in a matter of weeks I made the necessary decisions and spoke to the necessary people, and before the end of March I had moved into my boyfriend's Beacon Hill apartment. The nation was still two years shy of Stonewall, but clearly the logic of gay liberation had begun to reach me.

The hardest part of course was telling my wife. She had left her native Germany to come live with me and had patiently endured the deprivations of graduate student life for nearly three years. More important, we had a one-year-old child. Since I had got the Stanford job, she thought the family was about to move to California and properly begin our grown-up life. I think she may have had some inkling of what was amiss. But she was still shocked and angry. Nevertheless she agreed to a divorce, which committed me to pay about half my Stanford salary in alimony and child-support. We would suffer a few rough years, until she married another academic, who turned out to be a superb father to our daughter. Ute's liberality and fair-mindedness guaranteed that she would ultimately welcome me back into her life, and even after Susan had grown up we remained in close touch. In April 2006, some forty-two years after our marriage, she suffered a fatal heart attack. In one of our last conversations she told me she thought of me not as her former husband but simply as an old friend. It is an unsettling experience for a gay man to find himself suddenly widowed.

Telling my family was less daunting. I began with my brother, who was broadminded and affectionate and who of course gained a certain moral

authority as the last standing straight man in the family. I relied on him
to convey the news to our mother. I knew she would be unhappy, if only
because she was very fond of my wife. And, indeed, she was in a funk
for a few weeks before she succumbed to the family's almost congenital
liberalism. The truth is, I had a very easy time of it, at least compared to
the typical gay man coming out in the 1960s. Since I was the official family
genius and was about to get a Ph.D., everyone seemed to assume I must
know what I was doing.

Finally, I had to deal with Stanford. Not that I planned to tell my future
colleagues the truth. On the contrary, from the start I adopted a policy of
"out at home and closeted at work." But my new boyfriend, who was still
in school in Boston, was reluctant to pick up sticks and move to California. So I called David Potter, the department chairman, told him I was
getting divorced, and asked if I could delay my appointment for a year.
He said he sympathized and made reference to his own divorce (which
had in fact prompted him to leave Yale for Stanford), but he insisted that
I must take up my duties in the fall. So in the few months remaining before
I was to depart for California, I had to negotiate my divorce, persuade my
boyfriend to come with me to San Francisco, and find a place there for
him to finish school. In my giddy romantic abandon nothing seemed impossible. Somehow I also managed to finish all but the last chapter of my
dissertation, which I remember typing at the dining table in our one-room
apartment. Throughout this frenetic period I was deliriously happy.

*   *   *

I have a vivid recollection of the important events of my high school,
college, and graduate student years, and I have little trouble locating those
events in place and time. Just the opposite is the case with my now forty
years as an academic. Academic life is profoundly repetitive: one writes
books and teaches courses. In memory it all becomes a blur. I can still recall what might be considered "outside" events, such as my liver transplant,
which occurred in 1988 and about which I've published an essay ("My
Afterlife"). But the work you do writing a book or teaching a course is in-
distinguishable from the work on another book or course. Your life gradually turns into your bibliography: you become a list of publications more
than a living, breathing actor. That's why most academic autobiographies
are so uninteresting. If you want to make something readable of an aca-

demic life, the proper vehicle is the novel, where personal animosities and power struggles, rather than books and courses, can take center stage.

I lived in San Francisco my first two decades at Stanford. I thereby created a thirty-five-mile *cordon sanitaire* between my public and my private life. I had given up driving when I returned from Europe and no longer even had a license. So two or three times a week, at 7:00 in the morning, I took a charter bus from North Beach that brought me to the campus at 8:00. Living in San Francisco had a profound impact on my thinking. The city already had a substantial gay population when I arrived in 1967. But over the next two decades the numbers increased exponentially, and along with them the visibility of gay economic, cultural, and, finally, political institutions. Restaurants, bars, and bathhouses proliferated, the Castro was invented, a gay man was elected supervisor (and subsequently murdered), and, in the 1980s, the AIDS epidemic began. The psychological effects of living day in and day out in such a place were incalculable. Above all, it provided me with a deep sense of comfort and belonging. The personal confidence I derived from living in San Francisco fed inexorably into my confidence as a scholar and teacher. It also influenced the subjects I chose to write about, at first only implicitly, but then ever more directly.

I loved Stanford from the start. To my surprise I found I was especially drawn to my senior colleagues, men (there were no women) a generation older than I. The younger members of the department were nearly all social historians. We shared leftist politics, but they disapproved of my interest in the history of ideas, which, while not as regressive as diplomatic or military history, was nonetheless elitist in their view. By way of contrast, several of my older colleagues—notably Gordon Craig, Gordon Wright, and David Potter—were not merely accomplished scholars but highly cultivated individuals who knew a great deal about literature, art, and ideas. I felt a natural affinity with them, even though they had no particular interest in the figures, like Freud and his disciples, I was writing about. They were also more amusing companions than my earnest but generally humorless contemporaries. It did not hurt that many of these older men—like our Eastern European historian, Wayne Vucinich, and our Latin Americanist, John Johnson—were fond of me and invited me into their homes. They were perhaps tired of being patronized by the younger generation and found me a less critical spirit. Uncharitably, you could say that I had already become an old boy. A great sadness of the past decade has been watching this older generation die off. The last to go—and the one I felt closest to—was Gordon Craig, whom I visited every week in the "health center" where he spent the last year and a half of his life. He remained proud and funny to the end.

I am often asked what it was like being a gay faculty member at Stanford, especially in the early years. Technically I remained closeted at school until 1982, when *Salmagundi* published a correspondence I had with a gay undergraduate ("Dear Paul"—also reprinted in *Opera, Sex, and Other Vital Matters*). During that first decade and a half I felt I had a tacit agreement with my Stanford colleagues. They knew I was living with a man in San Francisco, and some of the younger ones even visited occasionally. I had to endure a certain amount of routine heterosexual chatter, but I never felt obliged to ogle the girls or talk about my romantic life. In other words, my senior colleagues treated me with considerable tact. At no time did I fear that my sexuality posed a threat to my professional advancement. Still, in retrospect I feel I should have come out sooner and more forcibly than I did. I now fully subscribe to the proposition that the closet is a form of self-imposed tutelage and that teachers have a particular obligation to quit it. But ambition and a certain faintheartedness persuaded me to keep my San Francisco and Stanford lives hermetically sealed until well after I had received tenure.

*   *   *

In my scholarship I have followed the principle that you should write about things that really matter to you. Writing is such a precarious undertaking that only genuine passion can sustain you through the long, lonely years it takes to produce a book, and even then the process is hedged about with anxiety and the possibility of failure. More than once, even when past the midway point of composition, I've been overwhelmed by the sense that my "text" was just one damn thing after another. Because I have always picked topics I hoped would sustain my enthusiasm, my writings have not added up to an easily identifiable scholarly profile. I think of myself as a European intellectual historian—and my meat-and-potatoes courses at Stanford have been about the history of thought since the Enlightenment— but I am sometimes identified as a psychoanalyst, sometimes as a sexologist, and sometimes as a historian of music. In my own mind my books are in fact united by certain common themes and assumptions. Over nearly four decades of writing, as I see it, I have had three great subjects: Freud, sex, and opera. All of them are grounded in the experiences of my early life, and at some level of my imagination they are all connected.

Freud has been my most conventional subject. He is after all a canonical figure in Western intellectual history. In this sense my interest in him is no different from my interest in other profoundly original and influential thinkers, like Marx and Darwin. Actually I have written less on Freud himself than on his interpreters and critics. In my dissertation—which with only minor changes became my first book, *The Freudian Left* (1969)—I addressed what I saw as the central issue in interpreting Freud as a social thinker or social philosopher. This Freud appeared to be a profoundly gloomy diagnostician of the human predicament, a man who argued that humanity must learn to live with an ever growing burden of sexual repression and hatred—Freud, if you will, as a kind of anti-Marx.

I felt instinctively that this view was wrong, or at least incomplete, and I set about to expound the ideas of three thinkers who disputed the consensus that psychoanalysis was fundamentally conservative—who insisted, on the contrary, that with a certain amount of intellectual tinkering one could find a way out of the pessimistic conclusions to which Freud's ideas seemed to lead. It was, I hardly need add, a project undertaken very much in the spirit of the 1960s—my modest contribution to the counterculture—and, however indirectly, it allowed me to register a protest against the reigning sexual dispensation.

The central inspiration for this project was Herbert Marcuse's book *Eros and Civilization*, to which the culminating chapter of *The Freudian Left* was devoted. But I preceded my treatment of Marcuse with an analysis of two earlier thinkers, Wilhelm Reich and Geza Roheim, who had anticipated Marcuse's revolutionary interpretation of Freud. Marcuse focused on what Freud himself called "genital tyranny," the way in which over the course of development the child's originally anarchic sexual impulses get subordinated to the genitals. He argued that Freud had wrongly seen this process as a biological inevitability and that we must strive to reverse the process and restore the body to its original "polymorphous perversity." The feature of Marcuse's analysis I found most intriguing was that he expressly presented the homosexual as a kind of psychological hero—a figure that had resisted the repressive regime of genital tyranny. How thrilling that a book published in America at the height of the homophobic 1950s should make the homosexual its psychological protagonist!

In *The Freudian Left* I hit upon a formal device that was to prove useful to me in the future. The book consists of a triptych, the portraits of three thinkers who, taken together, constitute an intellectual tradition. The virtue of the device was that it allowed me to tell the story of an evolving tradition but to devote most of my energy to what I do best as a scholar, namely, the close reading of individual texts. If I am absolutely honest, however, I will have to confess that I fell into the triptych accidentally. I had finished my chapters on Wilhelm Reich and Geza Roheim when, in March of my first year at Stanford, I got a letter from Stuart Hughes saying he expected the rest of the dissertation by May, in time for me to get my degree. I had intended to compose two further portraits, one of Marcuse and the other of Norman O. Brown, who advanced a very similar interpretation of Freud in *Life against Death*. But to finish by May, I decided I would have to reduce my discussion of Brown to a few pages within the Marcuse chapter. Thus did my planned four-part dissertation suddenly become a triptych. I somehow managed to complete the chapter on time, even though I was in the middle of inventing the lectures for my course on European thought. I have repressed all memory of what must have been the most unrelenting period of intellectual labor in my life—much of it, ironically, devoted to the proposition that we can look forward to a future of enhanced sexual freedom.

I always say you have to have luck with books. In the case of *The Freudian Left* I had better luck than I would enjoy with any other book. When I began the dissertation, Marcuse was an obscure professor of philosophy at Brandeis. He was an old friend of Stuart Hughes's (from OSS days) and a teacher of my fellow Harvard instructor Martin Peretz, and through Hughes and Peretz I got an interview with him. I found him a delightful man, with a splendidly dirty mouth. When, however, in the summer of 1968 he was attacked by the American Legion and reactionary congressmen and actually forced into hiding, he became, virtually overnight, a celebrity—"the philosopher of the New Left." Suddenly, and through no virtue of my own, I had a publishable book on my hands. Stuart Hughes put me in touch with his editor at Harper and Row, and within a year they published the dissertation virtually unchanged. The book came out in paperback almost immediately and sold over 20,000 copies. I can even boast that my coinage "the Freudian left" entered the discourse of the period. Significantly the book contains no dedication. In my own mind I had dedicated it to my lover (to use the term we all preferred in those days), and I even entertained the naïve idea that my omission would invite such an interpretation. It was a quintessentially closeted gesture. On the back of the jacket was a large photo of me taken at his family home in Boston.

I returned to Freud over two decades later in another intellectual triptych, only this time my three thinkers were not friendly interpreters seeking to give Freud a more progressive reading but three critics out to show that Freud was dishonest, cowardly, or simply wrong. *The Freudian Left* appeared in the twilight of Freud's midcentury American ascendancy. By the time *Freud and His Critics* appeared in 1993, Freud had suffered over a decade of unrelenting attacks on his character and ideas, and his reputation was in serious decline. Partly out of loyalty to him but also to weigh in on the current debates, I examined the writings of what I considered his three most impressive critics, the sociobiologist Frank Sulloway, the Sanskrit scholar and intellectual gadfly Jeffrey Masson, and the philosopher Adolf Grünbaum. My book provided a close reading of these critics with a view to showing where their arguments lacked cogency or their evidence was unpersuasive. It was necessarily a somewhat scholastic enterprise, though it won substantial praise from Freud's intellectual friends, like Peter Gay. Unaddressed in the book, but lurking on the margins, was the figure of Frederick Crews, whose scathing criticism of Freud was often on my mind. I've continued to teach Freud and occasionally write about him in the years since *Freud and His Critics*, and I've not lost my enthusiasm for him. As I said to Fred Crews when we rode in the same bus after a conference at Yale in 1998, you can't read Freud without falling in love all over again. And of course no one willingly gives up the intellectual heroes of his youth.

*   *   *

I said that sex was my second great subject, but then writing about Freud is already writing about sex. Still, I have managed to make the history of sexual thought, independent of Freud, the subject of three books. In *The Modernization of Sex* (1976) my goal was to show how the distinctively modern way of thinking about sex had developed. Again I settled on three figures: Havelock Ellis, Alfred Kinsey, and William Masters and Virginia Johnson. They represented a logical progression in both method and ideas. Havelock Ellis derived his ideas largely from his correspondents, whose sexual stories were often presented verbatim in the appendices to his volumes. I was especially interested in his study of homosexuality, *Sexual Inversion*, which made the case that homosexuality was not a crime but a congenital disorder. We are now inclined to complain about the "medicalization" of homosexuality in figures like Ellis, but he viewed the shift from a moral to a medical understanding as progressive and humane. Alfred Kinsey's two monumental volumes of the midcentury are based not on correspondents but on the interviews he and his associates conducted with thousands of subjects. He used his findings to disabuse his readers of their conservative sexual assumptions, showing that Americans led much more varied sexual lives—including a good deal more homosexuality—than our official sexual ideology allowed. For their part, Masters and Johnson carried the modern sexual tradition to its logical conclusion: for Kinsey's interviews they substituted the direct observation of human sexual behavior in the laboratory. Curiously, however, their sexual ideas were more conventional than Kinsey's. True, they advanced the cause of feminism by proving there was no such thing as a vaginal orgasm. But their conception of ideal sexual relations remained uncritically heterosexual, even marital. Unlike Kinsey, they were not the gay man's friend.

The Modernization of Sex, in contrast to *The Freudian Left*, was not a lucky book. It appeared in the same year as the English translation of Michel Foucault's *The History of Sexuality*. Imprudently, I wrote a hostile review of Foucault in *The New Republic*, suggesting that my own book was a more reliable guide to the history of sexual opinion than his. I was probably justified in my empirical criticisms, but I woefully failed to appreciate Foucault's conceptual power and originality. I have spent years trying to make amends, especially in my teaching. In any event, Foucault's book fully—and I'm inclined now to say rightly—eclipsed mine. Where my first book had caught a wave of the Zeitgeist, my second seemed curiously out of tune with the times.

In the past decade homosexuality has become the direct and fulltime subject of my writing, as opposed to the implicit and often glancing subject it was in my earlier books. *Gay Lives: Homosexual Autobiography from John Addington Symonds to Paul Monette* (1999) is a study of fourteen autobiographers, all of them intellectuals and artists. The book aims to show how the gay autobiographical tradition has evolved since the late nineteenth century. It is much longer than any of my other books, and with fourteen subjects it might seem to mark a break with my tried-and-true formula of examining thinkers in groups of three. But in fact the tripartite structure can still be detected in the book's organization: it sets six British autobiographers against three from France and five from America.

Gay Lives inspired me to create a Stanford undergraduate seminar on gay autobiography, which I have taught every year but one since 2000. It has been a revealing experience, as well as an entertaining one. We read nine autobiographies by gay men and women—and the occasional transsexual—and at the end the students write their own autobiographical essay. When I first taught the course it was taken exclusively by gay men and the women who love them (to borrow a phrase from the *New Yorker*'s Nancy Franklin). But over the years the constituency has changed in a heartwarming way: I now often have straight men in the course. They take it for what I would call political reasons: as progressives, they feel a kind of obligation to inform themselves about this particular form of oppression. Clearly the world has changed when twenty-year-old heterosexuals no longer feel any embarrassment about enrolling in such a course. True, Stanford is not Oklahoma, but I nonetheless take it as evidence that homophobia is in trouble, perhaps fatally so.

I followed up *Gay Lives* with a book on gay conservatives, *Queer Wars: The New Gay Right and Its Critics* (2005). In it I argue that the emergence of gay conservatism is the most striking recent development in the gay world—and a measure of the extent to which gays have been assimilated into mainstream society. *Queer Wars* focuses on four conservative intellectuals, the most prominent of whom is Andrew Sullivan. I show how these thinkers have broken with the central doctrines of the gay liberation movement of the late 1960s and early 1970s. Not surprisingly, they have been outspoken champions of gay marriage, which they have succeeded in making into the main gay issue of our time. *Queer Wars* also examines the critics of these conservatives—figures, like the literary scholar Michael Warner, who regret their betrayal of the movement's historic commitment to progressive politics, gender liberation, and sexual fulfillment.

*   *   *

Finally, opera. I am convinced that my writings on opera and its relation to intellectual history represent my most important and potentially enduring contribution. What pleases me most about them is the level of passion they achieve, something difficult to do in academic writing. My interest began to shift from orchestral music to opera at Yale. The shift was effected mainly by listening to recordings and to the Saturday afternoon broadcasts from the Met. Moving to San Francisco only increased my interest, and by 1970, despite my poverty, I had bought a subscription to the San Francisco Opera, where I saw around ten productions a year. As the decade progressed I became ever more persuaded that the works I was hearing on the San Francisco stage engaged the same issues I was teaching in my lecture courses on European thought at Stanford: opera, I concluded, was a constituent of intellectual history, just as was the history of painting or the history of the novel.

For a while I thought I would pursue this insight by writing a book on Verdi, who is the central composer in the operatic canon and whose music I found especially beguiling. I actually managed to write a substantial piece of my Verdi study before giving up on it and converting the results into a chapter of a very different book on opera. I figured out I wanted to write something similar to Joseph Kerman's *Opera as Drama*, which I still consider the best opera book I've read: Kerman assesses a handful of operatic masterpieces against the classical (Aristotelian) standards of drama. Only, in my book, the point of reference would be not drama but the history of ideas. I eventually settled on eight works, from Mozart to Strauss, that I related to the major developments in European thought from the Enlightenment to modernism. In each case my argument was based not on the libretto but on the music. I fully accepted Joseph Kerman's dictum that in opera the composer is the dramatist: ideas that do not find musical expression for all practical purposes cease to exist.

Opera and Ideas: From Mozart to Strauss appeared in 1985 and was the subject of a front-page review in the *New York Times Book Review*. It won several prizes and, in its paperback edition, quickly went through three printings. To my surprise it was received sympathetically by the musicological community, which I had feared would view me as a crass interloper. Happily, a younger generation of "new" musicologists, eager to liberate the discipline from its hermetic habits, embraced me as an ally in their campaign to link music to the wider intellectual world. *Opera and Ideas*, in other words, was another lucky book. As I've already intimated, its main strength lies not in the particular hypothesis it advances about opera and the history of thought but in the passion it manages to convey about the works it treats. No comment on the book pleased me more than one reviewer's observation that it was "white hot."

I should not leave the impression that my interest in opera is exclusively or even primarily intellectual. Much of what attracts me to opera is the same stuff that earlier attracted me to instrumental music: it is ultimately unanalyzable but has to do with such structural features as melody, harmony, form, and instrumental timbre. But the primary seduction of opera for me, as for most opera lovers, is still the human voice. If you are not charmed by operatic singing, you will never become devoted to the genre. Perhaps it is an intellectual embarrassment, but I have spent countless hours listening to voices. In the case of certain singers—Martinelli, Callas, Bjoerling, Janowitz—I've come to know the historical trajectory of their vocal evolution so precisely that I can judge within a matter of a year or two when particular recordings were made.

I don't want to end this discussion of the books I've written without saying something about writing itself. From the beginning I've been intensely conscious of wishing to write a certain kind of prose, of which clarity, economy, and elegance are the primary characteristics. I think of it as the plain style. Its bible is Strunk and White's *The Elements of Style*—a book I have recommended to generations of students—and it is embodied for me in a handful of writers I've taken as models, among them George Orwell, Lionel Trilling, and Freud. I've tried not to be dogmatic about the matter, and over the past few decades, as a more difficult and opaque language has invaded the academy, I've been prepared to allow that intellectual complexity sometimes requires a more complex literary manner. I also worry that in my own writing I have been more concerned about good sentences than good ideas. I spend as much time correcting and pruning as I do producing the original draft. My obsession with the plain style, I should add, does not extend to literature. On the contrary, my favorite novelist is Proust, to whom I have become ever more addicted as I've grown older and about whom I would someday like to write a book. If I do, however, it too will be in the plain style.

* * *

I began by raising doubts about my identity as a historian. I've noticed that, in comparison to my departmental colleagues, I have a much less proprietary sense about the discipline and about my subdiscipline within it. I do not worry about whether, when I retire, Stanford will replace me with another European intellectual historian. To be sure, I teach my graduate students about the history of the field, and I have closely followed the careers of its major practitioners: Stuart Hughes, Carl Schorske, and Peter Gay in the previous generation, Robert Darnton, Dominick LaCapra, and Martin Jay in my own. But perhaps because much of my writing has fallen outside the mainstream of European intellectual history (sex and opera have hardly been its central concerns), my narcissistic investment in the field has been relatively modest. And, in any event, disciplines and subdisciplines are ephemeral conventions. To set too much psychological store by their fate would be imprudent.

In the last chapter of *A Room of One's Own*, Virginia Woolf writes, "The truth is, I often like women." I want to echo her, despite the reservations I've expressed: I often like historians, and on the whole I am happy to have spent an intellectual career among them. Perhaps I would have been equally happy in other disciplines—like music or literature—in no small part because I enjoy the routines of academic life. Being a professor is the best imaginable job: you have no boss, you largely control your own time, you work on what interests you, and, not least, you get to spend a lifetime around attractive and eager young people. I find even the bureaucratic routines of the academy diverting: hiring and promoting, admitting graduate students, electing chairmen. About the only thing I dread is discussing "curricular reform."

Still, I admire historians and feel comfortable with them. What I admire most is their intellectual modesty and lack of pretension. The quality reveals itself in a number of ways. It is most obvious in their preference for the plain style, which guarantees that their work can be read beyond the confines of the profession. I also admire their respect for evidence: historians have an instinctive aversion to the categorical and unsupported pronouncements that often mar literary scholarship. A corollary of the respect for evidence is their healthy suspicion of abstraction. Finally, living among historians has the inestimable advantage of serving as an antidote to what I call "the provincialism of the modern." Most of us study things that, from the point of view of world history, happened yesterday and largely in our own backyards. Having colleagues who know about seventeenth-century Russia or ancient China serves as a corrective to this modern myopia. The pervasive spirit of the discipline is cosmopolitan and democratic.

History, then, has provided me with an accommodating home for my labors. Its ecumenical spirit has indulged my rather idiosyncratic passions. Its unpretentious intellectual manners have suited my own preference for clear argument and plain speaking. And the prevailing collegiality of its adepts—certainly at Stanford—has made "going to work" a highly agreeable experience for the past forty years.

Maybe I am a historian after all.

JAMES M. BANNER, JR.

Historian, Improvised

Some historians come by their immersion in the past by virtue of some particular characteristic of family, residence, or historical background. I didn't.

I came from circumstances possessing a history that no family members considered to be of much interest—to them or to me. Like members of many American families, especially those whose earliest members arrived in the United States in the nineteenth century, my grandparents and their parents, and taking after them my own parents, meant to put the past behind them. As a result, I was exposed throughout my childhood to information about the family's past but to no significant parental curiosity about it or its historical context. Until I put the basic facts together in my sixties, no family genealogy existed. History was something my family possessed but not something it had lived. Nor was history, as in so many other cases, something that the family had escaped, although evidence of my family's adaptation to the United States through purposeful assimilation was clear enough. Neither the great Irish famine behind one side of my family, nor the circumscribed opportunities open to most Jews in the nineteenth century on the other side, nor the renown of a German great-grandfather, Louis Bauer, who fled Germany after 1848 and helped establish orthopedic surgery in the United States, were presences in my life in the 1940s. Nor in any deep sense was the Second World War, even though I lost an older cousin at Anzio.

My father, after whom I was named, was the son of second generation, unobserving Jewish parents, Solomon Morrill Banner and Isabelle
Ranger, themselves the children of German and English Jews. An independent New York City businessman like his father before him, my father
was resolutely, if quietly, an American patriot. He rarely mentioned his
ancestry, although he was easy with answering questions about what he
knew. He had not been raised a Jew. Religion meant little to him, and he
ceded the family's religious associations to my mother. Because of his own
parents' assimilating goals, he had attended two schools, the Riverdale
Country Day School in New York City and (the first in his family to graduate from college) Yale, both of which, then more than now, helped compose and educate the northeast's Protestant institutional establishment.

My mother, née Dorothea Bauer, the daughter of a second-generation
German Protestant father, Otto Hudson Bauer, and a second-generation
Irish-American mother, Helen Cecelia Byrne, was raised a Catholic. She,
too, went to schools—Spence in Manhattan, then Abbot Academy in Andover, Massachusetts—desirable to new, as well as old, eastern families,
and she followed that schooling up with a year at Smith College. But true to
the assimilating impulse of her own family and my parents' desire not to
raise their children either as Catholics or Jews, my mother and father's marriage was celebrated not in church or synagogue but at my mother's parents'
apartment and officiated over by—whom else?—an Episcopal priest.

Not surprisingly, I was baptized in that same Episcopal way station
between Catholicism and Judaism and eventually confirmed in the starchy
Calvinism of the Dutch Reformed Church, in which my mother said her
prayers for fifty years. As a result of this exposure to religion, I emerged
steeped in Protestant music, language, and worship, yet I never became religious. With so many roots, my default identity, as we would now say, was
American. When asked of what religion I was, through college I answered
Dutch Reformed. A question about my ethnicity would have met with nothing but perplexity: I wasn't German, or English, or Irish, or Jewish; I was
American—or I was all those elements together and so none of them alone.*

History would thus arrive at the door of my consciousness from outside my own origins. For me, it was unlikely to arrive, as it does for many
historians, from a sense of place. I was not bathed in the storied reality of

* In conversation once with Michael Novak, shortly after he had launched his concept
of the "unmeltable ethnic" on its short career, I asked him how his idea of ethnicity could
encompass ethnic mongrels like me. He had no answer, nor of course did his theory.

a location, like the American South. Born in Manhattan, I spent the years from five through fifteen north of New York in Westchester County and just west of suburban Scarsdale, my childhood post office address. Mine was a diverse community, not nearly so economically homogeneous as more famous Scarsdale. My family's neighbors and my schoolmates were all white and of Western faiths and extractions, but working class children mingled easily with those from professional and commercial middle-class families in school-time and extracurricular camaraderie. If this community had any coherent identity, it took that identity from its proximity to Scarsdale and from the world metropolis only thirty minutes away by train. Manhattan was my lodestar; and in an era of greater ease of mind than today, by age twelve my friends and I were visiting New York City in each other's company.

Because I lacked a family or cultural introduction to the past, when history made itself known to my consciousness, it arrived in the daily news. For a young boy born in 1935, history came in the form of wartime dispatches from Europe and the Pacific (Ed Murrow's "This is London"), and, at war's end, the grand victory parade up Fifth Avenue and the armada of naval vessels in the Hudson. It also made itself known to me through home-front contributions during the war. My father had tried to join the armed forces shortly after Pearl Harbor; but because of a mild case of rheumatic fever as a child he was deemed unfit for military service, even in the stateside officer corps. So he enlisted in the American Red Cross and became a field commander responsible for meeting troop and hospital ships in New York. His involvement in wartime affairs was not the kind to drive home, at least to a child, the dangers of warfare, the sacrifice of family, even the world's peril. And because none of my father's family remained in Europe exposed to the Holocaust, neither the European nor Pacific wars were psychological or blood presences at home. Yet history had begun to seep into my consciousness from the fact that by the age of six my life was affected, however modestly, by air-raid drills, the installation of black-out curtains, and, most actively under my mother's guidance, community-wide drives to collect tin cans, newspapers, and used cooking fat. I joined the war effort as a tot in service to my country and to history—at least to history as that which happens to you until you can affect it yourself, if you can.*

---

* I suspect that, as for a few other historians like Lawrence Stone and Peter Gay, youthful experience with stamp collecting also helped broaden my horizons, give me a sense of

More formally, the past entered my life as knowledge at the Edgemont School (now the Seeley Place School), principally through Lyle L. Flick and O. Stanley Stonesifer. Like so many teachers, these two were far more influential for the men they were than for the history they taught. It's hard for me to summon any precise memories of them now, save for the pleasure they seemed to gain and transmit in what they taught me of government, civics, and the past. Energetic, good-natured, sly in their tributes, sardonic in their criticisms, quite unlike each other but similar in the impressions they left on me, they made history—dare a professional historian use the term today?—fun. At least fun for me. I was a bookish sort of boy, and my parents, while not readers of serious books, indulged my bookish ways and wisely never, then or later, tried to discourage me from following my own inclinations, professional or otherwise. Not naturally athletic or emboldened by the kind of natural good looks or athletic ability that some of my schoolmates could count on for popularity, I was forced back onto what few native strengths I had; and in school my chief strength was getting better grades than most. That ability did not ingratiate me with all my classmates, but it did win me a kind of grudging respect and made me work hard to maintain it. A reader then of fiction, much of what I read were the historical novels of Esther Forbes, Kenneth Roberts, and Walter Scott. While I've lost a taste for that genre now, the romance of "real" historical events held great attraction for this schoolboy, and no doubt that romance was in part responsible for my later attraction to formal knowledge of the past.

But memory of those years is hazy and general at best, and my sense now is that whatever then was drawing me toward history as a subject was oblique, not direct and specific. Not so with the next influence, however paradoxical it was. That influence was Sheldon Howe, a master at Deerfield Academy, the boarding school in western Massachusetts that I attended for the last three years of my schooling. A son of the Connecticut Valley, two of whose oldest family names he carried, Mr. Howe taught junior-year American history. Known behind his back as "Mumbles," not without affection, for his manner of speaking (the result, I later learned, of an injury sustained earlier in life), Mr. Howe was the kind of history teacher much recalled by too many students: a "facts man" who denatured

---

geography and of other times and places, send me to maps, and arouse my curiosity about the people and events depicted on those small bits of paper.

his subject with nothing but textbook explanations. Most would guess that Mr. Howe's teaching was precisely the kind that would turn me away from his subject. Yet no doubt in part because of his instruction, I became a professional historian. I suspect that Sheldon Howe, through his seriousness of purpose and his determination that we know the history of our own land, somehow conveyed to me a sense of the abiding importance of the subject. Still puzzled as to how he did it, I draw from the brute fact of his influence the lesson that teaching and learning remain in their nature great mysteries, different for each one of us.

Except in required English courses, books—entire books—were not part of the Deerfield ethos. In fact, I cannot recall reading a single work of history at Deerfield. The days of supplementary reading, or of lessons taught from documents or conflicting interpretations, or, in eleventh-grade American history, from reading entire works of interpretation, had not yet arrived at that school either. Deerfield in the 1950s—which meant Deerfield under the legendary leadership of Frank L. Boyden—did not much care to nourish the intellectual vigor of its faculty or students. No Henry Bragdon, Exeter's renowned scholar of American history, no Dudley Fitts, Choate's great classicist, ornamented its faculty. In fact, it would not be until the 1970s that the first scholars and artists—people who wrote books and poetry, painted and sculpted, and considered themselves members of the larger world of culture and the intellect—appeared on campus in any numbers. Like so many of those great New England schools, Deerfield meant to nurture character, not mind.

The school did, however, give me confidence in myself as a thinking person, perhaps a budding intellectual. This remembrance would therefore be incomplete were I not to record the effect on me of Bryce V. Lambert, a beloved teacher of English, who, though not a historian, was critically important to my becoming one. I find it something of a curiosity that a teacher who so affected me never taught me in class. Instead, this reserved, dry, and imperturbable son of Maine oversaw the corridor on which I spent my last year at school. Bryce Lambert set for me an example of seriousness and scholarly passion that I had never seen before.

That a teacher can affect you while not teaching you might seem strange to those people educated in American public schools, where teachers are associated with classes and subjects but, because we don't see them outside their classrooms, rarely with life. But in a boarding school, teachers might become your intimates of sorts, however formal that intimacy was, not just during class but the whole day through because you and they happened to live in close proximity. Bryce and I lived together for an academic year—he in his private lodgings at the end of the hall, I down the corridor from him. It was he who got his charges up in the morning, saw us to our desks for study in the evening, checked us into bed at night, and helped see us through the normal confusions and unhappy moments of adolescence. It was he who invited us in for cookies and milk, for conversation (always laced with moral and teacherly lessons), and, probably unconsciously on his part, for a view of how a teacher lived and to what he consecrated his days.

What I saw in Bryce was more than the demands he placed upon us. What caught my attention were the demands he placed upon himself, none of them greater, it seemed to me, than his efforts to stay intellectually alive and engaged through literature. He read a book a day, usually late into the night—classics of English and Continental literature, but also current works of fiction and poetry. "Have you read this?" he would ask, poking some volume into our hands. "You should." "Did you really read that entire book last night?" we would ask, incredulous. "Yes, and I'm going to read that one," he'd say pointing to another, "tonight." The sheer commitment involved in such repeated effort struck me with much force. We were, as others for over forty years were to become, his life. To help his "scholars" (as, significantly, he called us) grow into responsible and knowledgeable young men was his mission. His doing so by a bravura display of intellectual commitment among other faculty members not observably so inclined carried great, distinctive weight.

Yet if, except for one or two people, Deerfield Academy didn't have much direct influence upon my becoming a historian, the town of Deerfield, of which the academy was just one of many historic elements, I suspect did. On the school's ground was an ancient building whose door bore the marks of tomahawk blows struck during the massacre of 1704. The houses lining the street, many hauled in from elsewhere by Henry N. Flynt, then in the midst of his noted reconstruction of the village, were ever present in the lives of each boy. I was in these old houses frequently, and the Connecticut Valley names associated with them bore the authority of age. Each Sunday the entire school (save for the academy's observant Catholic and Jewish boys) gathered in the town's Congregational church whose stark white walls were raised two centuries earlier. More so thus than in my somewhat featureless hometown or rushabout New

York City, history was a presence in Deerfield and entered my youthful consciousness as something worthy of close attention.

*   *   *

Yet it was life's next stage at which history was finally borne in upon me in the formal way that professionals eventually experience it. As I look back now on my four years at Yale, the second stop on a privileged course of education whose good fortune is never far from my mind, I see that they were suffused with exposure to history. And if in Deerfield I absorbed the past through the physical environment of the place, in New Haven history was taught to me by tradition and the Gothic look of the place, by the names carried by its colleges (Jonathan Edwards! Berkeley! Calhoun!), and of course by its faculty members.

My mind had been trained at Deerfield. At Yale it was opened. Many look back on their college years ("bright college years" in the words of Yale's famous song of that name) as a time of football games, fraternity hijinks, and liberation from parental supervision, and so with misty eyes they open their pockets to alma mater in gratitude. My indebtedness to the place springs from its gift to me of four years of unrelieved intellectual excitement and discovery. I had been in museums but knew nothing of the history of art; for years I had played the piano and attended concerts but knew little of the history of music. Plato and Aristotle? I knew their names but had never read them, nor Sophocles and Euripides, Aquinas and Kierkegaard, Homer and Milton. At Deerfield, I may have scanned a line here and there of Coleridge or Keats, but no one had led me to Dickinson or Whitman, Eliot or Stevens, cummings or Pound. And where my schooling had kept me hawsered to study hall desks in preparation for tests and exams, here in New Haven free-flowing, directionless, all-night, and impractical discussions—serious ones—about Luther and Calvin, Freud and Jung, Camus and Sartre, McCarthy and Hiss, Reinhold Niebuhr and even Billy Graham made me alive to ideas I'd never before encountered. It was in college that I found that ideas need not be located only in classrooms or books. They were to be found in the air, in friends' heads, in debates, even in drink. I was awakening to the adventures of thought.

I was fortunate to enter Yale in 1953 during the heyday of a young experiment in undergraduate education, its Directed Studies Program, to which I was admitted. The program was designed to provide organization and coherence to each term's five courses, including mathematics and the sciences, during the first two years of study. Thus in the very first week of freshman year, we dug into Plato in philosophy, Sophocles in literature, and Praxiteles in the history of art. Particularly in freshman year, we proceeded historically through what were then taken to be the canonical works of Western thought, writing, and art—all of course by men, just as everything else at Yale in those days was almost uniformly male. (An introductory biology laboratory instructor of mine was Jane Van Zandt Brower, who became a distinguished biologist.) With the program's faculty members attending weekly lectures in all subjects before leading their own sections, the discussions fit together and gained propulsion from each instructor's involvement in the whole. Chronology was the linking principle, and integration came through the historical parallels between each form of achievement that the program's faculty, so deeply involved in the whole interdisciplinary enterprise, could draw.

One freshman-year instructor I recall in particular, and it's perhaps not surprising that he was the one who, because of his subject, had to hew most closely to historical principles. William H. Jordy, a spirited historian of art, later at Brown, opened up the world of painting and sculpture to me in the very first week of freshman year. I had been led earlier in life to understand that painting was Art and thus important. But I had never thought about art before, never been trained to see and interpret it, and surely I had not recognized that it had a history. Jordy's infectious enthusiasm, his excited explanation of slide images, caught me in the web of art in which I've ever since been happily ensnared. Proceeding chronologically from Mesopotamia to the works of Josef Albers, himself on the Yale faculty, Bill Jordy, revealed to me that aspects of life besides wars and elections had histories.

Yet it was only in the last two years of college that I began to focus my intellectual energies and interests on history—although not too much. I had decided to major in the subject. But such was my interest in philosophy, art, political science, literature, and even science that I was determined to take no more history courses than necessary for my degree. I look back on my junior year in college as key—a time of deeper intellectual, social, and emotional openness and of deepening, serious friendships than I had ever experienced before. And as always, I was keenly influenced by my teachers.

One of them (again) was not a historian, but the great scholar-critic Cleanth Brooks, with whom I studied modern poetry for two terms in ju-

nior year and later became friends. Cleanth was at the height of his powers and influence in the mid-1950s. Owlish through thick-lensed glasses,
avuncular, and soft-spoken, he quietly took us through most of the late
nineteenth and all of the twentieth century's American and British poets.
It was a joy to lose myself in a close reading of a Hardy or Eliot poem, to
hear Cleanth probe at us about structure and meaning. It has always been
a misreading of the New Critics, at least of Cleanth Brooks, to assume that
everything external to a particular poem was forbidden to be considered;
in fact, it was the very richness of metaphors, their furtive and buried allusions, that had to be teased out of poems through consideration of what
lay outside, as well as within, them. In this sense, the New Critics weren't
deconstructionists *avant la lettre*. Not for them Derrida's famous "Il n'y
a pas de hors-texte." Instead in their view, through concentration on the
packed language of a poem (*explication de texte* and "close reading" being the day's terms of trade), one discovered possibility and significance.
Cleanth made me read documents more deeply and carefully than anyone
who ever taught me history.

Similarly with Beekman Cox Cannon, musicologist and later founder
of the Glimmerglass Opera in upstate New York. Those who took his year-
long course in the history of music—a course that began with Gregorian
chant and ended with Bartok—experienced the kind of muscular, confident teaching characteristic of that age when a teacher didn't flinch from
offering up a course that covered over five centuries of history in a year.
"Beeky" was a distinctive man: tall, big, and big-headed, handsome in a
shaggy way, and possessed of a distinctive, upper-crust manner of speaking. He was always excited about music and couldn't help convey his enthusiasm. I recall extending myself mightily to write papers about one of
Haydn's last string quartets and Berlioz's *Symphonie Fantastique*. I suspect that what in part drew me to the subject was its historical nature as
much as the music itself. Almost unaware, I was turning into a historian.

In becoming more of a historian I was surely helped along by William
Huse Dunham, with whom I studied British constitutional history. An understated, matter-of-fact man, Dunham exemplified in his teaching and
scholarship one essential quality in a historian: the search for the most
basic and simplest explanation of any phenomenon. He would have made
a fine scientist. I cannot forget the moment in the first week of class after he'd assigned us a reading of Magna Carta and the relevant chapter in
our text. "What's the significance of Magna Carta?" asked Professor Dunham. After many minutes devoted to many answers, all unsatisfactory in

his eyes, we were vouchsafed his own. "It was written down," he declared. I remember even now being astounded and delighted by the clarity of the explanation—not, to be sure, the full one, but the kind that deserves to be the starting point of any others.

Yet the historian who had the most influence upon me was one I never came to know personally. He flouted most of the conventional tenets of instructional conduct that are now held up to be eternally valid and unfailingly effective. He lectured. He never smiled or told jokes. He held himself aloof and appeared to be unapproachable. No friendly demeanor toward undergraduates offered he. In fact, in the two senior-year semesters in which I sat directly below the stage from which he held forth, I never shook his hand or had a single word with him; and I never met the man. Yet more than any other single person, he made me a historian.

He was Franklin LeVan Baumer, and his year-long course covered the entire Western intellectual tradition from Plato to Camus. Tall, dark-haired, always in dark three-piece suits, his piercing dark eyes covered in dark horn-rimmed glasses, his entire aspect, in fact, entirely dark and forbidding, Baumer, presence and gravitas personified, offered inimitable, full-bodied introductions to the thought of single thinkers in fifty-minute lectures to a roomful of 250 students. Even though he never varied his manner, never tried to adopt himself to the different ideas or dispositions of his subjects, his genius was the ability to make us think that the ideas of each thinker, from however far in the past, were worthy of the deepest respect. Hobbes and Locke were no more or less important to him than Hegel or Nietzsche. Aristotle was as immediate to Frank Baumer as Sartre. What seems additionally remarkable about the course was that it met only twice a week for lectures. No sections, no discussions. Yet those lectures generated conversations among classmates late into the night and set me on my own to reading serious, difficult books with excitement and pleasure. The memory of those lectures remains with me to this day. I can quickly summon the sensation of anticipation with which I looked forward to them, the excitement of the discoveries Frank Baumer never failed to open to me, the pleasure of the struggles to master understanding of some thinker's ideas. If this was what the past was like, filled with such ideas and men (all men—although that fact never crossed my mind), then the past was for me.

Senior year was critical, not only because of Frank Baumer's course, but because it marked the start of the concentration of my historical interests. Save for Sheldon Howe's course at Deerfield, I had formally taken only one course before then in American history, a year-long lecture course in American diplomatic history with Samuel Flagg Bemis. Bemis was a typical unreconstructed teacher in the old mold: he lectured, and we listened. But unlike Baumer, who lectured as if his life and ours depended upon it, Bemis lectured from his own celebrated text. The same sentences about the Hay-Pauncefort Treaty or seals in the Bering Strait that I'd read the night before were rolled out the next morning from the lectern. Not that Bemis couldn't be witty, which he could be, or that his formal manner wasn't distinctive, if somewhat risible. Yet it was hard not to think that diplomatic history was about as dry as a laundry receipt and to conclude that perhaps working in the Foreign Service wasn't for me. Fortunately, the course was rescued by its two "section men," both then graduate students under Bemis's tutelage, John A. Logan and Theodore W. Friend, both of whom went on to distinguished careers as historians and college presidents and remained my friends thereafter.

The only Americanist with whom I studied closely was Winton U. Solberg, then a historian of colonial religion, who subsequently spent most of his professional life at the University of Illinois, where he became the great historian of that institution. For some of us majoring in history, Wint Solberg led a year-long seminar on the American past. Like Bill Dunham, but with more flair, he sought to make his students start with the basics. At the seminar's very first meeting, he handed out assignments to each of us. No choice. To my lot fell a three-page paper, due the following week, on the founding of Yale College. "I can't cover this subject in three pages," I protested. "But you will," came the unsurprising answer. And of course I did—handing in a text spared of all adjectives, nuance, and subtlety but bearing what I had to choose as the most important facts and their relationships.

Wint, with whom I have remained a friend since, took me on as a student in a moment of confusion. I was recovering from the breakup of my first love relationship, and I couldn't decide what I was prepared to do upon graduating. In fact, I didn't want to complete the course's required major paper, and I beseeched him to help me find some other means to gain a grade. With characteristic cleverness, he found a way to hold me to the task. "What current news most grips you these days?" he asked. I was then drenched in deep late-adolescent cynicism about religion and for some reason was groaning my way with some friends through Norman Vincent Peale's *The Power of Positive Thinking*. Wint suggested that I write a paper about Peale's kind of semireligious moralizing and set it in the context of American religion's past. Once I did so and produced a creditable essay, I had the sensation, I recall, that I had proved myself a tyro historian and had greatly enjoyed the work, grateful, as I have remained, for the understanding push of my teacher.

To what degree did I become a historian in New Haven? The nature of Ivy League undergraduate education in the 1950s was not designed to form students into professionals. Instead, some of the greatest practitioners of the liberal arts were still trying, at the end of the era of the confident, canonical arts and sciences curriculum, to form at least some of their students into men of letters. For all its limitations (especially the monochrome attitudes of so many of the university's humanities faculty members, none more implicated in cold-war practices than its historians), it was a glorious moment in collegiate education and, for me, exhilarating. Such a generalist's education, even as a history major, explains my rudimentary introduction at Yale to historiography, to debates among historians, to controversies over, say, the utility of the social sciences for history. History was either delivered to us as packaged knowledge, as Sam Bemis delivered it, or, more surreptitiously, offered as a way of thinking with distinctive characteristics—the manner in which I learned it from Bill Dunham, Frank Baumer, and Wint Solberg. Yet what also strikes me forcibly now is the degree to which history formed the foundation of so much instruction in Yale College. And so while I left Yale with my earlier affection for historical knowledge intact and deepened, paradoxically, because history suffused so much else in the curriculum, that love was not particularly greater than my love of music, art, and philosophy or my interest in the sciences. When I graduated in 1957, I was caught up in the witchery of all ideas, but in no sense could I have been termed a historian.

In fact, I was heading, although somewhat uncertainly, for the law and had been admitted to law school by the time I had my undergraduate degree. But in that era, a young man could safely avoid the linearity of education by joining the peacetime armed forces. So, apprehensive about being drafted and wishing to postpone a decision about law school, I enlisted in the regular U.S. Army for a three-year hitch with the chance of selecting my branch and place of service. That act, like so many in life, turned out to have unanticipated consequences. By good fortune, after basic training at Fort Dix, I spent six months in Baltimore preparing for counterintelligence service, another six months in Monterey, California, studying French, and then received orders to report for duty in France in the fall of 1958. It was my two years in that European country that turned me into a historian of the United States.

*   *   *

It has often enough been remarked that one's identity is thrown into sharp relief in a foreign country. That truism takes on the character of a principle if an American is set down among the French and lives among them, as I did, for two years—living as a civilian though serving in the military. These two peoples, each believing themselves to be exceptional, are not made to understand or accept each other easily, especially when one has recently triumphed in a global war and the other is still finding its way out from occupation, collaboration, and loss. France in the late 1950s remained a postwar nation, its people yet confused and struggling. Parisians had regained their celebrated vitality and sense of superiority, but those in bleak, poor, agricultural, northeastern France, where I was stationed in Verdun, were still not participating fully in the nation's late-1950s recovery from war. Wartime privation still lay everywhere on the land.

Verdun itself was the ravaged center of over a millennium of European warfare. The horrible scars of the First World War were all about; ghastly Douaumont was just over the hills, *La voie sacrée* just down the road. Frequently, *les anciens combatants*, many of them amputees, would gather at the war memorial just across from the apartment in which I lived. But who of my hosts had been complicitous in collaboration or the deportation of Jews? I couldn't very well ask, and they didn't say. In those years, no reckoning with France's recent past having yet taken place (as it still not fully has), a kind of dull suspicion and worry hung over many relationships. More immediately, one was then already surrounded in France by the growing agonies over Algeria, and my work had to accommodate the possibility of threats, however modest, of what we now call terrorism. All of this together meant that for the first time in my life I was drenched in the linked ancientness of the past and immediacy of the present. Not lost on me also was the fact that, serving in the cold-war armed forces and assigned to evaluate the quality of physical security in all American military bases in eastern France, in a small way I was now participating in history.

While I had traveled throughout Europe during an undergraduate summer and had become familiar with different historical cultures, I had never before absorbed other ways through a foreign language nor gained such fresh perspectives on my own country from outside. Now, living in France, I came to see myself as an American. After all, the French saw me as one. Previously, I had taken my nationality for granted. Now I realized how American I was. I was made intently aware of the Americanness of my character, beliefs, and disposition as they rubbed up against those of my hosts. I could take nothing for granted; everything had to be compared to everything else. I was also reminded each day of gaps in my knowledge about my own country as well as about France. The more I read French newspapers and books and traveled about the country for work and pleasure, the more I became fascinated by the differences between my own and this other culture. Yet as my knowledge of France and its history grew, so did the distance between that knowledge and what, comparatively, I knew of the United States. Thus when it came time to choose what I would do upon my discharge from active duty in 1960, I decided against law school and opted instead for a graduate degree in history.

I have since asked myself why I did not become a historian of France. I had become acquainted with much of France, deeply so in the case of its eastern provinces. I had come to speak French with decent fluency (even being accused, especially in Paris, of having *un accent Vosgesien*), and I read it with ease. I could readily have become a historian of that nation. It now seems to me, however, that in France I had come to think of myself deeply, perhaps too deeply, as American. Fascinated with the history of the land of my temporary residence, I had nevertheless been thrown back forcefully there upon my own nationality. On top of my earlier interest in the history of my native country, the power of my now keenly felt national identity seems in retrospect to have made my choice of historical concentration irresistible. Of course, I had no way of knowing how my study of history would affect the person I became and the way I thought. Only slowly would I come to that understanding.

So I left France in the spring of 1960, spent four months learning German in Munich in preparation for my language exams, and matriculated at Columbia in the fall of that year. That institution was then in the last years of its tranquility and at the height of its intellectual and institutional influence. No university in the country could equal its social science and history departments in the quality, range, and impact of what we would now term their public intellectuals—figures like Richard Hofstadter, Lionel Trilling, C. Wright Mills, Daniel Bell, and Robert K. Merton. Yet the university was administratively ossified, and its stance toward its graduate students undermined their loyalty to it. While no one could have predicted in 1960 the university's blowup in 1968, all was clearly not well on Morningside Heights.

Students in Columbia's graduate school of arts and sciences were expected to study and survive by their own wits—and on their own funds. In this, a Columbia graduate education came about as close as one could come to European-style preparation in the United States. You would succeed or fail on your own; and if you failed, no one would notice. A guide for graduate students written by Columbia's polymath Jacques Barzun made that clear. The university seemed determined to let you educate yourself and almost willfully refused to do it for you—a defensible enough stance if designed carefully to aid the maturation of scholars. While the approach worked well enough for me, it was carried to such extremes that it seriously injured other students and was slowly sapping the university from within.

In history, so large was the number of annual matriculants, most of them women pursuing their master's degrees to further their teaching careers and never to be seen again, that the department could hardly keep track of us; and many of its faculty members acted as if only those admitted to the doctoral program after a year's probation in master's study warranted attention. Most of the department's offerings were lecture courses with upwards of fifty students, and in that regard the quality of my early graduate education was lower than my education at Yale, where a higher proportion of courses were small. Especially in the second and third years of study, when one prepared for general examinations, the inattention of the faculty threw students back upon each other. The study group that a few of us pulled together for self-education was a kind of protective mechanism that offset the anomie of graduate student life while helping prepare us for our oral examinations. My cohort of Americanists—Gerald McFarland, Herbert Johnson, Norman Fiering, Daniel Leab, Linda Kerber, Alan Graebner, and my close friend from undergraduate days Otis Graham—became a kind of conventicle, a self-support seminar that met weekly to discuss specific topics, test us with mock examinations, and sustain us until we scattered to complete our dissertations.

I find it hard to imagine what trying to complete a Columbia course of study must have been like for those who didn't have the encouragement and friendship of fellow students. I recall my own evenings of confusion and self-questioning. Did I wish to devote my professional life to isolated, lonely research? Was I cut out for academic, rather than a more engaged public, life? Did I have the stuff to make it through graduate school and then to stick out the struggles for employment and tenure? I can't imagine that most graduate students, especially in the humanities, with their lonely roads of research and solitary writing, don't awaken to similar doubts, aren't assailed by similar anxieties about talent, perseverance, and life ahead. How different for me, at any rate, were those sometimes searing doubts from the exciting discoveries and unbounded confidence of undergraduate days.

Lest one think that, as it may often look to others, every historical scholar marches an unswerving course from matriculation to degree, such was not my case. I still harbored an interest in the law, as attested by the subject of my exercise-like master's essay on the jurisprudence of a Supreme Court justice. And so during the second term of my inaugural year of study I nearly stepped aside from history in favor of legal studies. I was demoralized by the nature of graduate work, unmoored in the impersonality of Columbia, not yet appreciative of the benefits of being left alone to learn, and not finding much satisfaction teaching various kinds of courses elsewhere in the city (despite help from the GI Bill) to make ends meet. Those few months of perplexity and unhappiness ended after I passed easily enough over the hurdles to a master's degree, but they alerted me to the fact that even the most confident graduate students that I later taught might well be hiding the same anxieties and confusion that I had felt.

Since those days on Morningside Heights I have come to believe that the inner turmoil of that first year of graduate study arose from the absence of the emotional fervor that, because of my undergraduate experience, I had come to assume attaches to all intellectual discovery. It does not and probably cannot. I was naïve in thinking that it might. The yearning for an extension into graduate school of the often-comforting instruction, friendships, and experiences of collegiate life now strikes me as natural. Yet on the road to becoming a professional, a concentration of mind and spirit upon the goal rather than the process seems inevitable. Rather than open itself up, a graduate student's mind must concentrate itself. Particularly on the lengthy road to a doctorate in history, a longer course to the senior degree than in most other disciplines, one must focus and do so all on one's own. This leaves little time or energy, little openness, for the discoveries that can attend the mind's flowering into adulthood during college. On the contrary: graduate study is depleting and exacting; it requires the postponement of much, often too much. I recall those few years of graduate study—years also of marriage—as a time of painful and injurious emotional flatness, anxiety, and uncertainty. I was learning, I was becoming a professional historian, but I cannot say that I gained much pleasure from doing so. Satisfaction yes, especially when it was built upon the acceptance and esteem of my teachers. But of the giddy excitement of undergraduate learning and life there was little.

Fortunately, at Columbia there were enough oases of seminar study, distinctive teaching, and student friendship to sustain me. I was introduced to the professional study of history in my first year of graduate school by Robert D. Cross, later president of Swarthmore College and, after that, a member of the faculty of the University of Virginia. Bob was smart, tough, even-tempered, and thoughtful—a prince of a man with an elegant and penetrating mind. What's more, he, above all others with whom I studied at Columbia, introduced me to the new social scientific history and seemed determined to train his students to be historians.* Only a few others on the faculty, and perhaps none more so than Richard Hofstadter, were absorbing the theories and findings of the social sciences to enrich their history. But had I been assigned to a seminar other than Bob Cross's, such was the nature of the department's faculty that I might never have heard of, much less read, any of that day's new social and political history. In fact, while it can be said that I was trained as a historian on Morningside Heights, I was not fully prepared in consonance with the discipline's contemporary developments. The university's history department, incorrectly thought of, because of Hofstadter's fame, as the seat of social science thinking, was nothing of the sort. Most of its senior members, all men, superb as they may have been, were traditionalists in their approaches to the past. You learned of historical thought there but were lucky to be exposed to its most exciting and influential contemporary currents. That would come later—and elsewhere.

One decisive, altogether positive offsetting quality of the department was its requirements for study. While preparing for general examinations in your principle field, you were expected to master a minor field. In Columbia's history department, that meant, for an Americanist, preparing yourself in two centuries of European history (my choice) as well as in all of American history—from the seventeenth century to the present. Such breadth of preparation was distinctive, perhaps unique, for its time. Soon, at Columbia and elsewhere, you could become an Americanist by

* Here I follow Alice Kessler-Harris's penetrating distinction between *having* graduate students and *training* them. I was never trained. My teachers taught me the results, never the process, of doing history; they showed what they and others had done, not how they had done it.

studying American history only—and then not even all of that; you could
get by with, say, only American history through the Civil War, or after
it. But in the early 1960s, the Columbia history department still sought
to force its students into breadth, even if breadth in its case had more to
do with geography and chronology than with the fresh intellectual waves
flowing through the discipline. Thus I studied with Garrett Mattingly, then
at the peak of his powers, Peter Gay, just making his mark, French economic historian Shepard B. Clough, Europeanist Walter L. Dorn, and
outside the department the great sociologist Robert K. Merton, as well
as with peppery colonialist Richard B. Morris, lively William E. Leucht-
enburg then in the early stages of a distinguished career, Henry Steele
Commager, visiting from Amherst, whose lectures were an unending tor-
rent of ideas and words, and, above all, Eric L. McKitrick.*

It may have been that my years in France had laid the groundwork
for my never becoming too narrowly an Americanist, but my study at
Columbia forced me to remain as broadly educated as any graduate curriculum could spur me to be. No longer is that the case, in large part because of the financial support that's now more readily available to graduate students than it was fifty years ago. At 1960s Columbia, if particular
graduate students in one of the humanities departments weren't asked,
as most were not, to teach a section of the university's famed undergraduate contemporary civilization or humanities courses, they had to fend
for themselves. Such was my lot. For a number of years I made my way
as fledgling historian by teaching current events to young women at a
fashion school downtown, a world history course at Bronx Community
College, the first half of the American history survey at Hunter College,
and a course, spanning the entire nation's history, at the Rosemary Hall
School, a private school for girls then in Greenwich, Connecticut, now
part of the Choate-Rosemary Hall School in Wallingford, Connecticut,
where my wife Lois was teaching. These experiences had two salutary
consequences. By instructing others in subjects beyond my emerging specialty, the history of the early American nation, I was able to deepen and

* Garrett Mattingly, not to live long after I took a course with him, warrants particular
mention for his distinctive manner of teaching. With a small notebook in hand, he leaned
standing against the desk in the front of the room and chatted about the past. The very first
day of class, he recommended that we not take his course. Why? Because, he said, we could
learn far more in the library in an hour than by listening to him for sixty minutes. Then he
began to talk about his subject—the late Renaissance—and held everyone in thrall for the
rest of the time. No library was ever so appealing.

broaden my historical knowledge in much of Western history. In addition, before I took full-time academic employment, I had taught a diverse range of students. I have ever since believed that those programs that too well fund their students and confine their students' teaching to limited areas of the curriculum are doing them a disservice.

One particularly distinctive influence, Eric McKitrick, was a former student of Richard Hofstader, and had joined the Columbia faculty the year I commenced graduate school. I registered for his first course—a lecture course—my very first term on campus. Within no time, I concluded that his was the most distinctive mind I had ever encountered, and I think that to this day. Possessing a ruminative intelligence, comfortable with counterfactual speculation, always indirect in expression, Eric was just enjoying the triumph of his superb work on Andrew Johnson. In addition, as the intellectual twin of his close friend Stanley Elkins, whom Eric had met when both were studying under Hofstadter, he was commencing his shift from the Civil War era back toward the early republic. Like Mattingly and Merton, he stood before a class and thought his way wonderingly through a subject. Rather than offering the results of a mind that had already settled an issue (the way most teachers present themselves), Eric's teaching offered a mind at work, one wrestling with a subject and thinking through the thickets of problems any intellectual endeavor presents. In full command of his subject—at that time the American Civil War and Reconstruction—he possessed the confidence and courage to risk exposure of his ignorance, puzzlement, and confusion where it might arise and to throw himself on the assistance of his students. Thinking the world slightly absurd, he had an intelligence that attacked problems obliquely and rarely head on. It was this quality that lent all his work both freshness and fascination. It was he, more than anyone else, who made me think like a historian.

But it was to the example of Richard Hofstadter that I set my compass. I was determined to study with him. Teachers' fame, not just their abilities as teachers or emollience of disposition, draws students to them. I could just as well have benefited from choosing Eric McKitrick or a number of others as my *Doktorvater*. But it was Hofstadter of whom I'd heard in college; it was Hofstadter whose name appeared in the occasional American magazine or critical journal that found its way to me in France; and so it was toward his office door that I aimed. And thus I came to study with him, and thus he, in close association with Eric McKitrick, came to guide the remainder of my doctoral studies.

It would be incorrect to say, as the convention has it, that one studied *with* Dick Hofstadter. Rather, one studied *to* him. One observed his mind at work, read his histories for their subtleties and manner as well as for their brilliant arguments. But one was not taught by him. His mind, as many experienced, was incandescent. Beyond their substance, what made his written works distinctive was their brilliant colloquial style and the flow of their informality. In social company, Hofstadter was witty and tart. In class he was almost inert. It was known that he gained little satisfaction from teaching. Surely that was true in his doctoral seminar, although, since I never heard him lecture, he may have come alive at the lectern. In a seminar with roughly ten students, including Linda Kerber and Otis Graham, he let us discuss the books he assigned without often intervening, probing, or inquiring. By 1961, he was becoming interested in the birth of political parties, and so the reading for his seminar started with literature about the pre-Revolutionary years and moved toward the Jacksonian era. But I don't recall his ever telling us that we were accompanying him on a fresh intellectual voyage, or that he wanted us to help him think through the history of the republic's early decades. Nor did he try to make our readings cumulative in their impact or significance. It was as if he and we were going through required motions. Interesting enough, but his great mind was rarely revealed to us. True to the university's ethos, we were on our own, even in his office.

If I were going to study with Hofstadter, what was I to do to satisfy him? On my own, I had become interested in the nation's early years, and so his seminar's readings had a particular importance for me. But a general interest is not a dissertation topic. The history of New England drew me in. "Why not write on the New England elite?" he suggested, clearly wanting me to do so for his benefit. After rooting around for some weeks in the existing literature on that subject, I decided it wasn't for me. But something—I don't now recall what—gave me the idea to focus on the origins of political parties in New England, an idea that eventuated in a more particular emphasis upon the Federalists. Fine with me, in effect he said. So, after passing my general examinations (before him and Eric McKitrick, Peter Gay, and Orest Ranum), off I went after all in pursuit of a portion of the New England elite, genus politicus. That was in 1963. Not until five years later, with characteristic Columbia "speed" (little financial aid, much extracurricular teaching), did I put an end to the dissertation and land my doctoral degree.

It was through the research and writing of my dissertation, with the help of an SSRC fellowship, that I took a giant leap toward becoming a historian. Traveling to archival collections, often in tiny local libraries and public records offices, amassing and trying to keep control of piles of notes, running (quite rudimentary) statistical calculations of voting results, excruciating (a nice eighteenth-century word) my eyes over microfilm readers, and doing all this on my own, with no supervision—"Show me your first three or four chapters," was Dick Hofstadter's direction—cast me back upon myself and on the succor and support of those similarly situated.

Writing a dissertation in history is, as is so much labor in the disciplines of the humanities, autonomous, lonely, and hard. Taking notes in archives, discussing your project with aspiring and experienced colleagues, learning from books, articles, and other sources—these are passive activities. By contrast, writing a book-length manuscript is active work. You're thrown in upon yourself, the limits of your own mind, the intractability of the sources. It isn't always fun, even if it provides many satisfactions. But I found in myself the disposition to write a book; I conquered the loneliness of the effort; I slowly gained some pleasure from what I was producing. And so when I received Hofstadter's nod of approval—an enthusiastic one—for the first half of the work, I finally knew that I could make the grade and before long seek a full-time academic berth.

No doubt because of Hofstadter's confidence in me, I found that berth in 1966. Two years before I had my degree in hand, I was offered an instructorship at Princeton. I could not have been fully aware until later of the extraordinary professional moment in which I had prepared myself to be a historian and was now seeking my first professional post. For my cohort, positions were plentiful; the old patronage-based, male way of placing students was still intact; the rank of instructorship existed; and you didn't have to have a published book in hand to land a teaching job. No doubt someone at Princeton placed a call to Hofstadter, who recommended me. Within a few days of a perfunctory interview, I learned that I had passed muster and been invited to join one of the world's premier departments. Little did I know that I was about to begin in earnest my real education as a historian and that at Princeton I was to become a professional.

* * *

While I cannot speak for the fifteen or so others who, within a year or two on either side of 1966 also joined the Princeton history department as instructors, I immediately found that what I began to learn from my senior colleagues, to say nothing of my fellow fledglings, put into the shadows most of what I'd learned at Columbia. Here was one of the most powerful and diverse collections of up-to-date historical minds in the world. Its diversity was what made it great; ideas of all sorts—traditional, Marxist, social scientific, theoretical—were being put to critical scrutiny by the members of that department in ways unsurpassed elsewhere. Where else could one have found such a diverse collection of historians as the tough, shrewd, old-style medievalist Joe Strayer who had built this great department after the Second World War, Woodrow Wilson's biographer and editor Arthur Link, historian of science Charles Gillispie, internationally influential theoretician Tom Kuhn, traditional narrativist Eric Goldman, Russianist and historian of modernization Cy Black, Europeanist Jerry Blum, historians of China Fritz Mote and Jim Liu, Near Eastern historian Carl Brown, Russian cultural historian Jim Billington, gentle and shrewd colonialist Frank Craven, diplomatic historian Dick Challener, radical Marty Duberman, historian of Japan Marius Jansen, Latin Americanist Stanley Stein, *marxissant* Arno Mayer, and, not long after I arrived, cultural historians Carl Schorske and Natalie Zemon Davis? And where else at the time could I have attended the kind of fast-paced, intense, critical, and wide-open discussions overseen by that acerb democrat Lawrence Stone but in the department's Davis Seminar—a seminar attended by graduate students and visitors, as well as by faculty members and Davis Center fellows? At that moment, there was probably no other department like Princeton's in the world. What made it particularly distinctive was that, because small, it was more cohesive and collegial than most, even while becoming increasingly diverse.*

---

* This is the place to recall the group of unsurpassed near contemporaries who populated the department in my years there: John Gillis, Jim McPherson, Sheldon Hackney, Bob Darnton, Jack Talbott, Don Mathews, John Schrecker, Ted Rabb, David Hammack, Jim Obelkevich, the late Gerry Warden, Dick Wortman, Bill Jordan, Fred Notehelfer, Nancy Weiss (now Nancy Weiss Malkiel and the department's first woman member), John Shy, David Bien, Dan Baugh, Charles McClellan, Stanley Coben, Ginny Yans-Mclaughlin, Gerry Geison (now deceased), John Servos, Greg Roeber, Bob Tignor, James Henretta, Bob Gilmore, Elain Tyler May, Lary May, Ted Brown, Bob Cuff (also now dead), Fred Starr, Jim Bell, Dorothy Ross, Lamar Cecil, John Jeffries, Richard Andrews, Jim McLachlan, Bill Leary, John Coverdale, Bob McKeon, David Flaherty, Peter Winn, Marty Sherwin, Estelle Freedman, Pat Geary,

To be sure, you had to have a tough hide to survive in that atmosphere. While the pressures and anxieties of completing my dissertation, seeing to its publication in revised form (as *To The Hartford Convention* [1969]), and waiting to learn if I might make it through to tenure in that department kept putting me to severe tests, somehow, also, there was exhilaration. It was a kind of bracing, heady involvement in the discovery of new ideas and perspectives that I'd never felt in graduate school, except for Eric McKitrick's class and during one three-week period—tellingly, outside Columbia—when in the summer of 1965 I attended the first seminar on statistical methods for historians hosted by the Inter-University Consortium for Political Research in Ann Arbor. While others recall the Princeton department as a place of intellectual tensions, backbiting, and unnecessary pressure, I recall it as a spirited intellectual community that I'd never found before. Not only was the department filled with great, mature historical minds, lively younger instructors, and some of the best graduate students in the country, it was also the temporary resting place of three or four Davis Fellows a year and the term- or year-long stopover point for the likes of Emmanuel Le Roy Ladurie and Pierre Goubert, as well as many others from France, Britain, and Germany; and it gained, as did I, from proximity to the members of the Institute for Advanced Study, like Felix Gilbert, and its annual fellows. Never, perhaps, was a single department the beneficiary per capita of so many historians in temporary residence. During a year I spent later at the Charles Warren Center for Studies in American History at Harvard, the members of that university's history department seemed to go out of their way to avoid the seven or eight of us temporarily there, and its public seminars were sleepy and pallid compared with those of Princeton. Many deride Princeton for its insularity, suburban isolation, and comparatively small size. Yet it was precisely that small size, the concentration of its intellectual resources in a small town, and the ratio of its faculty members and visiting historians to its students that made it so powerful and influential an institution.

I also gained from being married to a historian, Lois W. Banner, whom I had met when, like I, she was entering graduate study at Columbia. Lois brought different perspectives, especially knowledge of the history of women and professional involvement in women's affairs, into my professional life. Fighting in those early years of women's professional advancement

---

Tony Grafton, Mike Mahoney (now dead), Doug Greenberg, Jerry Siegel, and John Murrin. I may inadvertently have forgotten one or two.

to make her way as a Columbia graduate student and then as an irregular member of the Douglass College faculty, she strengthened my native disposition to be suspicious of conventional ideas and practices and to take a more sharply critical view of the attitudes and ways of my colleagues. It did our marriage, which eventually failed, no good to be subjected to the stresses of dual career advancement while raising a child, our daughter Olivia, later joined by her brother Gideon. The fact that we were involved in the same discipline meant that our home was too intensely focused around the same matters. Rarely was there a break from the pressures and, in Lois's particular case, the protracted battles and anxieties over her search for steady employment as a historian. Necessarily, I privately fought those battles with her, occasionally for her, and bore part of their emotional freight. I'm not sure that many marriages could have survived those complex stresses and the expenditure of emotional capital that ought to have gone into ourselves rather than into our work. Be that as it may, this is an appropriate place to salute my partner of those years for her fortitude and strength of character and to acknowledge the contribution she made to my own understanding of our discipline and of the academic setting in which I was then practicing it.

And practicing it as fully as I could: if Princeton was the place I came to intellectual maturity as a historian, it was also the place I became a professional teacher of history and a professional historian in most other ways, or at least as close to being a full professional as a traditional academic career then allowed. Not that that occurred by direction. On the contrary: as remains largely the case for historians and probably most academics, I became a self-taught teacher and professional. No one instructed me in classroom techniques and conduct; no one took me aside to initiate me into the mysteries of search committees, the institutions of the discipline, or the opportunities to serve as historian outside academia. As in so many other respects, I was left to learn about my professional world on my own.

Teaching took place at Princeton by immersion. You showed up for your first year, were told that you were going to "precept" for senior members of the faculty, and were dropped into those small classes to lead discussion and fend for yourself. While you attended each lecture of the course in which you were "precepting," your more senior colleague teaching the course never visited your own preceptorial classroom. So how did you learn whether you were teaching well, and how was your teaching evaluated? You learned by talking with other junior colleagues, recalling how others had taught you, watching how others lectured, and calling upon your own skills and temperament. You became a teacher of history by yourself.

As for other professional skills, these, too, I gained from doing, not from being taught. Most academic historians, especially those at a university like Princeton, defined, and still define, professional responsibilities narrowly. To serve on a committee of the American Historical Association, evaluate applications for fellowships to the American Council of Learned Societies or the National Endowment for the Humanities, read manuscripts submitted to presses for publication, review books for scholarly journals, and deliver papers at professional meetings then constituted the kind of activities that passed for "professional." Other, equally worthy professional activities, such as offering in-service instruction to school teachers, giving advice to the producers of historical films, or consulting, as I did with other historians in 1974 for the Impeachment Inquiry of the House of Representatives, were considered not really "professional," even if not actively discouraged.* Since the Princeton department, like most then, was composed of many historians who considered it inconceivable, irrelevant, or *infra dignitatem* to venture far outside academic walls with their historical knowledge, and who adhered to the invidious distinction between academic and public historian, on-the-job training in extramural history work had to stand in for a purposeful education in it. A cloistered virtue stood in the way, as it still too often stands in the way, of a full embrace of the entire professional world of the discipline.

Yet such were the opportunities that came from being a member of the Princeton faculty that all manner of diverse opportunities to contribute as a historian outside academia frequently came along. I found myself

---

* I don't recall ever being asked by colleagues to discuss or assess my contribution as historian to the Impeachment Inquiry. Far more significant was the treatment accorded Eric Goldman upon his return to the department in 1966, the year I joined the department, from leave in Lyndon Johnson's White House. To my knowledge, Eric was never asked by the department to make a presentation about his experiences in Washington. Worse, some of his young colleagues worked to keep students out of his previously oversubscribed course on modern America, and he learned of their subversion. What remains with me to this day is the sense of impotent shame—I was then but a powerless instructor on one-year appointment— as I watched colleagues turn their backs on Eric for his "complicity" with the Johnson administration and eventually drive that sensitive man into bitter seclusion. An analogous case: Joe Strayer's and Cy Black's deep and extensive involvement in national intelligence issues were considered private matters not for discussion with colleagues and certainly not useful for instructional or exemplary purposes with graduate students. I have to admit that I never asked them about their government work on my own. Perhaps they would have spoken willingly about it.

increasingly drawn toward accepting invitations to participate, as historian, in those extramural activities. I became increasingly convinced that the humanities in general, and history in particular, were institutionally underdeveloped and incapable of having the kind of productive cultural and intellectual engagement with the rest of late twentieth-century American society that was warranted for the good of all. With those convictions, I became restless and began to look beyond the groves of academe for satisfactions and new challenges. Having, after long effort, become an academic historian, I was no longer content to leave it at that.

I suppose that by temperament I could never have been fully fulfilled by only an academic career; I would have always needed to alloy its responsibilities with activities that might benefit history but not necessarily in its academic incarnation. I found great pleasure in imagining something and then trying bringing it into being. I see in retrospect that that had been my inclination since the early 1970s, when, with my colleague Frederick Starr, I had proposed the revitalization, through restructuring, of the AHA, something that was carried out with my participation under the leadership of Hanna Holborn Gray. And as a member of the national governing board of Common Cause for six years and deeply engaged in fighting the Nixon administration's illegal activities, I'd gained a taste for the kind of civic involvement in which public historians are always engaged. Yet to balance and mix my academic and scholarly responsibilities with extramural projects proved increasingly difficult, especially after, with my colleague Theodore K. Rabb, I founded an organization to try to provide to the humanities resources similar to those available to the disciplines of the sciences—resources they still do not enjoy. I have recorded elsewhere the history of the American Association for the Advancement of the Humanities. Let it be said here only that, having established that organization in Washington in early 1979 and directed it for eighteen months, before the Reagan administration came to office determined to reduce sharply the national budget and with it funding for the humanities, I was faced with the hard choice of either turning the organization over to someone else and thus in effect orphaning my child or resigning my professorship to continue my efforts. It was with no ease, either to myself or to my family, that, in 1980, after fourteen years at Princeton, I took the latter course. I have never regretted that decision, but I have always subsequently missed the great university and colleagues I left behind.

As it turned out, I paid a price for that decision. After four years of operation, I had to close the association's doors. As a result, in 1983 I was thrown out upon the professional world to make my way afresh and do so when the economy had greatly darkened and the world in which I moved had become excessively dispirited and fiscally weakened. Having written only a single book, resigned a tenured post as an associate professor, and without any significant campus administrative responsibilities, I was not considered promising material for another faculty position or for academic administrative posts, especially in a day of straitened academic employment for all historians. Discouraged, at a loss as to what to do, and without experience or training in what was just becoming known as "public history," I kept afloat with miscellaneous educational and consulting projects. After two years, I joined a research institute in Washington as its book publisher. There, in addition to becoming greatly attracted to scholarly book publishing, I was able to begin to reestablish myself as writer and historian and to begin projects that would occupy me for the remainder of my professional life.

Should this part of the story be read as a story of error—of a risk foolishly taken, of a mistake I might have avoided by remaining at Princeton? There were moments, especially as I struggled to regain my professional legs, when I thought it had been. Others have no doubt thought so, too—although courteously behind my back. But I now think that is not the way to understand my decision, just as I believe that my resignation was not necessarily courageous, as some have insisted. It turns out rather—and I surely didn't see this then—that I was one of an increasing number of historians responding as much to new, if then still weak, professional "permissions" to attempt new things as I was to my own restlessness.

*   *   *

Upon reflection, I also now see that in these years I was continuing the process of becoming a historian—but not the historian that I had earlier imagined myself to be or that others expected me to be. I had never, would never have, detached myself either from my discipline or the academic profession. I continue deeply to feel myself to be an academic historian. Yet I had effectively entered a second apprenticeship, one without established career paths or the supporting institutional structures available to academics. While it suited my disposition to be able to roam the larger world of learning and design my own life as historian from within my work as publisher and, in the 1990s, as director of academic programs at a federal fellowship foundation, I also knew the sting of being considered no longer a "real" historian. I also had to adjust myself to the loss of career predictability, a situation in which the support and bemused understanding of my nonacademic, long self-employed companion and now wife, Phyllis Kramer, was key. That new circumstance of professional independence, perhaps more than any other, would from then on define my life as a historian—and in an important way free me to pursue what I considered important. Professional achievement mattered to me as much as ever, but now I had to set for myself, and not let others set for me, the standards of determining what that achievement would be.

That process of defining what I wished to do was another step in my becoming a historian. The importance of a professional's fidelity to self is little considered by those who prepare aspiring professional historians; instead, they immerse their students in the discipline's literature but rarely in its larger life, promise, or needs. Nor in the hothouse, competitive atmosphere of graduate training do young historians confide in each other about their worries and hopes. Yet since senior historians are likely for one reason or another to withhold from their students much critically important professional guidance, it behooves students to try to learn on their own what the discipline offers by way of occupation, pleasure, and challenge outside academic walls and to think beyond the scholarly literature. And it behooves them also to be true to themselves.

I have come to this conclusion because, while I had roamed more widely than many other academics outside university walls during my early career, after 1983, I was left more or less on my own to improvise the rest of my professional life. I have invented it since then largely by devoting myself to creating institutions and practices in history that hadn't before existed and to writing some works that have brought me much pleasure if little recognition among my colleagues—all the while undertaking some conventional historical scholarship and writing of my own. In the early 1980s, soon after settling in Washington, I helped found the National Humanities Alliance, which has become the lobbying arm of the humanities in the nation's capital. Then I turned my attention to other institutional developments, especially trying to figure out how to make historical knowledge useful and used. With Joyce Appleby, in 1996 I founded the History News Service, a gratifyingly successful syndicate that distributes "op ed" pieces written by historians that try to set current events in their historical context. Having spent much of my life as a teacher in classrooms, I coauthored with classicist Harold C. Cannon two books, one for teachers, the other for students (*The Elements of Teaching* [1997] and *The Elements of Learning* [1999]). And in 1999, adopting a vision of J. Franklin Jameson, Julian Boyd, and other earlier historians, I set into motion what would eventuate in the founding of the National History Center in 2002. The Center, a nonmembership institution designed to bring new resources to the discipline, in its early stage is helping create new subjects of historical inquiry, make historical knowledge a more significant element of policy making, and intensify historians' endeavors to improve history teaching in the nation's schools. Throughout this period, I continued to teach history at various universities in Washington, as well as at Charles University in Prague as Fulbright visiting professor.

In pursuing these diverse projects, my concern about the deficiencies in the way we prepare younger historians for the full range of activities and capacities that constitute being a professional has only deepened. By "the full range of activities and capacities" I don't mean simply those connected to teaching, the principal recent focus of proposals to broaden graduate students' preparation for their professional world. However rewarding and privileged are teaching positions on American campuses, those positions now constitute a declining proportion of the professional berths that historians occupy. To continue to train historians only for academic appointments, to fail to prepare them to be citizens of their discipline in the broadest sense, now strikes me as a failure as critical as historians' postwar abdication of responsibility for keeping history alive in the classrooms of our schools and for making historical knowledge remain a vital part of the larger culture.

In considering what I have written here, a reader might well ask about the links between my career as a historian and the rest of my life, especially the life of the nation and world. My historical interests did not reflect the tumults of the 1960s and 1970s, in many of which (racial and gender integration, marching on the Pentagon during the Vietnam War, fighting the Watergate scandals) I participated on campus and off. Those of us men born in 1935 were already somewhat too old, already committed too deeply to careers and family and already decently formed as adults, to be as personally affected by the changes in American life that came with the 1960s as were those eight or ten years younger than we. While we had been born in time to avoid active service in warfare, we had been born too early to savor, as somewhat younger Americans could, the zesty fervor in public movements and idealism that so often accompanies the openness of adolescence and college years. The history I wrote was never "my history" as was that of so many women and African Americans. But for me that was precisely its fascination. My subjects were distant in time, attitude, place, and affect. That fact enabled me in some deeply satisfying way to bring those people and events into my life, and not the other way around. I learned from the past and tried to teach my students how to do so. I learned how to think of politics and institutions in my own day by studying minutely their practices sometimes two and more centuries earlier. In that sense, within me past and present merged, but in a way, I suspect, quite different from the way it did for many, perhaps most, of my contemporaries.

I've never thought that my life as a student of history and as historian should serve as an example to anyone else. I did not intend it to do so, especially since so much of my career has been episodic. I became a historian through no burst of inspiration. Instead, because of particular circumstances and opportunities and because of temperament (an often overlook dimension of professional growth and pursuit), I chose to become a historian. Yet if there's any lesson to be drawn from this intellectual and professional travelogue, it may be this: that we historians should try to prepare ourselves and to prepare others for the broadest range of intellectual and professional engagements we can. The pursuits and practices of history are among the most democratic of the arts; all humans, as Carl Becker long ago insisted, are their own historians. Trained historians are to be found in many professions. The histories they write and produce take many forms, reflect many dispositions, and yield many kinds of achievements. We fail as historians, as I was often failed by my teachers and, for a long time, as I failed my own students, when we limit the definition of professional historian to academic historian alone. Today's world is too multidimensional, too needy of historical knowledge and understanding, for us to immure ourselves within academic boundaries and wall ourselves off from our fellow citizens and from the tumultuous world in which we live. The professional universe of the intellect can tolerate no gated communities of the mind or pursuit.

Contributors

James M. Banner, Jr., is an independent historian in Washington, D.C., whose scholarly interests have focused on the history of the United States between 1765 and 1865. A leader in the creation of the National History Center and cofounder and codirector of the History News Service, he is writing a book about what it means to be a historian today.

John R. Gillis, who now lives in Berkeley, is professor emeritus of history at Rutgers, the State University of New Jersey. His recent work on islands has led him to ponder the changing meaning and condition of coasts in an era of global warming.

Linda Gordon is professor of history at New York University. Her early work focused on the historical roots of social policy issues, particularly as they concern gender and family issues. Her last book, *The Great Arizona Orphan Abduction*, won the Bancroft Prize for best book in American history and the Beveridge Prize for best book on the history of the Americas. She is now writing a biography of photographer Dorothea Lange.

David A. Hollinger is the Preston Hotchkis Professor of American History at the University of California, Berkeley, and a Fellow of the American Academy of Arts and Sciences. His books include *Cosmopolitanism and Solidarity* (2006), *Postethnic America: Beyond Multiculturalism* (1995, 2000, and 2006), *Science, Jews, and Secular Culture* (1996), and *In the American Province* (1985).

Rhys Isaac, long a member of the faculty of LaTrobe University, where he remains active, as he does at the College of William and Mary and the Colonial Williamsburg Foundation, holds B.A. degrees from the University of Cape Town and Oxford University. He has also held appointments at Johns Hopkins, Princeton, and Rutgers universities. In 1983 his first book, *The Transformation of Virginia, 1740 to 1790*, was awarded a Pulitzer Prize.

Temma Kaplan, a comparative historian, critic, and feminist activist, has written extensively about social movements, political culture, and the gendered nature of historical memory in Spain, Argentina, Chile, and South Africa. She is one of the founders of women's studies, later served as the director of the Barnard Center for Research on Women, and now teaches at Rutgers, the State University of New Jersey.

Franklin W. Knight is the Leonard and Helen R. Stulman Professor of History at the Johns Hopkins University, Baltimore. His research and writing range widely across Latin America and the Caribbean. He served as president of the Latin American Studies Association (1998–2000) and of the Historical Society (2004–6) and has been honored in Brazil, the Dominican Republic, and Jamaica for his scholarly work.

Maureen Murphy Nutting, a Manhattan native and Notre Dame Ph.D., resigned her first tenure-track position in 1975 to accompany her husband to a new Coast Guard assignment. Since then she has led an unpredictable life as an academic and public historian, military spouse, volunteer, and mother of four. Now tenured, Nutting teaches history at North Seattle Community College and promotes history initiatives locally and nationally.

Dwight T. Pitcaithley is professor of history at New Mexico State University. He retired from the National Park Service in 2005 after serving as chief historian for ten years. During his thirty-year career with the NPS, he served in Santa Fe, Boston, and Washington, D.C., where he focused on issues relating to historic preservation and the interpretation of historic sites. He holds a Ph.D. in history from Texas Tech University.

Paul Robinson is the Richard W. Lyman Professor in the Humanities at Stanford University, where he has been a member of the history department since 1967. He teaches courses in modern European intellectual history. He is a member of the American Academy of Arts and Sciences.

Joan Wallach Scott is the Harold F. Linder Professor of Social Science at the Institute for Advanced Study. Her most recent book is *The Politics of the Veil* (2007).